MW01195835

"In this imaginative and rapturous reading of D.H. Lawrence, Myron Tuman tunes in to the writer's "winter prose," or the interior fixation that drove his literary imagination, finding textual evidence of his complex erotic yearning to be the recipient of a virile male lover."

Rachel Cleves, *author of* Unspeakable, *a biography of Norman Douglas*

The Hidden D. H. Lawrence

The Hidden D. H. Lawrence is a new study of the psychological and literary aspects of a great writer's lyrical genius. It explores how Lawrence, when writing on his favorite subject, the relations between men and women, moved so quickly between heavy-handed exposition and deeply inspired prose, depending on the gender of the object of his attention. Nowhere is this clearer than in the three grand love scenes from *Lady Chatterley's Lover*, those cut from the first American edition of 1932. In these scenes, Mellors, Lawrence's usual alter ego, suddenly and almost magically becomes the object of attention, although now seen through the eyes of his female protagonist. It may seem as if Lawrence's purpose here is to probe a woman's psyche, until one realizes that it is only such moments—when his focus seems less on his female character than the erotic allure of a powerful man—that unlock Lawrence's lyrical genius. The claim here is that in his major novels and stories, Lawrence was less interested in exploring the emotional lives of women than in using his female characters (as well as many sensitive male protagonists) to explore his own psychic life, one marked by the persistent attraction to the image of a strong male—an inner life that for the last century has been hiding in plain sight.

Myron Tuman, with a PhD in Victorian literature from Tulane University, taught at universities in West Virginia, Alabama, and Louisiana. Since 2006, he has published a series of literary studies of major writers and the psychic strains of family life: *Melville's Gay Father*, on men and their sons; *Don Juan and His Daughter*, on women and their fathers; *The Sensitive Son*, on men and their mothers; and *The Stuttering Son*, on men and their fathers.

Routledge Studies in Twentieth-Century Literature

For more information about this series, please visit: www.routledge.com/Routledge-Studies-in-Twentieth-Century-Literature/book-series/RSTLC

The Hidden D. H. Lawrence

Unmasking a Lyrical Genius

Myron Tuman

Routledge
Taylor & Francis Group

NEW YORK AND LONDON

First published 2025
by Routledge
605 Third Avenue, New York, NY 10158

and by Routledge
4 Park Square, Milton Park, Abingdon, Oxon, OX14 4RN

Routledge is an imprint of the Taylor & Francis Group, an informa business

© 2025 Myron Tuman

The right of Myron Tuman to be identified as author of this work has been asserted in accordance with sections 77 and 78 of the Copyright, Designs and Patents Act 1988.

ISBN: 9781032784205 (hbk)
ISBN: 9781032800332 (pbk)
ISBN: 9781003495093 (ebk)

DOI: 10.4324/9781003495093

Typeset in Sabon
by Newgen Publishing UK

Contents

Preface

I have spent a lifetime reading, teaching, and thinking about D. H. Lawrence. I remember, for instance, the excitement of first reading *Lady Chatterley's Lover* in the mid-1960s from the Grove Press's Black Cat edition and, some ten years later, teaching *The Fox* to a class of juniors at an all-girls high school. Then, after two decades focused on computers and the plight of college composition, I explored Joyce Carol Oates's long fascination with Lawrence in my 2009 study *Don Juan and His Daughter*; ten years later still, there was a chapter comparing Lawrence with his near-contemporary F. Scott Fitzgerald in *The Sensitive Son and the Feminine Ideal*. In making this comparison, I soon realized that Lawrence, unlike Fitzgerald, was an ill fit in a volume focused on Jean-Jacques Rousseau and on other male authors who, like Rousseau, spent a lifetime erotically aroused by the images of a powerful, often distant woman. Indeed, the Lawrence of this current volume gradually came into view as the near-mirror image of these mother-obsessed writers.

I began this current volume on Lawrence following the completion of *The Stuttering Son* (2022), a study of the difficulties a series of male writers had with their fathers, to consider how Lawrence's marriage to Frieda Weekley might be seen as part of the emotional and erotic tensions that male writers faced married to strong-willed women, possibly as an extension or reworking of Jeffrey Meyers's intriguing *Married to Genius*. Over time, I realized that the defining relationship in Lawrence's life was not with his mother or wife but with his father—if not the historical Arthur Lawrence, then the image of an older male protector somehow modeled on him. As such, *The Hidden Lawrence* became a complementary work to *The Stuttering Son*, although one focused on an entirely different son–father dynamic.

Like my four previous literary studies, starting with *Melville's Gay Father* (2005), *The Hidden Lawrence* is another work exploring my sense of the nearly incalculable influence that early family life has on the imaginative lives of so many great writers—or, perhaps more accurately stated, another work focused on how great writers like Lawrence regularly rework these strains, even the trauma of their early family lives, into some of the world's most memorable imaginative literature. In the present volume, this effort has involved uncovering the connection between what I came to see as the largely buried erotic tensions in Lawrence's life and the lyrical genius that illuminates his most brilliant writing.

I want to thank those Lawrence scholars and friends who were all kind enough to respond to my queries: Hugh Stevens, Jeffrey Guss, Paul Poplawski, David Brock, Barbara Kearns, Ronald Granofsky, Judith Cohen, Bill Winkley, Susan Reynolds, Marina Vorontsov, Maria Rivas-McMillan, Stevan Dittman, Carol Siegel, Judith Ruderman, Patrick Scott, Keith Cushman, and a special nod to Gavin Gillespie for all his diligence in helping track down Gudrun and Gerald's path under the colliery railway. Finally, a special nod to Nigel Hamilton for his gentle encouragement and constant friendship through my recent trio of books focused on sensitive sons—their frequent trials and occasional triumphs.

1 Introduction

A Writer's "Winter" Thoughts

It may seem odd to begin a study of D. H. Lawrence by referring to Charlotte Brontë and specifically to a single passage in *Jane Eyre* that occurs immediately after Brontë's young heroine has survived a miserable winter at the Lowood boarding school—material based on Brontë's traumatic experiences as an eight-year-old. In the novel, Jane's closest friend has died from the harsh conditions, as did Brontë's two older sisters that winter. It is hardly a surprise that Brontë should open Chapter 9 by welcoming the change of seasons: "But the privations, or rather the hardships, of Lowood lessened. Spring drew on: she was indeed already come" (65).

There was indeed reason to rejoice, and Brontë does her best to celebrate the season of rebirth. The problem was that the pleasantries of spring—its softness, especially—were, for Brontë, no match for "the privations, or rather the hardships," of winter. It is not just that Brontë's emphasis remains on the pain that she experienced, but that there is something distinctly different in Brontë's writing itself, something radically unbalanced, in her account of the two seasons.

There is, for instance, Brontë's inability to ignore winter's pains—how "the frosts of winter had ceased [...] its cutting winds ameliorated"—even in welcoming spring. Thus, Brontë gives us this finely worded subject, "My wretched feet, flayed and swollen to lameness by the sharp air of January," ending with this banal predicate: "began to heal and subside under the gentler breathings of April"; or this sharp description of pain, "the nights and mornings no longer by their Canadian temperature froze the very blood in our veins," followed by the innocuous account of how spring allows us to "endure the play-hour passed in the garden." Brontë ends this opening paragraph with her most concerted attempt to sing spring's praises, noting how "flowers peeped out amongst the leaves: snow-drops, crocuses, purple auriculas, and golden-eyed pansies": "On Thursday afternoons (half-holidays) we now took walks, and found still sweeter flowers opening by the wayside, under the hedges."

DOI: 10.4324/9781003495093-1

Brontë continues this effort in her second paragraph, noting how with spring came the "pleasure [...] in prospect of noble summits girdling a great hill-hollow, rich in verdure and shadow"—only to change course suddenly. Enough with this silly talk about spring, she seems to say; let me tell you some more about what really interests me: "How different [this scene] looked when I viewed it laid out beneath the iron sky of winter, stiffened in frost, shrouded with snow!" Yes, winter—that real season, with Brontë's prose finally reflecting her genius: Winter,

> when mists as chill as death wandered to the impulse of east winds along those purple peaks, and rolled down "ing" and holm till they blended with the frozen fog of the beck! That beck itself was then a torrent, turbid and curbless: it tore asunder the wood, and sent a raving sound through the air, often thickened with wild rain or whirling sleet; and for the forest on its banks, *that* showed only ranks of skeletons.

Here is Brontë at her most intense, her most lyrical; nor is there anything surprising, out of line, for instance, with Lawrence's insight that "art-speech is the only truth"—that truth lies not in Brontë's honest, high-minded effort to praise the restorative property of spring. "An artist is usually a damned liar," Lawrence adds, with the truth of a work of art deeply embedded in the text itself. There are always two morals or truths to literature: the truth the writer is trying to sell us and the truth embedded in the tale itself, as suggested in Brontë's agitated, intense account of winter versus her mild, placid take on spring.

A writer's "novels and poems," Lawrence tells us, "come unwatched out of one's pen"; it is only in the works themselves that we can find "pure passionate experience," and then, as we shall see repeatedly in Lawrence, in some passages more than others. A writer's "metaphysic or philosophy"—the very ideas we try to live by or what Lawrence bitingly derides as "pollyanalytics"—"may not be anywhere very accurately stated and may be quite unconscious": "Men live and see according to some gradually developing and gradually withering vision. This vision exists also as a dynamic idea or metaphysic—exists first as such" ("Foreword" 65). Or, as he states more cryptically—and this is the message at the heart of this study—"Never trust the artist. Trust the tale. The proper function of a critic is to save the tale from the artist who created it" ("Spirit" 14).

Lawrence's insight here is so apparent in the life of Charlotte Brontë, one involving the difference between Brontë, the demure clergyman's daughter portrayed by her friend and first biographer, Elizabeth Gaskell, and that other Brontë, the wildly passionate soul reflected in her more profound *winter* thoughts—Brontë, the grand chronicler of the broken heart, who lived with the intense psychic pain of the unrequited love for her married professor from Brussels, Constantin Héger. Here is the writer whose career began with—and, in some ways, rarely transcended—her fierce determination to make her mark as a chronicler of that pain.

Thus, it can be said that the distant pain connected to her memory of the death of her two sisters some 20 years before was intimately connected with the anguish apparent in her letters from 1845 to her forsaken professor, letters fortuitously saved by his descendants and first published in 1913. It is the pain we see, for instance, in her admonition to herself against sending one of these letters without first rereading it—"dimly aware that there are some cold and rational people who would say on reading it—'she is raving.'" Her "sole revenge," she continues, "is to wish these people a single day of the torments that I have suffered for eight months—then we should see whether they wouldn't be raving too" (Barker 125).

Here is the same anguish we see in the opening pages of *Jane Eyre* (begun just months after the last of these letters to Héger), where we learn that the young Jane was most attracted to the desolate seabirds described in volume two of Thomas Bewick's *History of British Birds*, and specifically to another "winter" passage, one that highlights a great "rock standing up alone in a sea of billow and spray; to the broken boat stranded on a desolate coast; to the cold and ghastly moon glancing through bars of cloud at a wreck just sinking" (6).

This is the same anguished spirit we also see early on at the Lowood school, as Brontë uses her young heroine to lament life without the love and admiration of her professor. "No," she tells a friend, "I know I should think well of myself, but that is not enough: if others don't love me, I would rather die than live—I cannot bear to be solitary and hated" (60). Here is language better suited to the author's real-life grievances than the situation confronting her ten-year-old protagonist. "Look here," she warns her friend Helen Burns in another cascade of "winter" thoughts:

> to gain some real affection from you, or Miss Temple, or any other whom I truly love, I would willingly submit to have the bone of my arm broken, or to let a bull toss me, or to stand behind a kicking horse, and let it dash its hoof at my chest—.

This is the same inappropriate or at least unexpected tone of defiance, the same "winter" thoughts we see in perhaps the most famous lines from the novel—Jane's response to Rochester's efforts to patronize her, the culmination of his failure to recognize her true worth. Jane, we are told, was "roused to something like passion," as she explains her reasons for leaving Thornfield: "Do you think I can stay to become nothing to you?" she continues. "Do you think I am an automaton?—a machine without feelings?

and can bear to have my morsel of bread snatched from my lips, and my drop of living water dashed from my cup" (222)?

Here is Brontë in full flight, a great writer at her best, not according to some secret code a reader has to uncover, but because this moment, reenacted in fiction, represents one of the most intense, poignant moments of the author's life—the threat of losing the respect and admiration of the great love of her life. "Do you think, because I am poor, obscure, plain, and little, I am soulless and heartless? You think wrong!—I have as much soul as you,—and full as much heart!" What type of shortsighted, misguided criticism—in the name of some abstract, artificial ideal about the novel as art—would want to close its eyes to the vital connection between such magnificent writing and the author's own life, in the process failing to see an actual person's suffering at stake here?

> And if God had gifted me with some beauty and much wealth, I should have made it as hard for you to leave me, as it is now for me to leave you. I am not talking to you now through the medium of custom, conventionalities, nor even of mortal flesh;—it is my spirit that addresses your spirit; just as if both had passed through the grave, and we stood at God's feet, equal,—as we are!

Shouldn't the connection with Lawrence now be obvious? Yes, some readers may want to think that great writers like Brontë or Lawrence all have that Shakespearean quality that John Keats called "negative capability," that capacity to submerge their egos in their narrative, essentially hiding themselves while instilling fully conceived, separate lives into their various characters. Such thinking, however, leads to the notion that, with truly great writers like Shakespeare, it is difficult to discern the author's presence in the drama, making us unable to answer even the most basic questions about Shakespeare the man—his politics or sexual orientation.

Meanwhile, the situation for fiercely passionate writers like Brontë and Lawrence is, more often than not, just the opposite. The goal here is to show how Lawrence is often no different from Brontë struggling to praise spring when her heart was buried deep in winter. Hence, our thesis: that Lawrence, like Brontë, can achieve Shakespearean brilliance only when he is fully and passionately engaged with his material; that, as we hope to show repeatedly, starting with our next chapter on his most famous work, *Lady Chatterley's Lover*, Lawrence's writing soars or sinks, has its lyrical "winter" or prosaic "spring" moments only when the subject truly touches an otherwise hidden nerve in his psyche.

There is an obvious corollary to this thesis regarding the fixated nature of a writer's genius, one at the heart of Henry James's well-known story "The Figure in the Carpet," namely, that for a writer like Lawrence, his most significant, most lyrical work—and hence where the interest of this study lies—inevitably springs from a repressed or hidden desire. Such is the position that James has his stand-in, the famous author Hugh Verecker, enunciate regarding the "little point" that all his readers routinely miss, whether they are his fans or critics, or, as James explains with a wink, "with a perfection exactly as admirable when they patted me on the back as when they kicked me in the shins"—the "little point" being "the particular thing I've written my books most for." And finally, from Verecker, we get this beautifully rendered "winter" thought, although one posed by the ever wary James as a rhetorical question: "Isn't there for every writer"—and, we will add, for Lawrence especially—

> a particular thing of that sort, the thing that most makes him apply himself, the thing without the effort to achieve which he wouldn't write at all, the very passion of his passion, the part of the business in which, for him, the flame of art burns most intensely?

The basic idea here is the one motivating this volume—the notion that there is a core unifying element across the totality of a great writer's work, one likely connected to hidden aspects in an author's life—the metaphorical "figure in the carpet" in the title of James's story. It is also a position that, in typically elusive fashion, James immediately tries to undercut through the actions of his overly fastidious narrator and his mostly ridiculous cohorts. Luckily, we need not bother untangling how Verecker's elusive suggestion regarding a writer's hidden desire might be related to James's work, a connection that James certainly did his best to bury under the weight of his baroque prose.

Fortunately, our concern is neither with James nor Brontë but with Lawrence, a writer who openly acknowledged the need to confront "the problem of himself, of his own individuality and his own sex." Such, for Lawrence, is our common burden, our "own single, private, individual affair"—except, of course, when it is specifically a writer's burden, someone Lawrence sees as "fight[ing] it out with his own soul, alone, or with a book which is like his own self speaking, making him appeased in his aloneness" ("Foreword" 55).

And it is this "aloneness" that is our sole subject in the eight chapters that follow, with each offering a different take on the intimate connection between Lawrence's life and his most powerful work—his "winter" thoughts, "the very passion of his passion," those places where, in James's words, "the flame of art burns most intensely."

Chapter 2, "Lady Chatterley's Hidden Lover," looks at the tension between Lawrence's public persona and that other, *hidden* Lawrence that is the focus of this study—a tension visible in his last and best-known novel, *Lady Chatterley's Lover*, between the two different representations of the novel's principal male character, the gamekeeper Oliver Mellors. One is Mellors, the often crude, misogynistic ranter against women, primarily for their shortcomings as sexual partners, a complaint that, oddly enough, would seem to include Connie Chatterley, the novel's namesake and just recently his mistress. The other is Mellors, seen through Lady Chatterley's eyes as a patient, attentive lover. Two representations of Mellors whose depictions by Lawrence mirror Brontë's accounts of spring and winter— with Mellors' matter-of-fact renderings of some of their sexual encounters vastly different from the soaring lyricism of other encounters, including their three most extended accounts, as depicted mainly through Connie's perspective. How odd that one literary character can play two such disparate roles—when speaking as Lawrence's stand-in and, when mostly mum, as Lady Chatterley's near-perfect lover. Resolving this apparent contradiction entails recognizing Lawrence's success in hiding such a crucial part of himself in such a widely read novel.

Chapters 3 and 4, "Adolescence—Angst and Exuberance" and "The Other Three Women," offer a biographical overview of Lawrence, an account of the man and the writer coming to terms with what he sensed was his peculiar sexual nature. It is the story of a young man told in three acts: first, that of a lengthy, mostly happy, essentially asexual adolescence; second, a period in his early twenties where he was exceptionally eager for his first sexual experience, not realized until his twenty-fifth year; and third, the culmination of this brief, two-year period of sexual activity when, at age twenty-six, he met and eventually ran off to Europe with the married Frieda Weekley.

Lawrence's protracted adolescence, the topic of Chapter 3, focuses on his extended, complicated relationship with Jessie Chambers, portrayed as Miriam Leivers in his coming-of-age novel *Sons and Lovers*. Lawrence's account of these years reflects what will be the oft-repeated pattern of his writing life—his most lyrical writing when he was free of the pressures associated with being intimate with a woman. The biographical focus of Chapter 4 begins with Lawrence's other sexual relationship in *Sons and Lovers*, with the married Clara Dawes—an affair partially based on his only other sexual relationship before meeting his future wife in 1912. Next comes a look at the complications of Lawrence's first months with Frieda Weekley as they traveled to Germany and Italy. The chapter ends with Lawrence's brief involvement with Rosalind Baynes, possibly his last lover.

Chapter 5 presents a fuller account of the "hidden" Lawrence by looking at how different presentations of a single situation—the Pan-like shepherd embracing a maiden in the painting *An Idyll* by Maurice Greiffenhagen—elicited so much of his most intensely lyrical writing. Greiffenhagen's painting can tell two competing stories—one about male lust for a beautiful young woman and the other about that youth's fascination with a powerful male presence. It is this second reading that provides the key to revisiting several key scenes across Lawrence's works—starting with the two young lovers in Lawrence's first novel, *The White Peacock*, and culminating in the magnificent "under the colliery railway" love scene between Gudrun and Gerald in *Women in Love*.

Chapters 6 and 7, "Man-to-Man" and "Hiding in Plain Sight," form the literary heart of this study, showing how this notion of a "hidden" Lawrence can provide the basis for rereading some of his greatest works. The focus in Chapter 6, drawing on *Women in Love* and three short stories, shows the considerable constraints Lawrence often felt under in describing the erotic struggles of male protagonists, attracted to and sometimes touching another man. The chapter ends with a consideration of changes over time in Lawrence's thinking about male friendships.

Chapter 7 shows a far freer Lawrence in five brilliant works of short fiction—"Sun," *The Ladybird*, *The Fox*, "The Princess," and "The Woman Who Rode Away"—each presenting a female protagonist under emotional duress, responding in different ways to the attraction of an illicit male lover.

Chapter 8, "His Father's Body," returns to material covered in Chapter 5 to look at how his father's likeness came to play such a central role in Lawrence's imaginative life, starting with his early masterpiece, "Odour of Chrysanthemums." What we see there is what is present in nearly all of Lawrence's most memorable moments—a gentle, "feminine" soul coming to terms with a powerful male presence.

Chapter 9, "Man Alone," uses Lawrence's Australian novel, *Kangaroo*, to offer a final look at the other area of his experience that elicited his "winter" thoughts, the one topic about which Lawrence and his many alter egos could always speak freely and passionately—this was the excitement and wonder of feeling alone in the natural world.

Works Cited

Barker, Juliet. *The Brontës: A Life in Letters*. Overlook Press, 1998.

Brontë, Charlotte. *Jane Eyre: An Authoritative Text*. Ed. Richard J. Dunn. Norton, 1971.

James, Henry. *The Figure in the Carpet and Other Stories*. Ed. Frank Kermode. Penguin, 1986.

Lawrence, D. H. "Foreword: An Answer to Some Critics." In *Psychoanalysis and the Unconscious and Fantasia of the Unconscious*. Ed. Bruce Steele. Cambridge UP, 2003: 51–65.

———. "The Spirit of the Place." In *Studies in Classic American Literature*. Eds. Ezra Greenspan, Lindeth Vasey, and John Worthy. Cambridge UP, 2004: 13–19.

2 Lady Chatterley's Hidden Lover

A "Tender" Lover or a Reluctant One?

We begin with what seems to be a contradiction around the term *tenderness*, so crucial to Lawrence's best-known novel, *Lady Chatterley's Lover*, that he considered using it as the novel's title. Of immediate concern is Lawrence's use of the term in the final meeting between his two lovers, Mellors and Connie Chatterley. The scene begins with Mellors's observation—the same one Lawrence had long heard about himself, even as a youngster—that he had "too much of the woman in me." It is an accusation that Mellors immediately denies, even while acknowledging that "I like men, and men like me," although, as he says, only a particular type of man—specifically, the strong, quiet type—that is, one so different from the "twaddling bossy impudence of the people who run this world" (333).

Here, for once, we can see Lawrence speaking calmly and deliberately through Mellors, his stand-in for much of the novel, about his place in the world. Something rings true here in Connie's response as well when she tells Mellors what Lawrence might have remembered hearing from Frieda: that he had what "other men don't have, and [the one thing] that will make the future"—namely, "the courage of your own tenderness" (334). It is a point that seems related to one of the novel's central motifs—the call for a new, more loving relationship between men and women, and specifically between this man, Mellors, and this woman, Connie Chatterley—although it is a point that she seems to undermine, reducing Mellors's grand notion of tenderness to the moment "you put your hand on my tail and say I've got a pretty tail."

"Ay! [...] You're right," Mellors responds. "It's that really. It's that all the way through." Here, one senses we are dealing with a subject close to Lawrence's heart, as he then allows Mellors to expound on his special character, which he learned entirely from his military experience "with the men." "I had to be in touch with them, physically," he continues, "and not

DOI: 10.4324/9781003495093-2

go back on it. I had to be bodily aware of them. and a bit tender to them, even if I put 'em through hell" (334–35). The great Buddha, he admits, knew the importance of such awareness, but "even he fought shy of the bodily awareness, and that natural physical tenderness, which is the best, even between men; in a proper manly way."

This is a notion of a man's tenderness as standing in place of, even in opposition to, direct physical arousal. It suggests a higher purpose devoted to satisfying the other person's needs through warmth and touch, through a general show of concern for that person's well-being—that is, a concern like that we might expect in that universal symbol of tenderness: a mother's *tender* regard for her infant. As such, *tenderness* can be seen as the opposite of the father's sexual arousal in seeking his immediate physical satisfaction. Thus, it seems precisely this different sort of man—one with the capacity to forgo such sensual pleasure out of a *tender* concern for others—that both Mellors and Connie join in celebrating in the novel's closing pages. Here is praise for a new sort of man, one more like the father celebrated in the Parable of the Prodigal Son, a patriarch who greets his wayward son not with the punishment he has earned but with a kiss, that is, with a mother's *tender* regard.

Thus, it is in Lawrence as well, with tenderness promoted as the mostly passive affection that a real man offers a woman in place of the demand that she gratify his phallic needs—a notion of lovemaking touted by Mellors as the vital component of what makes men "really manly, not so monkeyish." Only such men, those who can be tender and loving, not just to women but to each other, can be good lovers, capable of possessing what Mellors labels "cunt-awareness." He then concludes this speech with an essential belief for Lawrence—that

> [s]ex is really only touch, the closest of all touch. And it's touch we're afraid of. We're only half-conscious, and half alive. We've got to come alive and aware. Especially the English have got to get into touch with one another, a bit delicate and a bit tender. It's our crying need.
>
> (335)

What a beguiling concept this is: that all lovers, and men especially, need to learn to touch instead of grab, a notion likely with an added appeal to women—this view of men as *tender* lovers, caring for their partners' well-being in the same *tender* manner that a mother cares for her infant. But—and here we get to Mellors's other side, and, as we shall see, Lawrence's as well—all this sermonizing coming from someone whose unabashedly proclaimed beliefs about men's sexual relations with women earlier in the novel seems anything but tender.

Indeed, even Lawrence recognizes how such high sentiments coming from Mellors might strain credulity, as he has Connie voice her suspicion that all this chatter about tenderness is just another sign of his reluctance to perform as a traditional lover, another reason—besides his already expressed displeasure over her wealth and the fact she is carrying his child—he has for ending their relationship.

"Then why are you afraid of me?" Connie asks, no doubt sensing in Mellors—for all his talk of touching—an underlying fear of intimacy. Perhaps Lawrence is using Connie's question here to signal a contradiction in his feelings—how Mellors's warm thoughts about tenderness may apply primarily to his relations with men and hence have little to do with the various complaints against women as sexual partners that we will soon see Mellors voicing earlier in the novel. Nor is it a surprise when it is Connie, not Mellors, who suggests one final act of intimacy, her erotic arousal signaled by what she senses is a "soft, pure look of tender passion" in Mellors—and, no surprise, it is Mellors who demurs, adding, "I ought to leave you alone" (336).

Mellors's protests notwithstanding, their final act of lovemaking soon begins, and, like their earlier acts seen mainly from Mellors's viewpoint, their interaction is both brief and uninspired. "Oh, you love me! You love me!" Connie responds, "in a little cry like one of her blind, inarticulate love cries." Then this single bland utterance—more in line with Charlotte Brontë's account of spring than winter: "And he went in to her softly, feeling the stream of tenderness flowing in release from his bowels to hers, the bowels of compassion kindled between them" (336).

Lawrence then allows Mellors to offer a forced, odd sort of pseudo-celebration of lovemaking, again one more in the spirit of Brontë's luster-less celebration of spring—Mellors realizing "as he went in to her that this was the thing he had to do, to come into tender touch, without losing his pride or his dignity or his integrity as a man." Here, Mellors sounds less like a lover swept away by passion than a good-hearted chap doing his duty, a man honoring his word. Despite his dislike of her wealth, Mellors tells Connie, he was "too proud and honorable to hold back his tenderness from her on that account"—reaffirming his commitment to "the touch of bodily awareness between human beings [...] and the touch of tenderness" (336–37). This is all that Lawrence gives us—no actual details of Mellors being tender, only abstractions about the importance of tenderness, precisely the sort of "pollyanalytics" we saw Lawrence disparaging in Chapter 1.

Lawrence has Mellors end this speech with what may well have been a gracious but hardly passionate nod to his life partner, Frieda: "She is my mate," Mellors notes, again effecting a kind of guy talk, before recognizing how this woman, nominally Connie, upheld her half of their bargain in Lawrence's long-standing struggle against "the money, and the machine, and the insentient ideal monkeyishness of the world":

> And she will stand behind me there. Thank God I've got a woman! Thank God I've got a woman who is with me, and tender and aware of me. Thank God she's not a bully, nor a fool. Thank God she's a tender, aware woman.

With that testament, Lawrence ends this last moment of intimacy between his famed pair of lovers with this strained, hardly pleasant image: "And as his seed sprang in her, his soul sprang towards her too, in the creative act that is far more than procreative" (337).

Later, in the novel's coda, Mellors now living safely apart from Connie, this "tender" lover subjects her to a rousing hymn to chastity, noting how "being chaste" now is something he loves "as snowdrops love the snow" (364). And, about lovemaking—nominally the principal topic of this novel—all Mellors can do is aver how "wearisomely" it is "to philander": "What a misery to be like Don Juan, and impotent ever to fuck oneself into peace." Alas, it is chastity, not fucking, that summons up a final, brief lyrical moment from Mellors, his praising chastity "like a river of cool water in my soul. [...] like fresh water and rain" (365).

Such praise should hardly surprise anyone who knows Lawrence's spirited defense of his much-attacked novel, "A Propos of *Lady Chatterley's Lover*," where we find a similar praise of chastity: that a "great many men and women today are happiest when they abstain and stay sexually apart, quite clean" (308). Nor does Lawrence seem capable of ending *Lady Chatterley's Lover* without giving his ever-reluctant lover one last crude, deflating thought about intercourse: "If I could sleep with my arm round you, the ink could stay in the bottle. We could be chaste together just as we can fuck together."

Mellors's stance as the reluctant lover at the novel's conclusion is one matter; there remains the more compelling matter of his extended rant against women earlier in the novel, a kind of misogynistic showpiece, which surprisingly occurs after he had already made love to Connie five separate times, including two of their most exalted sessions, their third and fifth, interactions that, as discussed below, clearly showcase Mellors's tender side, at least from Connie's point of view.

The rant itself is preceded by Lawrence using Mellors to offer a crude rehashing of his lengthy relationship with Jessie Chambers—a matter treated at length in the next chapter. She was his closest friend throughout adolescence and early adulthood—"The first girl I had, I began with when

I was sixteen," who "egged me on to poetry and reading" (240). Then, five years later, at his mother's urging, Lawrence agreed to stop seeing Chambers romantically, but the two remained friends, with Lawrence continuing to rely on her literary advice. It was another four years that Lawrence, then 24 and likely still a virgin, eventually convinced Chambers to be his first sexual partner, and three more years later, in 1913, when she became the model for Miriam Leivers, Paul Morel's one close friend in Lawrence's grand coming-of-age novel, *Sons and Lovers*.

There seems little reason for Lawrence to recount any of this history here in *Lady Chatterley's Lover*, nominally in Mellors's voice, except as part of a broader complaint he wanted to make against women. Thus, while acknowledging the immense support this unnamed friend provided him— "We were the most literary-cultured couple in ten counties"—Lawrence has Mellors quickly pivot to what was the main problem, sex ("the serpent in the grass"), cruelly adding, "She somehow didn't have any; at least, not where it's supposed to be." Mellors then admits to pressuring her into sex: "Then I said we'd got to be lovers. I talked her into it, as usual. So she let me. I was excited, and she never wanted it. She just didn't want it" (241).

Nor was she an anomaly, as Mellors adds that there were "lots of women like her," including the next woman he complains about, possibly based on Louie Burrows, Lawrence's fiancée for 14 months when he was in his mid-twenties—"a soft, white-skinned, soft sort of a woman, older than me" (200–01). "A demon," he calls her, who "loved everything about love, except the sex": "Clinging, caressing, creeping into you in every way: but if you forced her to sex itself, she just ground her teeth and sent out hate" (241).

Finally, settling into his topic, he turns to the woman he would eventually marry, admitting how, unlike all the other "pure" women of his youth—"women [who] had nearly taken all the balls out of me"—this woman, Bertha (possibly based on Alice Dax, the first of the three women treated in Chapter 4), was at least agreeable, even open to sex: "made no bones about it." "And I was as pleased as punch. That was what I wanted: a woman who *wanted* me to fuck her. So I fucked her like a good un." But even this was far from perfect, adding, "I think she despised me a bit for being so pleased about it" (242, emphasis in original).

Mellors's rant continues with what was a peculiar complaint of Lawrence's—that these women partners, partly out of a personal pique for him and partly a general deficiency of women as sexual partners, would "never come off when I did. Never! She'd just wait." Nor does Mellors here display any interest in the emotional satisfaction a man might receive in pleasing a woman sexually, in sharing her pleasure, or in the intimacy such an experience might involve—as we shall soon see, all essential components of his successful acts of lovemaking with Connie, at least in their crucial third and fifth interactions, both primarily narrated from Connie's perspective.

Instead, all we are given here is a kind of loose talk about sexual pleasure one might expect to hear in a men's locker room: "If I kept back for half an hour," Mellors continues, "she'd keep back longer. And when I'd come and really finished, then she'd start on her own account." As a result, Mellors had to force himself to "stop inside her till she brought herself off, wriggling and shouting, she'd clutch clutch clutch with herself down there, an' then she'd come-off, fair in ecstasy. And then she'd say: That was lovely" (242)!

Here is an account of lovemaking without the slightest pretense of affection or tenderness, lovemaking reduced to a kind of mutual masturbation—the man's sole interest, his orgasm; the woman's satisfaction, merely an imposition, and, for Mellors, an increasingly burdensome one. "Gradually," he adds,

> I got sick of it: and she got worse. She sort of got harder and harder to bring off, and she'd sort of tear at me down there, as if it was a beak tearing at me. By God, you think a woman's soft down there, like a fig. But I tell you the old rampers have beaks between their legs, and they tear at you with it till you're sick. Self! Self! Self! All self! tearing and shouting!

One thing is clear—that Mellors, a man whom Lawrence has already showcased twice as Lady Chatterley's near-perfect lover, had no interest in the clitoral arousal of his female partner nor, as we will eventually consider, even much interest in females generally as sexual partners, his complaint quickly reaching beyond his wife. "She got no feeling off it, from my working. She had to work the thing herself," then, adding the particularly unpleasant metaphor, had to "grind her own coffee." Nor was Bertha done. "And it came back on her like a raving necessity, she had to let herself go, and tear, tear, tear, as if she had no sensation in her except in the top of her beak, the very outside top tip, that rubbed and tore"—that is, "how old whores used to be, so men used to say" (243).

Nor is Mellors's misogynist rant over, as he broadens his attack from his wife to all women—here making no effort even to exclude Connie—dividing them into five groups, starting with "the mass of women," who really "don't want the sex, but they put up with it, as part of the bargain" (243–44), that is, "just lie there like nothing and let you go ahead"—a practice that Mellors rejects as a kind of male masturbation. While "most men like it that way," Mellors (and presumably Lawrence) hate it, especially when women pretend to be "passionate and have thrills" (203).

The three types that follow are no better, with the fifth and final sort, presumably the worst, described in especially crude language—this is the woman who "puts you out before you really 'come,' and go on writhing their loins till they bring themselves off against your thighs." Then, before concluding, Mellors mentions a sixth and final type, albeit one that exists for him more as an imagined ideal—that is, a woman who would have her orgasm simultaneous with his: "I could never get my pleasure and satisfaction of *her* unless she got hers of me at the same time." Alas, for Mellors, it seems that this ever-elusive simultaneous orgasm "never happened." The reason? "It takes two" (247–48, emphasis in original).

Four points seem especially important here. First, as already noted, is Lawrence's language here—just how crude and deflating it is in depicting the most basic aspects of heterosexual lovemaking; indeed, how reminiscent it is of the coarsest sort of male banter, focused as it is entirely on the man's orgasmic pleasure. Second, Mellors's rant represents the sort of quasi-analytic theorizing, or "pollyanalytics," that we saw Lawrence warning against in the last chapter—our trusting artists' ideas or conscious thoughts (often lies) instead of their deeply felt images. It will be crucial to see how such crude banter is entirely at odds with the language Lawrence uses to describe Mellors's third and fifth acts of lovemaking with Lady Chatterley, as noted, both narrated mainly from her point of view.

Third is recognizing how traditional literary critics might want to analyze Mellors's language in terms of the character's psychological makeup and the needs of the novel, seeing Lawrence here as the master novelist in complete control of his characters. One might claim, for instance, that Lawrence is here showing us the crude Mellors before somehow being transformed by his interactions with Connie, even though he has already had multiple lovemaking sessions with her and even though, as we have seen, he ends up falling back into some of these same attitudes in the novel's conclusion. In addition, such an approach overlooks the extent to which Mellors's complaints against women here are remarkably similar to those that Lawrence often made previously—for example, the complaint of his first groundskeeper, Annable, in his debut novel, *The White Peacock*, against his wife for wanting "her own way too much—I let her do as she liked with me." But even this compliance did not satisfy her: "it took her three years to be really glutted with me" (this last phrase toned down at the request of the publisher to "three years to have a real bellyful of me") (212, 422).

Finally, there is the crucial moment when Connie finally objects to being included in this rant, and Mellors turns to his one good trait as a lover, something seemingly that all his female partners lack: his "being warm-hearted in love, in fucking with a warm heart." Then adding, "It's all this cold-hearted fucking that is death and idiocy" (248), ignoring the apparent contradiction, still awaiting resolution, that, as we shall soon see, it is doubtful if anyone in all literature has fucked with a warmer heart than the person, or at least the literary creation, he was just then addressing.

Hence, this core contradiction at the heart of *Lady Chatterley's Lover*: that Mellors should be portrayed as this warm-hearted, "tender" lover of women, at least in some of his interactions with Connie, while otherwise appearing as a most reluctant lover, one who seems to dislike almost everything about making love to a woman, except for that rare occasion when both parties have simultaneous orgasms. It is a contradiction based, as we shall see, on his somehow excluding several tender interactions with Connie from his rant, ending things, oddly enough, by insisting that she was no different from all those other women who "like good, sharp, piercing cold-hearted fucking, and then pretending it's all sugar":

> Where's your tenderness for me? You're as suspicious of me as a cat is of a dog. I tell you it takes two even to be tender and warm-hearted. You love fucking all right: but you want it to be called something grand and mysterious, just to flatter your own self-importance. Your own self-importance is more to you, fifty times more, than any man, or being together with a man.
>
> (248)

Surprisingly, we can find these same misogynistic complaints about heterosexual lovemaking not just in Lawrence's first novel, *The White Peacock*, but expressed by Connie's first lover, the young Irish playwright Michaelis, in this novel, especially in their third and final act of lovemaking. Here again, Michaelis ejaculates prematurely, with Connie having

> to go on after he had finished, in the wild tumult and heaving of her loins, while he heroically kept himself up, and present in her, with all his will and self-offering, till she brought about her own crisis, with weird little cries.
>
> (61)

Michaelis then continues in the spirit of Mellors, crudely berating his partner for being unable to "go off at the same time as a man": "You'd have to bring yourself off! You'd have to run the show" (62)! When Connie is taken aback, Michaelis continues, almost like Mellors's double: "You know what I mean. You keep on for hours after I've gone off [...] and I have to hang on with my teeth till you bring yourself off, by your own exertions" (62).

Connie, Lawrence tells us, "was stunned by this unexpected piece of brutality," startled just as "she was glowing with a sort of pleasure beyond words." When she inquires about his interest in her satisfaction, even if it entails her finishing after him, his reply is again as vindictive as Mellors's and as lacking in tenderness: "That's good. I want to hang on with my teeth clenched, while you go for me," adding that, "All the darned women are like that": "Either they don't go off at all, as if they were dead in there [...] or else they wait till a chap's really done, and then they start in to bring themselves off, and a chap's got to hang on." Then, with Mellors's familiar lament: "I never had a woman yet who went off just at the same moment as I did."

Connie naturally again complains about wanting her "satisfaction," referring to Michaelis's "incomprehensible brutality," with Lawrence possibly intending to suggest a significant distinction between the cruel Michaelis and her future lover, the sensitive, nurturing Mellors. Nor is it a surprise that her "whole sexual feeling for [Michaelis], or for any man, collapsed that night. Her life fell apart from his as completely as if he had never existed" (64). Connie's repulsion here thus sets the stage for the sudden appearance of what is nominally a different sort of lover, the gamekeeper Mellors—a character, oddly enough, who, in between his mean-spirited, misogynist rants, will somehow prove to be the ideal lover of Connie's dream. Here we can see Lawrence's conundrum regarding Mellors, however—that he seems to possess two distinct personalities reflecting opposing attitudes toward women: the Mellors whom Connie will painstakingly depict as her grand and tender lover, and the reluctant lover, the Mellors whose views on women were hardly less callous than Michaelis's!

One path out of this conundrum might rely on literary analysis to suggest how Michaelis's crudity foreshadows Mellors's and possibly how both reflect a kind of male crassness that Connie will eventually subdue, transforming Mellors into something better, into a nurturing male lover, and so forth. The ever-inventive literary critic capable of taming many a textual hydra will hardly be dissuaded by this Janus-like Mellors.

The solution offered below is more in the spirit of Occam's razor, based on the notion that Mellors is less a unified fictional character than a vehicle for Lawrence to explore two distinct, almost opposing roles: one as his stand-in, a role in which Mellors freely and loudly expresses a host of Lawrence's familiar grievances against women and modern life generally; and a second role as the novel's romantic ideal, at least in those acts of lovemaking in which Lawrence focuses principally on Lady Chatterley's feelings. It is to a deeper look at these two contradictory Mellors— Lawrence's garrulous stand-in and Connie's ever-silent lover—that we now turn.

The Two Mellors

The collapse in Mellors's dual roles—as Lawrence's stand-in and Connie's romantic ideal—is already apparent at the start of their first romantic encounter. There, from the start, we first see Mellors mainly through Connie's eyes, as a strong but gentle lover, one whose hand "softly, gently […] began to travel down the curve of her back […] [there] softly, softly, strok[ing] the curve of her flank, in the blind instinctive caress" (136). Thus, it is Mellors who, "in a quiet, neutral voice," invites her in:

> And closing his hand softly on her upper arm, he drew her up and led her slowly to the hut, letting go of her till she was inside. Then he cleared aside the chair and table, and took a brown soldier's blanket from the tool-chest, spreading it slowly.

Again, Mellors speaks softly, instructing Connie to lie down, and already, the psychological core of their relationship is laid bare. "With a queer obedience, she lay down on the blanket," Lawrence tells us, subtly switching focus: it is primarily her inner life that matters, her role as the supplicant:

> Then she felt the soft, groping, helplessly desirous hand touching her body, feeling for her face. The hand stroked her face softly, softly, with infinite soothing and assurance, and at last there was the soft touch of a kiss on her cheek.
>
> (137)

Yes, Mellors is depicted here as the gentle provider, with the point of view now shifted, if only momentarily: "She lay quite still, in a sort of sleep, in a sort of dream. Then she quivered as she felt his hand groping softly, yet with queer thwarted clumsiness among her clothing."

The point of view may momentarily seem unclear, with his actions mentioned without clarification as to whose pleasure is at stake—the man's in the active role of undressing the woman, anticipating what is to come, or Connie's, in the passive role of being undressed: "Yet the hand knew, too, how to unclothe her where it wanted. He drew down the thin silk sheath, slowly, carefully, right down and over her feet."

This same ambiguity continues with the account of their first kiss: "Then with a quiver of exquisite pleasure he touched the warm soft body, and touched her navel for a moment in a kiss." With the following sentence— the account of the moment of penetration—the focus finally seems clear: on the man's pleasure in "enter[ing] the peace on earth of her soft, quiescent body. It was the moment of pure peace for him, the entry into the body of a woman."

This perspective, however, lasts only a single sentence, at which point Lawrence again shifts to the woman's pleasure and her emotional life: "She lay still, in a kind of sleep, always in a kind of sleep." Yes, the "orgasm was his, all his," but with none of the rancor toward women that Michaelis and Mellors had previously demonstrated regarding their partners' lack of coordination. Nor do we see the disappointment Connie experienced with Michaelis when he finished first. Instead, we are told, "she could strive for herself no more":

> Even the tightness of his arms round her, even the intense movement of his body, and the springing of his seed in her, was a kind of sleep, from which she did not begin to rouse till he had finished and lay softly panting against her breast.

It is easy to argue that Lawrence has written a novel from a woman's point of view, so it makes sense for him to dwell on Lady Chatterley's response, particularly her confusion and delight over what it is like finally to have an actual male as a lover. "The man lay in a mysterious stillness," Lawrence tells us, and again, we see Lady Chatterley's erotic puzzlement: "What was he feeling? What was he thinking? She did not know" (137–38)—although, as is made clear in his rant, the only female lover Mellors sanctions is the one who, as Connie has surely failed to do this first time, would ensure that she has her orgasm simultaneously with his.

What is apparent here and will be amplified repeatedly in their subsequent meetings is Lawrence's focus not on Connie's fitness as Mellors's lover but the opposite, Mellors's fitness for Connie; indeed, less his fitness than his near perfection—a pattern already established in this first interaction.

"He was a strange man to her," Connie continues to muse; "she did not know him. She must only wait, for she did not dare to break his mysterious stillness." This "mysterious stillness" seems like an odd way to refer to a man who has seemingly just ended this bout of lovemaking as abruptly as Michaelis had previously ended his—only now, without a whisper of complaint from Connie. Here we see something almost magical happening—Mellors, the voluble ranter, being transformed into the very model of quiescence—someone now described through Connie's eyes as lying there "with his arms round her, his body on hers, his wet body touching hers, so close. And completely unknown. Yet not unpeaceful. His very silence was peaceful."

Here again we see the apparent contradiction of our two Mellors: one, a voluble misogynist with only limited interest in making love to a woman, who, as we shall see in some detail below, will not once in their 11 separate acts of lovemaking memorialize Connie as the ultimate object of his desire; and a second Mellors, this man lauded here, nominally by Connie, as a near-perfect lover, a man of "mysterious stillness" whose very "silence was peaceful." We say "nominally" in this context for the one reason suggested in our first chapter: that while this first Mellors, as we will repeatedly see below, speaks gruffly in prose, it is only as "Connie," the person being loved by this other Mellors, that Lawrence finds his lyrical, "winter" voice.

It is this other Mellors whom we see again in their second encounter, presented almost entirely through Connie's feelings, an episode that starts with Mellors gently "put[ting] the blankets down carefully, one folded for her head," then "[drawing] her to him, holding her close with one arm, feeling for her body with his free hand." Meanwhile, Connie "heard the catch of his intaken breath as he found her" (148).

"Eh! what it is to touch thee!" Mellors exclaims in dialect, with Lawrence briefly focusing on the man's actions. It is his finger that "caressed the delicate, warm secret skin of her waist and hips"; he is the one who "put his face down and rubbed his cheek against her belly and against her thighs, again and again." Yet Lawrence tells us nothing about how these actions may have felt to Mellors or any indication as to the pleasure any male initiator might experience from such intimacies. Instead, Lawrence's focus remains entirely on the other party, that of the passive recipient, as "the glide of his cheek on her thighs and belly and buttocks, and the close brushing of his moustache and his soft thick hair"—with the result, "her knees began to quiver"; or, as a means of suggesting that this new narrative voice, one so enamored of Mellors, is not as clear-cut and definitive as it appears, with the result, "*my* knees began to quiver."

Likewise, the following sentence—"Far down in her she felt a new stirring, a new nakedness emerging"—can be readily transformed to capture this new narrative perspective: "Far down in *me* I felt a new stirring, a new nakedness emerging." For what purpose, one might ask, when Lawrence clearly intended these to be Connie's thoughts? Only to suggest, without changing Connie's gender here, Lawrence's active presence in this scene as well—or, more accurately, in the spirit of our title, his *hidden* presence, a presence palpable in the conclusion of this marvelous paragraph: "And she was half afraid" becoming "And *I* was half afraid," with the rest rewritten as well: "Half *I* wished he would not caress *me* so. He was encompassing *me* somehow. Yet *I* was waiting, waiting."

The puzzlement of the two Mellors can be partially resolved here by seeing how he has been subtly transformed, from the petulant, dissatisfied lover of women to Connie's near-perfect lover, with Lawrence essentially changing places in the narrative as well. Our first Mellors is best seen as a stand-in for one side of Lawrence, namely, the historical or *public* Lawrence, the person who, in his real life and via his fictional stand-ins like Mellors, proved to be a reluctant lover, someone who rarely refrained from expounding on the incompatibility of the sexes and especially the difficulties men face in living with women. Our second Mellors, meanwhile, is essentially a creation of Connie's imagination or, as we shall see, her erotic trigger, someone we see only through her eyes or, stated differently, someone who is the creation of a substantially different or *private* Lawrence, one who has quietly taken up residence, as it were, in the voice and feelings of his new implicit narrator—this other Lawrence whom we identify here for the first time as the *hidden* Lawrence of our title.

Hence, the reason for suggesting the tenuous nature of the gendered pronouns Lawrence uses when referring to Connie's feelings—to alert us to Lawrence's presence in these scenes, to the possibility that the voice speaking to us in their first two love scenes is Lawrence's as much as Connie's. More important still will be the recognition, developed below, that Lawrence's hiding has less to do with the speaker's gender—his hiding as a woman—than with the gender of the person the speaker desires. Hence, the core thesis of this work—that Connie Chatterley is the first of a series of stand-ins for the *hidden* Lawrence we will be considering, all sharing the common fate of being drawn to the power of a strong, aloof, often menacing male presence.

It is their third act of lovemaking, however, and the first of the three extended lovemaking scenes in the novel, where Lawrence's focus shifts almost entirely to Connie's point of view, or, worded differently, to that of the bedazzled recipient of an active male lover. Once again, we see Mellors gently preparing the scene, leading Connie "through the wall of prickly trees": "He threw one or two dry [boughs] down, put his coat and waistcoat over them [...] [H]e was provident—he made her lie properly, properly," but inadvertently "broke the band of her underclothes," before "he too had bared the front part of his body." It is only after this brief introduction that the focus of Lawrence's narration permanently shifts so that what we witness is less a couple making love than the transformation experienced by this male lover's partner—with Connie now feeling "his naked flesh against her as he came into her" (157).

It is here that we finally see Lawrence's full lyrical description of lovemaking: "For a moment he was still, inside her, turgid there and quivering"; or, again, more radically, from the perspective of the *hidden* lover: "For a moment he was still inside *me*, turgid there and quivering."

Then as he began to move in the sudden helpless orgasm, there awoke in her new strange thrills rippling inside her, rippling, rippling, like a flapping overlapping of soft flames, soft as feathers, running to points of brilliance, exquisite, exquisite and melting her all molten inside. It was like bells, rippling up and up to a culmination.

(158)

When it was over, we are told that Connie, our new narrative voice or, as we will suggest here, Lawrence in *hiding*, "lay unconscious of the wild little cries she uttered at the last," except that, in what would be such an essential matter for Mellors in his rant, as presumably it was for Lawrence, Connie had not finished—alas, for her, "it was over too soon, too soon," even as she could not "force her own conclusion with her own activity."

Here, for the first time, we can see in Connie the emergence of a new sort of lover, the receptive sexual partner entirely attentive to the needs of her active male lover, someone prepared to act entirely differently than the women Mellors ranted against when she could "no longer harden and grip for her own satisfaction upon him." Now, alas, she "could only wait, wait, and moan in spirit as she felt him withdrawing, withdrawing and contracting, coming to the terrible moment when he would slip out of her and be gone"—or, in the first person, "slip out of *me* and be gone."

Yet, instead of Mellors's fierce recriminations or even those of Connie's response to Michaelis, Lawrence now gives us this wondrous account of the penetrated partner's post-coital bliss—all "open and soft and softly clamouring like a sea-anemone under the tides, clamouring for him to come in again and make a fulfillment for her"; altogether expressing a level of sexual satisfaction eons removed from what Mellors, as a stand-in for the public Lawrence, will experience anywhere in the novel playing the traditional role of the penetrative male:

> She clung to him unconscious in passion, and he never quite slipped from her, and she felt the soft bud of him within her stirring, and in strange rhythms flushing up into her, with a strange, rhythmic growing motion, swelling and swelling till it filled all her cleaving consciousness. And then began again the unspeakable motion that was not really motion, but pure deepening whirlpools of sensation, swirling deeper and deeper through all her tissue and consciousness, till she was one perfect concentric fluid of feeling.

Then, Lawrence's summation—our speaker, nominally Connie Chatterley, "lay[ing] there crying in unconscious inarticulate cries" (158).

While this moment of bliss—what Lawrence calls "the voice out of the uttermost night, the life!"—is solely the woman's, Lawrence does note

Mellors's amazement here in listening to the sounds "beneath him with a kind of awe, as his life sprang out into her." However, there is little doubt regarding Lawrence's focus in this post-tumescence moment, with Mellors described as "lay[ing] utterly still, unknowing, while her grip on him slowly relaxed, and she lay inert." Then, the ending—as the two of them "lay and knew nothing, not even of each other, both lost."

It is difficult to overstate just how much the tone changes and how much the writing deepens with the shift in point of view from the ever-reluctant Mellors, a stand-in for the public Lawrence, to the *hidden* voice of the beloved. For instance, right after their third bout of lovemaking, Lawrence focuses on Connie as she slowly returns home, "realising the depth of the other thing in her." And, again, the language has that lyrical, "winter" edge:

> Another self was alive in her, burning molten and soft and sensitive in her womb and bowels, and with this self, she adored him. She adored him till her knees were weak as she walked. In her womb and bowels she was flowing and alive now, and vulnerable, and helpless in adoration of him as the most naïve woman.
>
> (160)

Yes, we must recognize the extent to which Connie's concerns seem to be solely those of a woman, as, for instance, with her reference to "feel[ing] like a child in me": "And so it did, as if her womb, that had always been shut, had opened and filled with new life, almost a burden, yet lovely."

But our speaker's concerns here can also be seen more generically as those of someone newly in love, surprised to recognize the depth of her (or his) submissive nature. How even the gender-specific line quoted above about the feelings "in her womb and bowels" can be easily altered to refer to anyone's growing slowly comfortable in seeing oneself as the beloved recipient of a virile partner—that is, "flowing and alive now and vulnerable, and helpless in adoration of him as the most naïve *lover.*"

Nor do matters change in the rest of this passage, even with the gender-specific reference to "womb"—as Lawrence leaves us with thoughts about how anyone might be rendered dumbstruck with fear confronting a never-imagined depth of feeling: "It was not the passion that was new to her. It was the yearning adoration." What this person was experiencing was the very thing she (or could it be Lawrence?) "had always feared": "For it left her helpless; she feared it still, lest if she adored him too much, then she would lose herself, become effaced, and she did not want to be effaced"—did not want to be "a slave [...] must not become a slave."

What our speaker seemed most to fear was the depth of her "adoration":

> Yet she would not at once fight against it. She knew she could fight it. She had a devil of self-will in her breast that could have fought the full, soft, heavy adoration of her womb and crushed it. She could even now do it, or she thought so, and she could then take up her passion with her own will.

Next, we are given more "winter" thoughts, this time in praise of the male phallus, again, albeit with the recognition that not all phallic idolaters are women:

> To call on Iacchos, the bright phallos that had no independent personality behind it, but was pure god-servant to the woman! The man, the individual, let him not dare intrude. He was but a temple-servant, the bearer and keeper of the bright phallus, her own.
>
> (161)

The speaker here is admittedly marked by Lawrence as female—the Bacchae, after all, tearing down the male, the "mere phallos-bearer." However, such destruction, "known and barren, birthless," is not the outcome the speaker wants. What this speaker wants, her "treasure," is finally not gender specific; it is instead to delight in a level of "adoration" that is equally open to a man or a woman—one that is "so fathomless, so soft, so deep, so unknown."

And the key to this adoration? An eagerness to submit that even surprises our speaker—something that, despite the earlier reference to "womb," is less a matter of gender than the acceptance of a new, less rigid sense of personal autonomy, specifically, a willingness to surrender one's "hard bright [...] [individual] power." Here is a speaker who seems eager to have her distinct sense of personhood inundated by the power of a new male lover, a speaker ready to "sink in the new bath of life, in the depths of [...] her bowels that sang the voiceless song of adoration."

A Tale of Two Bodies

There is always the possibility that the lyrical writing we find in this third act of lovemaking results from Lawrence's adopting a woman's point of view. After all, *Lady Chatterley's Lover* is a novel about a woman's intense affair with the gamekeeper on her husband's estate. Yet, as we shall soon show, what triggers Lawrence's lyricism has less to do with the speaker's gender than the gender of the person being observed, indeed, as we will suggest, often observed as an object.

One place to begin is with Lawrence's rendering of Connie's thoughts earlier in the novel, as she undressed and "looked at herself naked in the huge mirror." Nor should one be surprised at the deflated language that Lawrence uses in showing us Connie examining such an imperfect object: "And she thought, as she had thought so often, [...] what a frail, easily hurt, rather pathetic thing a human body is, naked; somehow a little unfinished, incomplete" (80)!

Her matter-of-fact examination continues:

She had been supposed to have a rather good figure, but now she was out of fashion: a little too female, not enough like an adolescent boy. She was not very tall, a bit Scottish and short [...] Her skin was faintly tawny, her limbs had a certain stillness, her body should have had a full, down-slipping richness; but it lacked something.

Where previously we had Connie's praise for her male lover, we now get only her self-condemnation: "Instead of ripening its firm, down-running curves, her body was flattening and going a little harsh. It was as if it had not had enough sun and warmth; it was a little greyish and sapless." Her focus then shifts to her unpleasant breasts—"rather small, and dropping pear-shaped [...] unripe, a little bitter, without meaning hanging there. And her belly had lost the fresh, round gleam it had had when she was young" (80–81). Connie, like Lawrence's wife, Frieda—a large, 33-year-old woman with three children when he first met her—also once had a German lover.

Indeed, what Lawrence shows us in Connie's self-examination seems less like the 27-year-old heroine of his novel than someone far closer to what Lawrence might have seen in Frieda, who was 47 at the time of the novel's composition. Thus, we are given a woman who sees herself as "going slack, and a little flat, thinner—but with a slack thinness." Her thighs, which once were "so quick and glimpse in their female roundness," were no better, indeed, with her whole body seemingly "going meaningless, going full and opaque, so much insignificant substance."

Only her backside—with its "long-sloping fall of the haunches from the socket of the back, and the slumberous round stillness of the buttocks"—held out any hope, this one moment eliciting a rare lyrical simile: "Like hillocks of sand the Arabs say, soft and downward-slipping with a long slope. Here the life still lingered, hoping." Still, the passage ends with the harsh self-assessment that she was "going unripe, astringent" and the conclusion that "the front of her body made her miserable" (81–82).

Certainly, one can make the case for psychological realism here, noting how Lawrence is merely describing how unhappy even an attractive young woman might feel when examining herself in a mirror. The best response to such a claim would be to note how quickly and thoroughly matters change, with Lawrence's writing again becoming intensely lyrical in the scene we will examine next—one where he shows us Connie examining a different body, not that of a relatively young woman but one belonging, oddly enough, to a middle-aged man.

Just one chapter earlier, Lawrence depicts Connie out for a walk, drawn toward Mellors's cabin. When no one answers her knock, she walks to the rear, where "[i]n the little yard two paces beyond her," she saw "the man [...] washing himself, utterly unaware":

> He was naked to the hips, his velveteen breeches slipping down over his slender loins. And his white, slender back was curved over a big bowl of soapy water, in which he ducked his head, shaking his head with a queer, quick little motion, lifting his slender white arms and pressing the soapy water from his ears: quick, subtle as a weasel playing with water, and utterly alone.
>
> (76)

Connie turns away, puzzled by her reaction: "In spite of herself, she had had a shock. After all, merely a man washing himself; commonplace enough, Heaven knows!"

A man bathing—commonplace, for sure, unless it is not, as is the case here and, as we will see in Chapter 8, in an extended description from the short story "The Daughters of the Vicar." Meanwhile, we learn how, for Connie, this bathing scene was "in some curious way [...] a visionary experience[, one that] hit her in the middle of her body." Lawrence's further account of her thoughts has the elan of Brontë's winter reverie:

> She saw the clumsy breeches slipping away over the pure, delicate, white loins, the bones showing a little, and the sense of aloneness, of a creature purely alone, overwhelmed her. Perfect, white solitary nudity of a creature that lives alone, and inwardly alone. And beyond that, a certain beauty of a pure creature. Not the stuff of beauty, not even the body of beauty, but a certain lambency, the warm, white flame of a single life, revealing itself in contours that one might touch: a body!
>
> (76–77)

Here, Lawrence seems caught between two needs. On the one hand, there is his obvious delight in the reverie itself, in what appears to be the unalloyed scopophilic pleasure we will repeatedly see in Lawrence (especially in Chapter 5)—scopophilia being the erotic pleasure one experiences from gazing at a pleasing object, often in secret, although in popular culture more often thought of as the delight that men receive in looking at women on display in paintings and films. Here, at least on the surface, things seem to be reversed, with the intense gaze nominally of a female, although one unquestionably directed toward a male's half-naked, lathered torso.

On the other hand, there were the psychological demands of Lawrence's narrative—specifically, how long he could let such a reverie continue. Indeed, given the needs of his story, Lawrence has no reason to allow his 27-year-old woman to be thrown so topsy-turvy merely by watching a middle-aged man bathe. "Oh, come on!" Lady Chatterley seems to be telling herself, "Get a grip!"—although in Lawrence's language:

> Connie had received the shock of vision in her womb, and she knew it. It lay inside her. But with her mind, she was inclined to ridicule. A man washing himself in a back yard! No doubt with evil-smelling yellow soap!—She was rather annoyed; why should she be made to stumble on these vulgar privacies?
>
> (77)

Lawrence's difficulties—caught between a kind of scopophilic fascination with this reverie and the needs of his story—are even more pronounced in the earlier draft of his novel *John Thomas and Lady Jane*, only published in 1972. There, it is Parkin, the earlier iteration of Mellors, who is "washing himself to go out on his Saturday evening," and with the emotional connection to Lawrence's youth as the son of a coal miner underscored:

> He had stripped to the waist, as the colliers do. His velveteen breeches sagged low on his hips. And he was ducking his head repeatedly into the warm, steamy, soapy water, rubbing his hands over his brown hair and over the reddened back of his neck, while the water ran from his face and over his close-shut eyes.
>
> (*The First* 263)

In this earlier version, Constance starts to flee this scene, then stops as she tries to understand her shock. What follows is a scene that Lawrence, at least in this second of three drafts of his novel, cannot resist expanding into an extended scopophilic reverie of pure delight. Someone—Lady Chatterley or Lawrence—is clearly in love with this particular vision of the male form: this "white torso of the man had seemed so beautiful to her, opening on the gloom":

> The white, firm, divine body, with its silky ripple, the white arch of life, as it bent forward over the water, seemed, she could not help it, of

the world of gods. There still was a world that gleamed pure and with power, where the silky firm skin of the man's body glistened broad upon the dull afternoon. Never mind who he was! Never mind what he was! She had seen beauty, and beauty alive. That body was of the world of the gods, cleaving through the gloom like a revelation. And she felt again there was God on earth; or gods.

Nor can there be doubt why Lawrence had to excise this passage in his revision, curtailing the excess delight triggered by his imagination.

A great soothing came over her heart, along with the feeling of worship. The sudden sense of pure beauty, beauty that was active and alive, had put worship in her heart again. Not that she worshipped the man, nor his body. But worship had come into her, because she had seen a pure loveliness, that was alive, and that had touched the quick in her. It was as if she had touched God, and been restored to life. The broad, gleaming whiteness!

(263)

It should be clear that, at least in this early draft, Lawrence is going far beyond the psychological needs of his novel, doing so, one surmises, less to help us understand his heroine than for the sheer erotic joy it brought him as the author.

This passage should also clarify an even more compelling point: that the brilliance of Lawrence's writing in revealing Connie's fascination with Mellors here and elsewhere, such as in their third interaction we have already reviewed, is far less the result of who is the implicit speaker—in this case, Lawrence's female protagonist—than what is the object being described, in this case, a beautiful, partially clothed man.

Just as Charlotte Brontë could not help describing winter when it was already spring, here Lawrence's literary imagination seems to have gotten the better of him, coupled as it was for Brontë, with deeply embedded erotic feelings—here, for a gamekeeper, "a common man," with his whiteness an obvious erotic trigger:

That did not matter. He did not own his own body. His body was among the beautiful gods. She thought of it, as it arched over in an arch of aliveness and power, rippling then with movements of life, from the fallen sheath of those dead breeches, and her whole life paused and changed. How beautiful. How beautiful! And with what power of pure white, rippling, rapid life!

As in the published version of *Lady Chatterley's Lover*, Lawrence eventually tries to tie all this adoration back to the needs of his fictional character by noting how Connie herself was dumbfounded at her over-the-top response—how she was so "very angry with herself!" "A mere gamekeeper!" Lawrence has her say. "Didn't he always have a body! If it had really been anything wonderful, of course she would have sensed it through his clothes," and this had never happened: "So that obviously it was all the effect of her disordered imagination" (264).

Yet even here, Lawrence cannot overcome what seems to be his aroused feeling for an alabaster male: "But it seemed to her wrong," he adds, "that, being a commonplace individual, he should have that pure body, that arch of white, living power."

Lawrence wrote this eroticized description of the Mellors bathing in 1927 in the second draft of his last novel. Nearly 20 years earlier, in his first novel, *The White Peacock*, we find a similar scene—as another surprised observer, Lawrence's stand-in, Cyril Beardsall, finds himself, like Connie, intruding on yet another outdoorsman, his friend, George Saxton, a character based on Jessie Chambers's older brother, Alan. Although George is nominally courting Cyril's sister Lettie, his outstanding characteristic, from his initial entry, is the impact that his rugged bearing—"a young farmer, stoutly built, brown eyed, with a naturally fair skin burned dark and freckled in patches"—has on Lawrence's effeminate stand-in, Cyril.

Early in the novel, an activity as innocent as George's reading a book readily distracts Cyril—or, as Lawrence writes, how "very annoying" it was for Cyril

watch[ing] him pulling his brown moustache, and reading indolently while the dog rubbed against his leggings and against the knee of his old riding-breeches. [...] Round and round twirled his thick fingers, and the muscles of his bare arm moved slightly under the red-brown skin.

(3)

Later, Lawrence has his first chance to show his outdoorsman in a state of partial undress akin to Mellors'. Here, we see him entering the parlor "straight from washing in the scullery" and standing behind his sister playing the piano—"unconcernedly wiping the moisture from his arms." "His sleeves were rolled up to the shoulder," Lawrence continues, "and his shirt was opened wide at the breast." What follows is Lawrence using the same device in his first novel that he uses again in his last and, as we shall see, in many other works in between—that is, expressing his sexual attraction through the eyes of his female protagonist. So it is Lettie here, and not Cyril, who "was somewhat taken aback by the sight of him standing with legs apart, dressed in dirty leggings and boots, and breeches torn at the knee, naked at the breast and arms" (14).

An even stronger connection with Mellors's bathing scene occurs later in *The White Peacock*, in the much-praised chapter "A Poem of Friendship," when Lawrence finally brings his two friends together for an impromptu summer swim. Here, Cyril describes the robust George as "floating just beside me, looking up and laughing, *and his white breasts and his belly emerged like cool buds on a firm fleshed water flower*" (with the italicized words here and below from Lawrence's draft, eventually deleted in the toned-down published version):

> We stood and looked at each other as we rubbed ourselves dry. He was well proportioned, and naturally of handsome physique, heavily limbed, *and supplied with muscle, unlike me, whom Nature seems determined to reduce to a physical minimum—save in height, for I am taller than he; so that he says I am like Aubrey Beardsley's long, slim, and—he says—ugly drawings.*
> "Nevertheless," *I say, "I can show my body muscles better than you"—whereupon I put my rib muscles into prominence, and we laugh at one another.*
>
> (222, 386)

Then, even stronger echoes of Lady Chatterley, although this time from a male point of view but, as with Connie, still with the focus on a beloved male object:

> But I had to give in, and bow to him, and he took on an indulgent, gentle manner. I laughed and submitted. For he knew how I admired the noble, white fruitfulness of his form. As I watched him, standing up like a white cameo against the mass of green. He polished his arm, holding it out straight and solid; he rubbed his hair into curls, while I watched the deep muscles of his shoulders, and the bands stand out in his neck as he held it firm; I remembered the story of Annable.
>
> (222)

Annable, Lawrence's first gamekeeper, whom we have briefly met, was a man whose wealthy wife, as noted, "wouldn't let [him] out of her sight" (150).

Meanwhile, it is uncanny how Cyril's reveries, which Lawrence began composing when he was just 20, continue to mirror Connie's, written some 20 years later:

> He saw *me watching him, in my admiration forgetting* to continue my rubbing, and laughing he took hold of me and began to rub me briskly, as if I were a child, or rather, a woman he loved and did not fear. I left

myself quite limply in his hands, and, to get a better grip of me, he put his arm round me and pressed me against him, and the sweetness of the touch of our naked bodies one against the other was superb. It satisfied in some measure the vague, indecipherable yearning of my soul; and it was the same with him. When he had rubbed me all warm, he let me go, and we looked at each other with eyes of still laughter, and love was perfect for a moment, more perfect than any love I have known since, either for man or woman.

(222–23)

Although there are widely recognized homoerotic strains throughout Lawrence's writings, the most noted examined in Chapter 6, it is questionable whether he ever wrote anything as openly confessional as this scene from *The White Peacock*, not even the wrestling scene in *Women in Love* prominently featured in Ken Russell's 1969 film—an attitude Lawrence sums up in the concluding reference to his having known then a love "more perfect than any love I have known since."

Some ten years after the appearance of *The White Peacock*, a friend of Lawrence's would remember his saying that "the nearest he had ever come to 'perfect love' [...] was with a young coal miner when he was about sixteen" (Kinkead-Weekes 551)—the miner reference, likely the result of the friend's misremembering, as everything else in Lawrence's life and writings, points to the importance of his idyllic moments in the fields with Alan Chambers.

For our purposes, what matters most is the broad continuity within Lawrence's writings—one might call it something akin to Henry James's "figure in the carpet." Nor is such continuity surprising, given the inherent stability in a person's erotic life—an observation in line with what Lawrence had to say after rereading his first novel 15 years after its completion. Though the novel seemed "strange and far off and as if written by somebody else," he noted, there was still the recognition that "I'd come across something that showed I may have changed in style or form, but I haven't changed fundamentally" (Nehls 414).

Nor is there any reason to be surprised at the underlying similarity in the erotic lives of these two otherwise opposite protagonists from either end of Lawrence's life: Cyril Beardsall, Lawrence's effeminate alter ego in his first novel, and Constance Chatterley, the wealthy mistress of Wragby Hall, in Lawrence's last novel—opposites in so many ways, yet each sharing the similar fate of being besotted by an alabaster outdoorsman.

Our broader contention here has two parts. First, in noting how many of the most poignant moments in Lawrence—his "winter" moments—are the product of hidden or repressed feelings, perhaps seen most clearly or, in a sense more fitting with Lawrence's temperament, most tenderly, in his various accounts of his relationship with Jessie Chambers's older brother, Alan. Second (and the subject of Chapter 7, "Hiding in Plain Sight"), in noting how Lawrence often seems more comfortable expressing such feelings—as he does with Lady Chatterley's adoration of her gamekeeper and not as he did in his first novel—through his female characters.

Indeed, Lawrence having his alter ego Cyril aroused while swimming with his alabaster friend—the high point of this splendid chapter, "The Poem of Friendship"—was immediately seen by several early readers of *The White Peacock*, including the closeted gay novelist E. M. Forster, who called this one chapter "most beautiful," as a rare and open expression of homoerotic desire (Kinkead-Weekes 803), even while panning the rest of the novel. Likewise, Lawrence's having another character aroused by an outdoorsman in *Lady Chatterley's Lover* can be seen as the expression of the same homoerotic desire, at least if these two novels—Lawrence's first and his last—can be seen as products of a single historical person, a single libido.

What is at stake here is an expansion of Frieda Lawrence's observation that "the terrible thing" about this novel is that Lawrence identified himself with both Mellors and Clifford—that is, with both the virile lover and the impotent husband. "That took courage," Frieda continued, "that made me shiver, when I read it as he wrote it" (Ellis, *Dying* 675)—with Frieda, as she mentioned elsewhere, seeing herself as Lady Chatterley. Yes, as already noted, Lawrence used Mellors as a vehicle for voicing many of his grievances, and yes, as Frieda suggests, given his impotence brought on by his advanced tuberculosis, he likely also identified with Clifford Chatterley, the disabled mine owner. What we are proposing here—and what Frieda either could not see or, for her own reasons, ignored—is how Lawrence also identified even more closely with Lady Chatterley, an insight grasped by Linda Ruth Williams when she wrote how gender differences "can easily be elided" in Lawrence, with "a woman's gaze act[ing] as the channel of homoerotic desire" (122).

At the most basic level, our conclusion here is quite radical: namely, that we experience the most intense acts of lovemaking in Lawrence's last novel from Connie Chatterley's point of view, less because Lawrence wanted to write a novel about a woman's desire than because, consciously or not, he wanted to write one about his own; because, late in his short life, he wanted to describe the highest form of sensual pleasure he could imagine, including graphic accounts of the experience of being penetrated by a potent male lover—even though, it must be underscored, there is no biographical evidence to suggest that such an experience was for Lawrence anything but imaginary. More succinctly stated, it is in Mellors that we see the *public* Lawrence, the man who rants against women as lovers, but in Connie that we see the *hidden* Lawrence, the writer and the man who could only experience the rapturous feeling of love for, or, more accurately, from, another man in the recesses of his literary imagination.

This repeated switching back and forth between these two roles—between Mellors as Connie's ever-reluctant lover and Mellors as the rapturous object of Connie's desire—is played out in all the novel's lovemaking scenes, with their fourth and fifth interactions occurring immediately after Mellors' misogynistic rant. It is to these two scenes that we now turn.

The Two Mellors, Continued

As with their previous interactions, their fourth act of lovemaking (chapter 12) begins by focusing briefly on the solicitous actions of the stronger partner, here his "spread[ing] the blankets, putting one at the side for a coverlet": "Lie down then!" he tells Connie, while she "obeyed in silence." He then kisses her breasts "softly, taking the nipples in his lips in tiny caresses"—speaking here in dialect: " 'Eh, but tha'rt nice, tha'rt nice!' [...] suddenly rubbing his face with a snuggling movement against her warm belly" (205).

As we might expect, Connie's response is far more fulsome: "And she put her arms round him under his shirt, but she was afraid, afraid of his thin, smooth, naked body, that seemed so powerful, afraid of the violent muscles. She shrank, afraid." Then, as if a brake had been thrown, something inside Connie "quivered, and something in her spirit stiffened in resistance: stiffened from the terribly physical intimacy, and from the peculiar haste of his possession." Instead of showing us Connie as the adorer of this beautiful man, Lawrence, at least momentarily, has her assume an entirely different role, one we saw briefly in her response to Michaelis—that of the debunker of men as ridiculous lovers. "[T]he butting of his haunches seemed ridiculous to her, and the sort of anxiety of his penis to come to its little evacuating crisis seemed farcical" (171–72). What was the point of all this, Connie asks—"this ridiculous bouncing of the buttocks, and the wilting of the poor insignificant, moist little penis. This was the divine love!"

Here, for reasons that are not at all clear, Lawrence casts Connie as the mocker of sexual intercourse, the role previously played by Mellors, only now directed entirely against men, and specifically on how pitiful a man appears during lovemaking. "[T]he God who created man must have had a sinister sense of humour, creating him a reasonable being, yet forcing him to take this ridiculous posture and driving him with blind craving for this humiliating performance." And then, in a less satirical addendum, capturing what we will repeatedly see elsewhere in this study, Lawrence's persistent misgivings about the value of heterosexual lovemaking generally—the observation that "[m]en despised the intercourse act, and yet did it"—something seemingly out of place in a section ostensibly recording the thoughts of his female protagonist.

What an odd, misshapen novel Lawrence has written! One that has Connie praising Mellors as the paragon of male beauty as he is washing in Chapter 6 and then, here in Chapter 12, now wanting only to "escape his ugly grip, and the butting over-riding of his absurd haunches"! The beautiful body from a few chapters back, now reduced to "a foolish, impudent, imperfect thing, a little disgusting in its unfinished clumsiness" (206).

Of course, one could claim that something has changed inside Connie, possibly because of something Mellors has done, or that Lawrence intends to show us Connie's fickle nature. Still, how odd it must seem that Connie's critique of intercourse here should sound so similar to what we have already heard from Mellors or even from Michaelis or, for that matter, what we will again see from Mellors in the following two chapters! Nor does there seem to be a compelling reason to have Connie join in this critique now other than the sense that such grievances never seemed far from Lawrence himself.

Nor is it surprising that their attempt at lovemaking following these reflections goes terribly awry, with the added observation, also presumably from Connie's point of view, that "surely a complete evolution would eliminate this performance, this 'function,'" that is, would eliminate intercourse altogether—or a rewording of the very sentiment in praise of chastity with which Lawrence will end this novel, although there, at least, more appropriately uttered by Mellors.

Their actual lovemaking here ends almost as soon as it begins, only now with yet another change in Connie, who again becomes the impassioned lover lamenting the ache of her partner's withdrawal:

> And yet, when he had finished, soon over, and lay very, very still, receding into a silence, and a strange motionless distance, far, farther than the horizon of her awareness, her heart began to weep. She could feel him ebbing away, ebbing away, leaving her there like a stone on the shore. He was withdrawing, his spirit was leaving her.
>
> (206)

There is a change in Mellors as well, as he continues to speak in dialect, but now with a soft reassurance for his female partner, who again could not experience an orgasm:

> "Ay!" he said. "It was no good that time. You wasn't there" ... "It's once in a while that way." ... "Ta'e th' thick wi' th' thin. This wor a bit o' thin for once." ... Dunna fret thysen about luvin' me! Tha 'lt niver

force thysèn to 't. There's sure to be a bad nut in a basketful. Tha mun ta'e th' rough wi' t' smooth."

It is at this disappointing moment that Lawrence begins the transition to their fifth and altogether most rapturous act of lovemaking. Nor is it a surprise that it is presented almost entirely from Connie's point of view, focused on what it is like to be loved by a man or, more to the point, what it is like to submit totally to a man in the act of lovemaking. "He took her in his arms again," it begins, "and drew her to him, and suddenly she became small in his arms, small and nestling" (207). Or, if we allow Connie to address us directly: "He took *me* in his arms again and drew *me* to him, and suddenly *I* became small in his arms, small and nestling."

From the outset, what seems crucial for Lawrence is the erotic tension arising from this disparity in size and power—certainly what one might expect in the difference between a man and a woman. Still, something else is at stake here, closely tied less to the speaker's actual physical size than to the sharp psychological edge of losing one's sense of self in becoming an instrument for someone else's pleasure.

Thus, we are told, "It was gone, the resistance was gone, and she began to melt in marvellous peace":

And as she melted small and wonderful in his arms, she became infinitely desirable to him, all his blood-vessels seemed to scald with intense yet tender desire, for her, for her softness, for the penetrating beauty of her in his arms, passing into his blood.

This loss of boundary, moreover, becomes the core element of this particular, rapturous act of lovemaking—the possibility that our speaker seems to mark as a new form of touching, unlike any she has ever known before:

And softly, with that marvellous swoon-like caress of his hand in pure soft desire, softly he stroked the silky slope of her loins, down, down between her soft, warm buttocks, coming nearer and nearer to the very quick of her. And she felt him like a flame of desire, yet tender, and she felt herself melting in the flame. She let herself go.

One matter worth considering is the hyperbolic quality of the language here—lovemaking that seems to be described as something entirely new yet comes from a woman who has made love with multiple men already, including a handful of times already with this same man, Mellors. One explanation is that the purpose of the hyperbolic language is to enhance the value of this one act, to make it seem almost magical, far better than all those other times: "She felt his penis risen against her with silent amazing force and assertion, and she let herself go to him."

Yet there is another explanation here, and that is that we take Lawrence's language here literally, meaning that our speaker here, nominally Connie, in "yield[ing] with a quiver that was like death," was indeed experiencing something for the first time—specifically the taboo act of opening an otherwise hidden part of herself, exposing a deeply hidden vulnerability: "And oh, if he were not tender to her now, how cruel, for she was all open to him and helpless!"

Which reading—metaphorical or literal—is the proper one for this passage? A metaphorical reading does support the sense that these are Connie's thoughts, with Lawrence using heightened language to describe what his heroine found to be an especially riveting episode of the same sort of vaginal intercourse she had experienced many previous times—that Lawrence, in other words, is exaggerating here solely for effect.

A literal reading, on the other hand, suggests that the speaker here is truly experiencing something for the first time—in this case, what it might be like to open up an otherwise tightly closed part of one's body to that perfect male lover. With this literal reading, Lawrence's key term *tenderness* takes on a new meaning, perhaps closer to Lawrence's psyche and one that he could only hint at in the novel's last chapter: that is, *tenderness* both as the solicitous regard of the penetrating male partner in proceeding with care, and as the quiet, even grateful acceptance—the *tenderness*—of the penetrated partner, the one who "quivered again at the potent inexorable entry inside her, so strange and terrible."

> It might come with the thrust of a sword in her softly-opened body, and that would be death. She clung in a sudden anguish of terror. But it came with a strange slow thrust of peace, the dark thrust of peace and a ponderous, primordial tenderness, such as made the world in the beginning. And her terror subsided in her breast, her breast dared to be gone in peace, she held nothing.
>
> (208)

The speaker here, Lawrence tells us, "dared to let go everything, [...] and be gone in the flood."

Two possible readings—metaphorical or literal! What cannot be denied is the sweeping, lyrical power of Lawrence's prose here, describing not a man and woman making love but only half of that—what is it like to be made love to by a man or, even more precisely, what it is like to be the passive, receptive partner, to give oneself up entirely, in the act of love-making: "And it seemed she was like the sea, nothing but dark waves rising and heaving, heaving with a great swell, so that slowly her whole darkness was in motion, and she was ocean rolling its dark, dumb mass."

This brilliant passage continues, Lawrence's presence barely hidden by the third-person pronouns:

> Oh, and far down inside her the deeps parted and rolled asunder, in long, far-travelling billows, and ever, at the quick of her, the depths parted and rolled asunder, from the centre of soft plunging, as the plunger went deeper and deeper, touching lower, and she was deeper and deeper and deeper disclosed, and heavier the billows of her rolled away to some shore, uncovering her, and closer and closer plunged the palpable unknown, and further and further rolled the waves of herself away from herself, leaving her, till suddenly, in a soft, shuddering convulsion, the quick of all her plasm was touched, she knew herself touched, the consummation was upon her, and she was gone.

"She was gone, she was not, and she was born: a woman"—so ends this paragraph, but even this gender-specific passage can be readily transformed: "*I* was gone, *I* was not, and *I* was born: *myself.*"

This fifth act of lovemaking—"Ah, too lovely, too lovely!"—continues: "In the ebbing she realized all the loveliness. Now all her body clung with tender love to the unknown man, and blindly to the wilting penis, as it so tenderly, fraily, unknowingly withdrew, after the fierce thrust of its potency." And, "As it drew out"—that "secret, sensitive thing"—leaving the beloved's body, the speaker "gave an unconscious cry of pure loss, and she tried to put it back. It had been so perfect! And she loved it so!"

> And only now she became aware of the small, bud-like reticence and tenderness of the penis, and a little cry of wonder and poignancy escaped her again, her [...] heart crying out over the tender frailty of that which had been the power.
>
> "It was so lovely!" she moaned. "It was so lovely!" But he said nothing, only softly kissed her, lying still above her. And she moaned with a sort of bliss, as a sacrifice, and a new-born thing.

Before proceeding to the conclusion of this fifth act of lovemaking, this might be a fitting place to consider other issues involved with questioning the gender of Lawrence's narrative voice in this rapturous fifth act of lovemaking, why one might be tempted to read this last line above: "And *I* moaned with a sort of bliss, as a sacrifice, and a new-born thing."

Why imply ambiguity, in other words, about what Lawrence so clearly presents as heterosexual lovemaking, focusing as he does specifically on a woman's deep satisfaction in being penetrated by her male lover? One counter might be to note how odd it is that such a passionate account of love-making can be so readily opened up to such a radically alternative reading, not by altering Connie's gender but merely by allowing her to speak in the first person. Nor is there any reason to suppress the more significant issue here, the implication that what we are reading—and, at some level, what Lawrence must have imagined himself writing—is a celebration of gay sex.

While there is hardly anything groundbreaking in suggesting a distinct homoerotic strain in Lawrence's life and writing, much of the work on this topic has been confined to two different methodological approaches. One, led by biographers like David Ellis (*Love and Sex in D. H. Lawrence*), has sought to locate possible partners for actual homosexual interactions in Lawrence's life, with the most likely candidate being his Cornish neighbor from 1916, William Henry Hocking (briefly considered in Chapter 6). For most biographers, the highly inconclusive evidence for any intimacy with Hocking pales next to the grand sweep of Lawrence's heterosexual love life, especially the story of his first meeting with his professor's wife, Frieda von Richthofen Weekley, in March 1912 and their subsequent elopement to Germany two months later, all followed by 18 years of marital fidelity, at least on Lawrence's part. (Lawrence's complex relationship with Frieda and his two prior heterosexual partners is the subject of the following two chapters.)

The other approach, led by literary critics such as Jeffrey Meyers, has focused mainly on the handful of scenes in Lawrence's novels involving direct male–male physical interactions, one of which we have already considered, "The Poem of Friendship" chapter from *The White Peacock*. It hardly needs stating that none of these male-to-male interactions (the other three considered in Chapter 6) comes close to the wondrous account of the glory of being penetrated by a male lover, albeit nominally narrated from a female's point of view, that we have just recounted from *Lady Chatterley's Lover*.

The implication here, and at the heart of this monograph, is that under-mining the gender of Connie's voice in this fifth act of lovemaking gets us closer to something essential for Lawrence in the text about which he could not speak openly. The suggestion here is that the controlling narrative voice in this scene is finally not Connie's but Lawrence's, or, as indicated in our title, that of the *hidden* Lawrence. To be clear, this is a claim that it is not remotely possible to prove, even if we could put Lawrence himself on the witness stand—our desires being the most chal-lenging matter about which any of us can be forthcoming. Or, as Lawrence put it in his oft-cited stricture, it is only the tale we can trust, not the teller. Why? Because, as previously noted, he believed the artist to be "a damned liar" ("Spirit" 14).

Still, the strongest argument in its favor might well involve the crux of our study: this contrast in Lawrence's writing between the prosaic, often contorted passages enumerating the various difficulties a man faces in loving a woman—that side of Lawrence we have already seen in Mellors's misogynistic rant—and the grand lyrical accounts of lovemaking, such as those in *Lady Chatterley's Lover*, oddly enough involving this same man, only now seen through the eyes and the voice of the person, nominally a woman, who is the recipient of his lovemaking.

Here, we contend, is a reworking of the same winter/spring contrast we first saw in Charlotte Brontë, and, as with Brontë, a contrast finally with a distinct erotic trigger, in Lawrence's case, one having to do with his imagining himself not as a man making love to a woman but as that vulnerable, *tender* person eagerly accepting one's vulnerability, one's *tenderness*, while being made love to by a strong, silent man.

Why even worry about gender at all, some might argue, especially in our gender-fluid age? Except for the contention that the era in which Lawrence lived, especially his working-class Midlands background, created a host of prohibitions against not just gender fluidity but, at least for much of his life, against the very possibility of homosexual fulfillment (a topic treated further in Chapter 6, "Man to Man"). Fortunately, there was no such constraint on Lawrence's imagination, at least if we accept the argument that he could express his feelings most fully through his female characters (the subject of Chapter 7, "Hiding in Plain Sight").

Perhaps our central contention can be stated more affirmatively: that questioning the stability of the third-person pronouns Lawrence uses to recount Connie's experience in this fifth sexual encounter with Mellors—as well as elsewhere in this novel and eventually in other novels and stories—finally brings us closer to how Lawrence himself may have experienced these scenes, closer to that unacknowledged or *hidden* sense of who he was, closer to an understanding of how he felt compelled to express his vision of the world, including his erotic desires, through the imaginative lives of his vulnerable, often female characters. Such is close to what Lawrence says about "the creative, spontaneous soul" in his Foreword to *Women in Love*—how it "sends forth its promptings of desire and aspiration in us. [...] promptings [which] are our true fate, which is our business to fulfil" (485). Or, as he adds in his poem "The Work of Creation," where he calls truth-telling ("the mystery of creation") "a great strange urge, [...] not a Mind." No artist, he continues, no doubt speaking about himself, ever "thought" the work through "before it happened." Instead, "a strange ache possessed him," and "in the spell of the urge / his work [...] came to pass, it stood up and saluted his mind" (*Delphi* 7734).

One benefit in questioning the stability of the third-person pronouns associated with this narrative voice, therefore, is in allowing us to feel closer to this other, *hidden* Lawrence: to Lawrence the unconscious creator and living paradox; to Lawrence the writer capable of writing so expansively about Connie's experience in this fifth encounter—describing the absolute joy someone felt in being a beloved sexual object—while, as we shall in the following section, having considerable difficulty writing anything positive about subsequent lovemaking sessions in his novel described by her male lover.

Before returning to Lawrence's conclusion to Connie's wondrous fifth episode, we now turn to a brief look at these other perfunctory, uninspired accounts of lovemaking—all described mainly from Mellors's point of view.

Mellors and Connie's next interaction, their sixth (Chapter 14), occurs immediately after his misogynistic rant. Hoping to end the bad feelings he has just aroused, Mellors proposes a mock oath, in dialect: "Heart an' belly an' cock." The abbreviated account of the lovemaking that follows is typically uninspired. Connie was "silently weeping," we are told, while Mellors "lay with her and went into her there on the hearthrug, and so they gained a measure of equanimity. And then they went quickly to bed, for it was growing chill, and they had tired each other out" (250).

Their more extended seventh interaction begins with Mellors and Connie taking turns undressing each other, and Mellors offering this slightly ludicrous, juvenile take on Connie—noting how "she sat there with bare shoulders and longish breasts faintly golden," which Mellors "loved making [...] swing softly, like bells" (251). Then, a brief glimpse of Connie's "winter" thoughts: "Save for his hands and wrists and face and neck he was white as milk, with fine slender muscular flesh. To Connie he was suddenly piercingly beautiful again, as when she had seen him that afternoon washing himself."

This praise of the male body continues as Connie asks Mellors to get out of bed to draw the curtains. With Mellors at the window, turned from her, she comments on his "back [...] white and fine, the small buttocks beautiful with exquisite, delicate manliness, the back of the neck ruddy and delicate and yet strong"—ideas repeated in the following sentence: "There was an inward, not an outward strength in the delicate fine body."

On returning to bed, Mellors tries to cover his erection with his shirt; Connie protests, and she is then described—as if Lawrence cannot forgo something negative in speaking about a woman's body—as "holding out her beautiful slim arms from her drooping breasts" (252). Alas, while a woman's breasts may droop—indeed, in this novel, Connie's breasts always seem to do so, even though she is supposedly a young woman—her lover's penis is always erect and, in this case, exalted. "The sun [...] sent in a beam that lit up his thighs and slim belly, and the erect phallos rising darkish and hot-looking from the little cloud of vivid gold-red hair."

Connie is "startled and afraid": How strange he stands there! So big! and so dark and cock-sure! Is he like that?" Connie continues, " 'So proud! [...] And so lordly! [...] Like another being! A bit terrifying! But lovely really! And he comes to *me*!—' She caught her lower lip between her teeth, in fear and excitement." *Fear* and *excitement*—two terms that we will repeatedly see in association with the erotic needs of nearly all of Lawrence's alter egos.

After mild banter about his penis, for the first time deemed "John Thomas" by a satiric Mellors, he initiates this final stage of intercourse with the curt retort: "Lie down! [...] Lie down! Let me come" (253)! Here again, with Lawrence writing about intercourse from the male point of view, we are told, "He was in a hurry now"—this "he" possibly also referring to Lawrence, both men eager to conclude this act.

After this orgasm, Mellors's penis becomes erect again—"in slow soft undulations filled and surged and rose up, and grew hard, standing there hard and overweening, in its curious towering fashion"—thus beginning their eighth interaction. Only this time, the prose describing their encounter again becomes lyrical—the experience of intercourse, now given, as we would expect, mainly from Connie's point of view:

And she quivered, and her own mind melted out. Sharp soft waves of unspeakable pleasure washed over her as he entered her, and started the curious molten thrilling that spread and spread till she was carried away with the last, blind flush of extremity.

(254)

And what might Mellors or any male have felt in his orgasm? Lawrence says not a word but does offer, in dialect, these uninspired thoughts in praise of Connie, in response to her asking if he thought they could ever live as a couple:

A woman's a lovely thing when 'er 's deep ter fuck, and cunt's good. Ah luv thee, thy legs, an' th' shape on thee, an' th' womanness on thee. Ah luv th' womanness on thee. Ah luv thee wi' my ba's an' wi' my heart.

(255)

Before leaving to return home that morning, Connie asks to borrow a comb, offering a master painter with words like Lawrence, at least when his heart is moved, a scene that would have inspired a Renoir—that special, post-coital moment of a beautiful woman lovingly brushing her hair in the morning light. It is, of course, at least as engaging as the picture of a middle-aged man bathing that Lawrence could hardly stop describing, with this one difference—here, there is no desire. The result is this cryptic account of Connie as she "followed him into the scullery, and combed her hair before the handbreadth of mirror by the back door. Then," Lawrence adds, "she was ready to go" (256).

Their next meeting, their ninth (Chapter 15), begins dramatically, with Connie running out into the rain and dancing—something Frieda was known to enjoy. While more detailed than the novel's other descriptions of the female body, it is hardly more adulatory:

> It was a strange pallid figure lifting and falling, bending so the rain beat and glistened on the full haunches, swaying up again and coming belly-forward through the rain, then stooping again so that only the full loins and buttocks were offered in a kind of homage towards him, repeating a wild obeisance.
>
> (266)

Nor, as we might expect, given the exclusive male point of view here, is there anything erotic or especially pleasurable in the subsequent account of their lovemaking, one that begins with Mellors catching up to her and "[flinging] his naked arm round her soft, naked-wet middle." Connie then calls out, as "the heap of her soft, chill flesh came up against his body." Mellors, Lawrence writes, "pressed it all up against him, madly, the heap of soft, chilled female flesh that became quickly warm as flame, in contact." Next comes a line, alas, reminiscent of Brontë at her most prosaic: "The rain streamed on them till they smoked."

Indeed, some might consider the writing here, as well as the sentiment, genuinely dreadful, with Lawrence laboring to describe a man making love to a woman as their lovemaking spirals to its conclusion:

> He gathered her lovely, heavy posteriors one in each hand and pressed them in towards him in a frenzy, quivering motionless in the rain. Then suddenly he tipped her up and fell with her on the path, in the roaring silence of the rain, and short and sharp, he took her, short and sharp and finished, like an animal.
>
> (266–67)

We have already looked at their eleventh and final interaction (ch. 18) at the start of this chapter when considering the problematic nature of Mellors's self-proclaimed tenderness, and will save a discussion of their tenth interaction (ch. 16)—one that rivals their fifth encounter in terms of its importance—for the final section below, "On Sodomy."

All that remains here is a brief return to the conclusion of the grandest of all their interactions, their fifth.

> And now in her heart the queer wonder of him was awakened. A man! The strange potency of manhood upon her! Her hands strayed over him, still a little afraid. Afraid of that strange, hostile, slightly repulsive thing that he had been to her, a man.
>
> (209)

So begins the conclusion to this most memorable of lovemaking scenes, like all that came before, a paean to the wonders of a male lover, a song of praise of what it is like to be made love to by a near-perfect man. Indeed, one would think, here speaking hyperbolically, closing her eyes to the fact that the man in question is the otherwise prosaic Mellors, and our implicit narrator the same woman who had already made love with this man on four different occasions.

As hyperbole, however, it rings hollow and untrue, a high-test formulation of the regular gush of a lover. But, of course, the marvel of the passage is that Lawrence has created a speaker for whom this marvelous praise of the male form strikes us not as hyperbolic flattery but as a genuine cry of the heart, the outburst of someone discovering something extraordinary for the first time: "And now she touched him," this speaker tells us—"How beautiful he felt, how pure in tissue! How lovely, how lovely, strong, and yet pure and delicate, such stillness of the sensitive body! Such utter stillness of potency and delicate flesh! How beautiful! How beautiful!" Words spoken by someone for whom such intimacy with a man— here, more likely an unnamed, idealized male of Lawrence's imagination than the Mellors who serves as his stand-in for so much of this novel— strikes us as a revelation!

Perhaps most revelatory of all is this speaker's adoration of her lover— of "the soft, smallish globes of the buttocks":

> Beauty! What beauty! a sudden little flame of new awareness went through her. How was it possible, this beauty here, where she had previously only been repelled? The unspeakable beauty to the touch, of the warm, living buttocks! The life within life, the sheer warm, potent loveliness.

And then one final erection, with the speaker's "heart melt[ing] out with a kind of awe," and one more glorious moment of passive reception, of praise for the wonder of being penetrated: "And this time his being within her was all soft and iridescent, purely soft and iridescent, such as no consciousness could seize. Her whole self quivered unconscious and alive, like plasm." Nor could she know "what it was," the passage continues—"could not remember what it had been": "Only that it had been more lovely than anything ever could be. Only that" (209–10).

The aftermath that follows reveals the partners in near-perfect union, one where Mellors seems worlds removed from his earlier fixation on the mechanics of simultaneous orgasm or, at the novel's close, his parting sophomoric bromide about keeping his "ink [...] in the bottle."

But, then, who is this other man, we might ask, this new Mellors, here at the end of their fifth act of lovemaking, now garnering his lover's enraptured praise? Lawrence calls him *Mellors*, but is he not just as likely an unnamed, idealized male of Lawrence's imagination?

"And afterwards," Lawrence continues, Connie "was utterly still, utterly unknowing, [...] not aware for how long": the two of them—that most beloved of beings and her lover—unmoving "in an unfathomable silence."

And then this last sentence: "And of this, they would never speak"— a sacred oath that Lawrence himself never broke, at least not directly. Instead, his was a writer's life, a life not unlike the one lived by Charlotte Brontë or by the American frontier novelist James Fenimore Cooper, an artist whom Lawrence so harshly criticized for his duplicity: Cooper, the overly refined snob who, had he been true to himself, Lawrence believed, would have opted to live with his Deerslayer, the backwoodsman Natty Bumpo, the character whom Lawrence saw as not just the hero of Cooper's novels but also the object of his deepest desire. Cooper, the seemingly happily married author pictured by Lawrence as lying in bed "in a Louis Quatorze hôtel in Paris, [...] looking up at the painted ceiling, dreaming passionately of the naked savages, yearning for them" (53). The takeaway here Lawrence adds as a codicil—simply, "Men live by lies."

Cooper then joins Brontë and Lawrence as writers whose lives were filled with miraculous yearnings, if not deeds, eventually woven into the rich, elusive tapestry of their most lyrical ("winter") prose. Three writers who might all agree with Lawrence's famous cry of the heart: "My great religion is a belief in the blood, the flesh, as being wiser than the intellect. [...] [W]hat our blood feels and believes and says, is always true" (*Selected Letters* 53). Three writers, each with a complex erotic life mainly hidden from their readers—hidden, at least for Lawrence in *Lady Chatterley's Lover*, by a slender string of third-person pronouns.

On Sodomy—A Coda

"It was a night of sensual passion, in which she was a little startled, and almost unwilling: yet pierced again with piercing thrills of sensuality, different, sharper, more terrible than the thrills of tenderness, but, at the moment, more desirable" (297)—the beginning of Mellors and Connie's tenth act of lovemaking and the third one described mainly from her point of view.

It was a scene that had little chance of being included in the "authorized American edition" of 1946, involving, as it does, an account of anal sex, albeit in the veiled form that was required for a subject no author, not even Lawrence, could speak about openly, even in the heterosexual form described in his novel. This reluctance was still shared by the prosecutor in the 1960 British obscenity trial against *Lady Chatterley's Lover*, 32 years after Lawrence had the novel privately published—a reluctance apparent in the prosecutor waiting until his closing statement before referring to this tenth interaction, and then only obliquely, as sodomy was still a criminal offense, just as it had been 65 years earlier when Oscar Wilde had been convicted of gross indecency in that same courtroom and sentenced to two years of hard labor in Reading prison.

Lawrence's focus on this last of Connie's three extended scenes is decidedly different from the start, beginning with our speaker's admission that, "though a little frightened, she let him have his way, and the reckless, shameless sensuality shook her to her foundations, stripped her to the very last, and made a different woman of her"—or, with a non-gendered narrative voice, "a different *person* of *me*." And the strangest aspect of this new "sensuality"? That it was "not really love. [...] not voluptuousness. It was sensuality sharp and searing as fire, burning the soul to tinder."

Here is how Lawrence describes the resulting penetration, so different from their nine previous encounters: "Burning out the shames, the deepest, oldest shames, in the most secret places." Nor is it surprising that this activity was neither easy nor immediately pleasurable: "It cost her an effort to let him have his way and his will of her." The speaker, the recipient,

> had to be a passive, consenting thing, like a slave, a physical slave. Yet the passion licked round her, consuming, and when the sensual flame of it pressed through her bowels and breast, she really thought she was dying: yet a poignant, marvellous death.
>
> (297–98)

Such an account of lovemaking is reminiscent of Michel Foucault's reference to sodomy as an "erotics of truth"—something

> transmitted by magisterial initiation, with the stamp of secrecy, to those who have shown themselves to be worthy of it, and who make use of it at the very level of their pleasure, to intensify it, and to make it more acute and fulfilling.
>
> (Miller 269)

Lawrence's speaker, in turn, is focused on "what Abélard meant, when he said that in their year of love he and Heloïse had passed through all the stages and refinements of passion"—had passed through all that was "necessary, forever necessary, to burn out false shames and smelt out the heaviest ore of the body into purity. With the fire of sheer sensuality" (298).

How radically different was that night's lovemaking: "She would have thought a woman would have died of shame"—anyone might have died, given the moral taboo associated with such an act. "Shame, which is fear: the deep organic shame, the old, old physical fear which crouches in the bodily roots of us, and can only be chased away by the sensual fire, at last it was roused up and routed by the phallic hunt of the man," with Lawrence's speaker coming "to the very heart of the jungle of herself."

Again, how similar this sounds to Foucault's celebration of the profoundly transformative nature of sodomy—its role in the "creation of anarchy within the body, where its hierarchies, its localizations and designations, its organicity, if you will, is in the process of disintegrating. [...] This is something 'unnameable,' 'useless,' outside of all programs of desire. It is the body made totally plastic by pleasure: something that opens itself, that tightens, that throbs, that beats, that gapes" (Miller 274)—a topic to which we return at the end of Chapter 7.

Likewise, here is Lawrence's speaker celebrating "com[ing] to the real bed-rock of her nature," surprised to find herself "essentially shameless." This was her "sensual self, naked and unashamed." Lawrence's speaker "felt a triumph, almost a vainglory": "So! That was how it was! That was life! That was how oneself really was! There was nothing left to disguise or be ashamed of. [...] [having] shared [one's] ultimate nakedness with a man, another being."

Then comes the celebration of the speaker's partner, praised here as that "reckless devil." While nominally Mellors, although with no recognizable traits, all that seems to matter now is this "devil's" role as the "phallos-bearer"—the possessor of the one organ capable of penetrating to "the core of the physical jungle, the last and deepest recess of organic shame." And the role of the speaker—no longer referred to as *she*—is also fittingly reduced: "One had to be strong to bear him."

As before, there is the question of how best to interpret Lawrence's poetic language, which again seems less hyperbole than another genuine cry of the heart—the cry of someone who has spent a lifetime both fearing and desiring just such a moment. It is the fear that the speaker would have "hated it," only to discover the opposite: "how she had really wanted it!"

Here is someone who has just passed through a trial by fire and only now realizes that "at the bottom of her soul, fundamentally, [that] she had needed this phallic hunting out, [...] had secretly wanted it," and then this puzzling remark—this fear that "she would never get it"—an admission that may make more sense coming from a male author than his female character. "Now suddenly there it was, and a man was sharing her last and final nakedness"—with Connie, Lawrence concludes, "shameless" (298–99).

That arch-rationalist Sigmund Freud knew something was amiss when we humans seemed capable of finding such intense satisfaction in what struck him as the abandonment of the pleasure principle—people acting, as Lawrence's speaker appears to be here, "as though the watchman over our mental life were put out of action by a drug" (159). With the watchman off duty, Lawrence's speaker seems content to occupy what theorist Julia Kristeva refers to as that "fragile border [...] where identities (subject/object, etc.) do not exist or only barely so—double, fuzzy, heterogenous, animal, metamorphosed, altered, abject" (207). Or, finally, as Lawrence proclaims far more directly, albeit here speaking through his female protagonist: "What liars poets and everybody were! They made one think one wanted sentiment. When what one supremely wanted was this piercing, consuming, rather awful sensuality" (299).

It should hardly come as a surprise that, as with numerous issues involving sexuality, Lawrence would be of two minds concerning sodomy, reflecting the same two Lawrences we have already encountered: a *hidden* Lawrence we have just seen, capable of speaking so effusively about sodomy through a feminine persona, and a *public* Lawrence who, when speaking in his own voice, would sound more like the ranting Mellors. Here, for instance, is that censorious Lawrence, from the essay *Pornography and Obscenity*, leveling a tirade against the "great pornographical class" (242) of men who know all sorts of deviant ways to get themselves aroused. These are men who "tell dirty stories, carry indecent picture post-cards, and know the indecent books"—men who fall prey to what Lawrence saw as the two great sources of perversion: thinking about sex, aided by those "indecent picture post-cards" and other such paraphernalia, and direct phallic stimulation of the sort that might lead to that other great bugbear, masturbation. Opposed to such depravity was that open, healthier attitude toward sex that Lawrence tries to express through Mellors at the end of *Lady Chatterley's Lover*—the celebration of those rare men committed to "tenderness," men who believe in the supremacy of touching and, presumably, a kind of intimacy without words, thoughts, or, if possible, direct phallic stimulation.

In this same essay, Lawrence acknowledges St. Augustine's dictum "Inter faeces et urinam nascimur" (We are born between shit and piss), a notion Freud uses to show the hidden interconnectivity and ultimate ambiguity of our deepest desires. Lawrence, however, seemed to have less tolerance for such ambiguity. While admitting that "the sex functions and the excrementory functions" work closely together, he remains adamant that they are fundamentally distinct, "utterly different in direction":

> Sex is a creative flow, the excrementory flow is towards dissolution, de-creation, if we may use such a word. In the really healthy human being the distinction between the two is instant, our profoundest instincts are perhaps our instincts of opposition between the two flows.

This distinction, however, only seems to work in healthy men like Lawrence or Mellors at the conclusion of *Lady Chatterley's Lover*—that is, in men who do not seem especially interested in phallic pleasure. In the vast majority of men, what Lawrence calls those "degraded human[s]," those "really vulgar people," he sees these "two flows"—one concerned with sexual pleasure and the other with excrement—"becom[ing] identical." Such is the fate of men solely interested in their phallic pleasure, men in whom "the profound controlling instincts [have] collapse[d]": "Then sex is dirt and dirt is sex, and sexual excitement becomes a playing with dirt, and any sign of sex in a woman becomes a show of her dirt."

This is the same censorious Lawrence who experienced such fright during his famous visit to Cambridge in March 1915, where he met a group of openly gay men, including the young John Maynard Keynes, who, to Lawrence's everlasting horror, was still lounging in his pajamas at midday. In the days and weeks afterward, Lawrence ranted, often uncontrollably, about this visit to multiple correspondents. To Bertrand Russell, for instance, he complained about being unable to rid himself of the "smell of rottenness, marsh-stagnancy." He felt sickened, he complained, as if ill with "a melancholic malaria." "How can so sick people rise up? They must die first" (*Letters* 309). Or, later to another friend, more complaints about "these horrible little frowsty people, men lovers of men, they give me such a sense of corruption, almost putrescence, that I dream of beetles. It is abominable." (323). And to a third friend, David Garnett, the son of his editor and a friend to these abominable Cambridge men, a warning that

> when I meet [these friends of yours], I simply can't bear it. It is so wrong, it is unbearable. It makes a form of inward corruption which truly makes me scarce able to live. Why is there this horrible sense of frowstiness, so repulsive, as if it came from deep inward dirt – a sort of sewer [...] I begin to feel mad as I think of it—insane. [...] I feel as if I should go mad, if I think of your set.

Then another reference to this visit causing him to "dream of beetles" (320–21).

A month before he visited Cambridge in February 1915, Lawrence had gone off, only slightly less, after a weekend visit from E. M. Forster, already the author of four well-regarded novels and, as already noted, a closeted gay man. Forster's problem, Lawrence diagnosed, resulted from his lack of physical intimacy—perhaps an insightful observation considering that Forster, although 36 at the time of this visit, would remain a virgin for another two years. "His implicit manhood," Lawrence wrote to Russell in another manic letter upon Forster's abrupt departure, "is to be satisfied by nothing but immediate physical action. He tries to dodge himself—the sight is pitiful" (283). But Forster's solution, Lawrence argued, might entail his going to a woman for sexual release, even though doing so would be a form of "sensationalism," much as he would later argue in *Pornography and Obscenity*— that is, men acting like the women whom Mellors ranted against, those who misused intercourse for their selfish pleasure, seeing their partners merely as a masturbatory aid. Or, as he wrote to Russell, "When [such] a man takes a woman, he is *merely* repeating a known reaction upon himself, not seeking a new reaction, a discovery" (emphasis in original).

Then, this unexpected twist from Lawrence—the assertion that when a man uses sex for his phallic pleasure, "there is always Sodomy" (285). From this remark, we can see what so upset Lawrence about those gay young men at Cambridge and homosexuality generally—that, at least in Lawrence's mind, he saw such activity as inherently selfish, involving men interested solely in phallic stimulation, thus necessarily a sexual activity akin to masturbation. Nor was phallic pleasure much of an issue for Mellors in *Lady Chatterley's Lover*, who ranted so against women and often seemed so listless in his lovemaking; nor, as we shall see in the following two chapters and as heretical as it may sound, did Lawrence himself ever show much interest in sexual activity involving direct phallic stimulation. Instead, what was essential for Mellors and his creator was a different sort of lovemaking—one that Lawrence seems to have seen as the opposite of "sodomy" and to which he referred by that crucial but vague notion of *tenderness*.

And just what constituted *tenderness* in lovemaking for Lawrence, we might ask, at least in *Lady Chatterley's Lover*? In what sense could *tenderness* be seen as the opposite of sodomy, even when one of the three grand love scenes seems to involve the celebration of anal sex? And the answer seems to be that a "tender" lover is neither Connie's "reckless devil"— "the mere phallos-bearer"—that is, a man interested in phallic pleasure but, instead, a different sort of lover, one attuned to the more profound, more "feminine" pleasure only available to the receptive sexual partner.

We close this section on sodomy by looking at Lawrence's other fully realized account of anal sex, from the "Excurse" chapter in *Women in*

Love. This chapter opens with Lawrence's stand-in, Rupert Birkin, and his partner, Ursula Brangwen, struggling to establish a harmonious sexual connection. While Ursula had "a passion" for Birkin, Lawrence tells us, this feeling was something that Birkin found "not finally interesting." The source of this problem seems to have been something we will see repeatedly in Lawrence—the woman's need to feel emotionally intimate with her sexual partner, something that Birkin criticizes as Ursula's making matters "always so abominably personal" (296).

What it seems he wanted instead was what we have already seen in Connie Chatterley's three great lovemaking scenes and what we will see again in our next two chapters on Lawrence's own love life—and that was a desire to experience "depths of passion" free of any such emotional entanglements, for a different sort of lovemaking where "one became impersonal and indifferent, unemotional." Here seems to be the source of Birkin's confession, what looks like a wish wrapped in a cry of regret, of his having "taken [Ursula] as he had never been taken himself"—that is, "taken her at the roots of her darkness and shame-like a demon, laughing over the fountain of mystic corruption which was one of the sources of her being, laughing, shrugging, accepting, accepting finally."

It is hardly a surprise that the lovemaking sequence that follows later in this chapter would play on this fascination with the "roots of [...] darkness," even though this physical exchange begins, as if in a dreamscape, with the fully clothed couple awaiting tea in a public inn. It is a situation involving obvious logistical complexities that Lawrence, so focused on Birkin's unfulfilled desire, never seems concerned with unwinding. Instead, the dreamlike quality of what follows gives Lawrence the chance to play with the notion of Ursula's somehow fulfilling Birkin's wish for his being taken as he has already taken her—with Lawrence doing this imaginatively, as he had with Connie in *Lady Chatterley's Lover*, by again narrating the main elements of a couple's subsequent lovemaking from the woman's point of view.

Their physical interaction begins with Ursula "trac[ing] with her hands the line of [Birkin's] loins and thighs, at the back," in the process releasing the "dark fire of electricity that rushed from him to her, and flooded them both with rich peace, satisfaction" (305–06). With Birkin on top, Ursula reaches for his buttocks, "clos[ing] her hands over the full, rounded body of his loins [...] seem[ing] to touch the quick of the mystery of darkness that was bodily him." At this, both "seemed to faint," again as if in a dream, he on top, she on the bottom:

> It was a perfect passing away for both of them, and at the same time the most intolerable accession into being, the marvellous fullness of

immediate gratification, overwhelming, outflooding from the source of the deepest life-force, the darkest, deepest, strangest life-source of the human body, at the back and base of the loins.

Then, as we might expect, Lawrence's focus shifts from the couple's pleasure to Ursula's, and here, not surprisingly, the writing becomes more lyrical:

After a lapse of stillness, after the rivers of strange dark fluid richness had passed over her, flooding, carrying away her mind and flooding down her spine and down her knees, past her feet, a strange flood, sweeping away everything and leaving her an essential new being, she was left quite free, she was free in complete ease, her complete self.

As with Connie in *Lady Chatterley's Lover*, Lawrence now seems to be fully inhabiting his female character, intent on admiring in her lover not an actual person, neither Birkin nor Mellors, but an idealized male presence, described by Lawrence as a form that

stood there in his strange, whole body, that had its marvellous fountains, like the bodies of the sons of God who were in the beginning. There were strange fountains of his body, more mysterious and potent than any she [or possibly Lawrence] had imagined or known, more satisfying, ah, finally, mystically-physically satisfying.

Lawrence next gives us this odd acknowledgment from Ursula regarding her mistake in ever assuming that, regarding sexual pleasure, there was "no source deeper than the phallic source." Why, we want to know, should Ursula here be comparing her current pleasure in being sexually penetrated, not with the more common form of vaginal penetration—her obvious point being that this current experience is so much more compelling—but with what for her could only be a hypothetical notion, although likely a real concern for Lawrence: how her essentially passive pleasure as the recipient might compare with her partner's active or phallic pleasure?

Why such surprise that her pleasure as a woman could be greater than that of her male partner?

And the best answer here may be that, with feelings as heightened as they are, Lawrence's control over his material may have momentarily slipped, giving us this unexpected glimpse into his thoughts on the two different levels of pleasure afforded a man during sex, the anal pleasure of the bottom versus the phallic pleasure of the top—that is, here too, it seems as if Lawrence is voicing his thoughts through his female character.

Finally, could anyone doubt it is Lawrence and not Gudrun who is speaking in the final prophetic sentence of this wondrous passage—this unexpected and, at least in terms of character development and the action that has just been narrated, misdirected praise of the lower male torso as the source of our deepest sexual pleasure? "And now, behold, from the smitten rock of the man's body, from the strange marvellous flanks and thighs, deeper, further in mystery than the phallic source, came the floods of ineffable darkness and ineffable riches."

Works Cited

Brontë, Charlotte. *Jane Eyre: An Authoritative Text*. Ed. Richard J. Dunn. New York: Norton, 1971.

Ellis, David. *D. H. Lawrence: The Dying Game, 1922–1930*. Cambridge UP, 1998.

———. *Love and Sex in D. H. Lawrence*. Clemson UP, 2016.

Freud, Sigmund. "The Economic Problem of Masochism (1924)." *The Standard Edition*, Vol. 19. Hogarth P, 1961: 155–70.

Kinkead-Weekes, Mark. *D. H. Lawrence: Triumph to Exile*. Cambridge UP, 1996.

Kristeva, Julia. *Powers of Horror: An Essay on Abjection*. Columbia UP, 1982.

Lawrence, D. H. "A Propos of *Lady Chatterley's Lover*." In *Lady Chatterley's Lover*. Ed. Michael Squires. Cambridge UP, 1993: 303–35.

———. "Appendix 1: Foreword to *Women in Love*." In *Women in Love*. Eds. David Farmer, Lindeth Vasey, and John Worthen. Cambridge UP, 1987: 483–86.

———. Delphi Collected Works of D. H. Lawrence. Delphi Classics, 2015.

———. "Fenimore Cooper's Leatherstocking Novels." In *Studies in Classic American Literature*. Eds. Ezra Greenspan, Lindeth Vasey, and John Worthen. Cambridge UP, 2003: 52–65.

———. *The First and Second Lady Chatterley Novels*. Eds. Dieter Mehl and Christa Jansohn. Cambridge UP, 1999.

———. *Lady Chatterley's Lover*. The Orioli edition, privately printed in Italy in 1928.

———. *The Letters of D. H. Lawrence, Vol. 2: June 1913–October 1916*. Eds. George J. Zytaruk and James T. Boulton. Cambridge UP, 1981.

———. *Pornography and Obscenity*. In *Late Essays and Articles*. Ed. James T. Boulton. Cambridge UP, 2004: 233–53.

———. *The Selected Letters of D. H. Lawrence*. Ed. James T. Boulton. Cambridge UP, 1997.

———. "The Spirit of the Place." In *Studies in Classic American Literature*. Eds. Ezra Greenspan, Ezra, Lindeth Vasey, and John Worthy. Cambridge UP, 2004: 13–19.

———. *The White Peacock*. Ed. Andrew Robertson. Cambridge UP, 2002.

———. *Women in Love*. Heinemann, 1971.

Meyers, Jeffrey. "D. H. Lawrence." In *Homosexuality and Literature, 1890–1930*. McGill-Queen's UP, 1977: 131–64.

Miller, James. *The Passion of Michel Foucault*. Simon & Schuster, 1993.

Nehls, Edward D. H. *Lawrence: A Composite Biography: Volume 2, 1919–1925*. U Wisconsin P, 1958, 1977.

Williams, Linda Ruth. *Sex in the Head: Visions of Femininity and Film in D.H. Lawrence*. Wayne State UP, 1993.

3   Adolescence
Angst and Exuberance

The Great Friend of His Youth

Our initial concern here is with the different ways that Lawrence's attack on the great friend of his youth—unnamed by Mellors in *Lady Chatterley's Lover* but a clear reference to Jessie Chambers—appears in his early writings, both in several stories that we will look at later in this chapter and especially in his third novel and first great success, the coming-of-age saga, *Sons and Lovers*. Published in May 1913, when Lawrence was 27, it is a work in which he appears as Paul Morel and Chambers as Miriam Leivers. The focus of Lawrence's complaint regarding Chambers, as spelled out in *Lady Chatterley's Lover*, was what Mellors called "the serpent in the grass" (240), a euphemism for Chambers's hesitancy in becoming his first sexual partner as Lawrence became increasingly lascivious in his early twenties. Nor was Chambers the only woman to resist the blandishments of the youthful Lawrence, putting Lawrence, who seems to have detested both prostitutes and masturbation, in a difficult position. One result of this bind was that he seems to have remained a virgin until he was 24.

As with Brutus, the fault may have been less in the stars—or in this case, with these earnest young women—than in Lawrence himself, but here we are getting ahead of ourselves, something easy to do if we follow Mellors's unfortunate phrasing by which he introduces Chambers in *Lady Chatterley's Lover* as "the first girl I had, I began with when I was sixteen," that is, "had as a friend." What a world of turmoil inside the young Lawrence is glossed over here in his eliding the nine years between the spring of 1901, when, at 15, he first met Jessie Chambers, and the spring of 1910, when, as a 24-year-old virgin, he pressured her into becoming his first sexual partner, an experience described in considerable detail in the chapter "The Defeat of Miriam," in *Sons and Lovers*.

Lawrence's initial impression of Miriam Leivers, his fictional stand-in for Chambers, is largely positive—"a rosy dark face, a bunch of short black curls, very fine and free, and dark eyes"—but also, as with nearly

DOI: 10.4324/9781003495093-3

all of Lawrence's descriptions of women and so unlike that of Mellors bathing, not one without a whiff of criticism, with this initial account referring to her "dirty apron" and to Miriam as someone who was "shy, questioning, a little resentful of [...] strangers" (124–25). Lawrence's most detailed physical description of Miriam has a tinge of coldness, even cruelty. Again, there is praise for her eyes—"All the life of [her] body was in her eyes"—but perhaps less so in the simile that follows, noting how hers "were usually dark as a dark church" (153).

One area where Lawrence was least critical of Chambers involved their shared love of literature—something that shows up again in Mellors's comments about how she "egged me on to poetry and reading [...[[how] I read and I thought like a house on fire, for her," or how the two of them became "the most literary-cultured couple in ten counties." Unfortunately, the one scene from *Sons and Lovers* most clearly featuring this shared enthusiasm between Lawrence and Chambers, cast as Paul and Miriam, was cut by Lawrence's editor, likely for not advancing the story, and restored in the Cambridge edition (CE) of 1992. The scene itself shows the young Lawrence (Paul) making his weekly Thursday evening trip to Bestwood's "decent little library," to which his family and Miriam's had both subscribed "when their children were growing up." As Chambers recalled in her memoir, she always considered this evening "the outstanding event of the week" (CE 93), and here, for once, Lawrence almost matches her enthusiasm. His account adds a touch of nostalgia for the library's "two small rooms, with books all around the walls. ... [and] a great fire in the corner" and even for the librarian, Mr. Sleath, with his "white whiskers round his child-like face": "He was tall and inquisitive, but very affectionate, knew everybody and everybody's affairs" (CE 191).

Next comes small talk with the librarian about Paul's mother and her chapel attendance, but Paul's thoughts are elsewhere. For once, we see Paul anxious over Miriam's presence. "The youth knew everybody, and everybody's history," Lawrence writes, but "[t]hey did not interest him." What did interest him was the thought that Miriam might not come "because of the rain": "There were noises of people going, but no one entered. If she did not come? Then, at the thought, he could see the night ahead, dreary and profitless." His feelings here evoke if not love, then friendship or, at least, companionship—someone with whom he could discuss books. "It still felt warm and rich, just in front," then maybe the kindest line Lawrence ever wrote about Chambers: "and night went no further than the moment when she would arrive."

Here, Lawrence shows us an adolescent boy, lonely and a tad insecure, valuing his good friend, if not as his equal, then at least as valuable to him as a sounding board—for being "so dependable"—when he had no one else. "One of her great charms for [him]," Lawrence continues, "was that she was not held by conventions. If she wanted to come, she would come in spite of rain" (CE 192).

Such thoughts, although admirable, seem a long way from love. Still, Lawrence was at least honest about Paul's need for someone able to meet his immediate emotional needs, a situation similar to the one he will face a few years later regarding his burgeoning sexual desire. Yes, "[s]he *would* come," he continues. "He clung to the hope of her. He could feel her, across the night, wanting to come." And then her one true asset—that "she never failed him"—couched in praise tinged with criticism: "With her, the inner life counted for everything, the outer for nothing" (emphasis in original).

Finally, Miriam arrives: "He heard her step in the hall, and his suspense relaxed." Then, a few compliments, far different from Connie's praise for Mellors but also initially less judgmental than Paul's other accounts: "Her red cap was glistening with rain, her hair was revelling in dewy curliness, her face glowed." Still, we get this carping observation about her "short-sighted eyes [meeting] his," before being told, "A flame came up in her that burned him too."

As is often the case with the young Jessie, at least as Miriam, nothing can stay positive for long. "Come and see what books I have found for you," Paul eagerly directs, with Miriam "follow[ing] him implicitly": "Books did not matter to her. But he insisted on her approving." Of course, Lawrence is writing this scene in his late twenties, almost ten years after their weekly trips to the library, but also after years of relying on Chambers as his first and most important reader, after she assisted in his revisions for *The White Peacock* and *Paul Morel* (the earlier draft of *Sons and Lovers*) based in part on her recommendations, and after Chambers had been instrumental not just in encouraging Lawrence's early compositions but in sending off his first works to be published.

Still, Lawrence shows Chambers's value to him in this library scene, albeit mainly as a listener. As they headed home together, their conversation started—"quick and vigorous, and immediately it was a discussion of a book" (CE 193). It is here that Lawrence comes close to Chambers' description of "the magical quality of our association" that she recounted in her memoir, *A Personal Record*—how when they were "alone together we were in a world apart, where feeling and thought were intense, and we seemed to touch a reality that was beyond the ordinary workaday world" (58).

Lawrence then describes the adolescent Paul holding forth "passionately," while Miriam "listened and her soul expanded": "From the book, they inevitably came to a discussion of beliefs, very intimate"—here about religion and whether, in the grand scheme of things, individuals matter or just the fate of the larger group. Not unexpectedly, Lawrence's narcissistic bent keeps the focus on the impression he is making: "[T]o hear him talk was like life to her: like starting the breathing in a new-born baby."

In a later chapter, as part of a different incident, Lawrence describes Miriam looking up at Paul "with her dark eyes one flame of love," while Paul "laughed uncomfortably":

> There was for him the most intense pleasure in talking about his work to Miriam. All his passion, all his wild blood, went into this intercourse with her, when he talked and conceived his work. She brought forth to him his imaginations.

And then, as expected, the put-down—how "she did not understand, any more than a woman understands when she conceives a child in her womb. But this was life for her and for him" (202).

Lawrence seems accurate in portraying at least one aspect of this situation—that he and Chambers both seemed in love with the same person—adding this one insight as Paul and Miriam walk home from the library that night: "What we are inside makes us so that we ought to go one particular way, and no other." Then, when questioned over whether we always know our "true course," Lawrence has the young Paul respond, "Yes! *I* do. I know I'm following mine" (CE 193, emphasis in original).

As one might expect, Chambers's account of this same scene depicts a greater sense of balance, although with Lawrence still in the lead— his asking "in his abrupt way what I thought of such and such a character"—but with more give and take, as they would "compare notes and talk out our differences." "The characters interested us most," Chambers continued, "and there was usually a more or less unconscious identification of them with ourselves," before adding how it was "Scott's novels in particular [that] we talked over in this way," with "the scenes and events of his stories [...] more real to us than our actual surroundings" (93–94).

It is fitting that Chambers refers to Scott's novels, as those are the same works that Lawrence uses to reprove Miriam's character at the start of the ironically titled chapter "Lad-and-Girl Love." Her primary difficulty for the young Paul was that she seemed too much under the influence of Scott, too eager to see herself as "a Walter Scott heroine being loved by men with helmets or with plumes in their caps." Whereas a sympathetic friend may have seen a sensitive young girl who wanted something better out of life than farm work, Lawrence is all too ready to put Miriam down for seeing herself ("in her own imagination") as "something of a princess turned into a swine girl" (142).

So begins the chapter "Lad-and-Girl Love"—although what might more accurately be titled "The Struggle with Miriam"—with the central issue being what we have already seen in the library scene: Lawrence's keen sense of his special destiny awaiting him. Yes, he "looked something like a Walter Scott hero, who could paint and speak French, and knew what algebra meant, and who went by train to Nottingham every day," but, no, Miriam was mistaken in seeing their futures as intertwined. While Lawrence might eventually see Chambers as more than a "swine-girl," he would never entirely "perceive," or at least sexually respond to, "the princess beneath."

This chapter thus ends with what will be a significant turning point in Lawrence's emotional development, one that will occupy Lawrence's interest in the remaining chapters of *Sons and Lovers*, as well as nearly everything he would write afterward—that is, how to cope with his late-developing sexual awareness, something that Lawrence admits was slow to develop in Paul. For instance, just before telling us that Paul was by then 19, Lawrence notes how neither he nor Miriam "would have acknowledged" any signs of love between themselves—Paul being "too sane for such sentimentality, and she [...] too lofty." As Lawrence adds, "They both were late in coming to maturity, and psychical ripeness was much behind even the physical" (162). Perhaps this is also about when, in her memoir, Chambers notes Lawrence's reluctance "to admit that boyhood was over. [...] [even] to begin shaving, and was hurt when people chaffed him about the pale hairs on his chin." Chambers's assessment, far removed from Mellors's rant, was that he "found the present so good, he wanted it to last" (43).

Yet, as Lawrence would often proclaim, the body has its own course, and thus, by the end of this "Lad-and-Girl Love" chapter, he describes the onset of sexual desire in Paul while he was on a family vacation that included Miriam. In this single paragraph about Paul's consciousness, we can see three of Lawrence's most characteristic traits. First is the absolute mastery of his prose—apparent in the cadences of the opening sentences:

> One evening he and she went up the great sweeping shore of sand towards Theddlethorpe. The long breakers plunged and ran in a hiss of foam along the coast. It was a warm evening. There was not a figure but themselves on the far reaches of sand, no noise but the sound of the sea.
> (178)

Second is the closely related narcissism we have already noted in the library scene. Here, we can see it in Paul's delight in an immediate, physical connection with nature—how, for instance, he "loved to feel himself between the noise of it and the silence of the sandy shore."

Third is his treating a universal occurrence in young men, here the onset of sexual desire, as something quasi-mystical: "The whole of his blood seemed to burst into flame, and he could scarcely breathe. An enormous orange moon was staring at them from the rim of the sandhills. He stood still, looking at it." Later, regarding Thomas Hardy's driven protagonist Jude Fawley, Lawrence would promulgate an equally grim account of male sexual desire: his picture of a man wanting "that which is necessary for him if he is to go on"—that is, his "physical, sexual relief." And for once, Lawrence skips the loose metaphysics of desire to speak directly: "For continually baulked sexual desire, or necessity," he continues, "makes a man unable to live freely, scotches him, stultifies him. And where a man is roused to the fullest pitch, as Jude was roused by Sue"—and as he was eventually, although not clearly, by any one woman—"then the principal connection becomes a necessity, if only for relief" (*Study of Thomas Hardy* 115).

Miriam, not surprisingly, is alarmed by his change of mood; for Lawrence, however, it is a repetition of how the chapter opened—with Miriam being too spiritual here, possibly too worried about the sentiments associated with love. He could see she "was brooding. [...] slightly afraid—deeply moved and religious." What he calls, with a touch of sarcasm, "her best state," against which he was "impotent"—that is, powerless, but also what becomes increasingly important in their relationship, unable to be aroused. "His blood was concentrated like a flame in his chest"—how could she not feel the same urge he was feeling? "There were flashes in his blood. But somehow she ignored them." Exactly where some of Mellors's vaunted tenderness may well have worked wonders, bringing about the proverbial happy ending, there is only vituperation—the claim that she "was expecting some religious state in him" (178), a poetic moment, if you will, like her own.

In her memoir, Chambers also describes this scene—how they "set off light-heartedly enough" to see the moonrise that night, "but gradually some dark power seemed to take possession of [him], and when the final beauty of the moonrise broke upon us, something seemed to explode inside him." Then she describes two similar events, the second "much more severe," with Lawrence "skipp[ing] from one white boulder to another in the vast amphitheatre of the bay until I could have doubted whether he was indeed a human being." His actions created a feeling not of death, Chambers continues, but of the "utter negation of life, as though he had become dehumanized," adding that "always, somehow or other, it was my fault, or partly my fault" (*Personal Record* 128).

This crisis soon passes, and Lawrence, the master of indirection here, continues by noting how Paul "did not know himself what was the matter. He was naturally so young, and their intimacy was so abstract, he did not know he wanted to crush her on to his breast to ease the ache there"—if indeed that was what he ever wanted. Still, he continues blaming larger cultural forces for "suppress[ing] into a shame" the idea that "he might want her as a man wants a woman." And the fault here falls mainly on Miriam, who "shrank in her convulsed, coiled torture from the thought of such a thing," thus causing him to "[wince] to the depths of his soul" (178–79). In a sense, it all can be seen as a preparation for that momentous meeting when he was 26 with the woman who would be his third and possibly final sexual partner—Frieda Weekley, a sexually liberated woman six years his senior, with a husband, three children, and a handful of ex-lovers.

Yes, in the future, there would no longer be any shame attached to sex, even if sex itself, as we will see in Chapter 4, may be far from perfect. For the moment—at the end of the "Lad-and-Girl" chapter, there are only recriminations about "this 'purity' prevent[ing] even their first love-kiss." Surely, it was the young girl's fault—Miriam's or Jessie's: "It was as if she could scarcely stand the shock of physical love, even a passionate kiss." Yes, maybe all would eventually be solved by the open-minded Frieda— but Lawrence wisely adds the cautionary note that "he was too shrinking and sensitive to give it." Nor is it surprising that in early 1910, when the still horny 24-year-old Lawrence is reengaging with Chambers as a candidate to end his virginity, he confides to another female correspondent how he and Chambers have such an unusual history, having had "fine, mad little scenes now and again, she and I—so strange, after ten years, and I had hardly kissed her all that time" (*Letters* 154).

This initial stage of Paul's painful relationship with Miriam continues for two more chapters, "Strife in Love" and "Defeat of Miriam." The old antagonism continues, exacerbated by the allure of spring ("the worst time"), with Lawrence recalling one particular incident in March that begins with Paul lying on a riverbank with Miriam and unable even to look at her: "She seemed to want him, and he resisted. He resisted all the time." Then, anticipating what Mellors would declaim as his one consolation as a lover, his desire "now to give her passion and tenderness," even as he realized that "he could not" (194). The problem here is hardly that different from that faced by many young couples—that as a prelude to sex, Miriam seems to expect a level of intimacy from her would-be partner, something akin to the tenderness for which Mellors was so proud but which Lawrence's young persona in *Sons and Lovers*, despite his protestation, seems incapable of providing. Nor can Lawrence explain this situation without using the mystical language to describe human sexuality that will become his hallmark—language more focused on male sexuality, even his own peculiar sexual needs—namely, his sense that what Miriam wanted was something other than physical intimacy that he was more than eager to provide. Instead, she seemed to want "the soul out of his body," that is, a level of emotional intimacy, recognition, even tenderness that he could not give.

And Chambers's one fault here? Only that she was reluctant to engage in intercourse—"man and woman together"—without feeling this need for intimacy or, again in Lawrence's demeaning language, without "want[ing] to draw all of him into her," that is, without wanting Paul to feel that loss of self that so exhilarated Connie Chatterley, that so defined Lawrence's sense of the perfect sexual, at least as imagined with a male lover. Instead, Lawrence shows us Paul's resulting frustration, perhaps exacerbated by overstimulated hormones—the result, a drive that "urged him to an intensity like madness, which fascinated him, as drug taking might" (194).

One problem for Paul was that Miriam was physically unresponsive. We soon learn about what Lawrence claims was an even more considerable difficulty, and that was his mother's dislike of Miriam. The involvement of Lawrence's mother, of course, is part of a broader Oedipal reading of both the novel and Lawrence's life—this notion, which Lawrence expanded in his final revision of the novel under the active encouragement of Frieda, who was abreast of the latest currents in psychoanalytic theory, that it was Paul's attachment to his mother, or conversely, his mother's attachment to him, that made his ability to love Miriam, or possibly any woman, so difficult.

"[C]oming home from his walks with Miriam," Lawrence tells us, Paul was "wild with torture. [...] torn so, almost bewildered, and unable to move." And one reason? His mother was "at home and suffer[ing]," seemingly because of Miriam. Then, a clear statement about this connection: "If Miriam caused his mother suffering, then he hated her—and he easily hated her" (193). Or, as he states elsewhere in the novel, he was like "a good many of the nicest men he knew [...] [who were] bound in by their own virginity, which they could not break out of." The problem, according to Lawrence, was not a lack of desire—we will continue to see Lawrence in the throes of concupiscence, although sometimes without a clear object choice—it was that they

> could easier deny themselves than incur any reproach from a woman; for a woman was like their mother, and they were full of the sense of their mother. They preferred themselves to suffer the misery of celibacy rather than risk the other person.
>
> (279)

Such a self-serving observation overlooks how many other young men, some possibly also momma's boys, just as readily follow the path of Lawrence's older brother Ernest (William Morel in the novel), who moves to London and becomes engaged at 21, seeking sexual fulfillment with a woman, seemingly without a moment's hesitation.

It is a subject that stayed with Lawrence, one he reprises in the opening chapter of *The Rainbow*, written in the early years of his marriage. Here he describes the unfortunate situation of a similar young man, upset that he was "thinking of women, or a woman, day in, day out": "But when he had a nice girl, he found that he was incapable of pushing the desired development," unable to "think of her like that," to cope with the thought "of her actual nakedness": "She was a girl and he liked her, and dreaded violently even the thought of uncovering her." And, with a "loose girl," things were even worse, with his not knowing "whether he was going to get away from her as quickly as possible or whether he were going to take her out of inflamed necessity." It was the sex itself that "he despised," the confusion it caused in him: "he despised it deeply and bitterly" (21–22).

The problem with Chambers is that whatever "misery of celibacy" Lawrence shows us was offset, at least concerning Miriam, by an almost equal lack of desire for her. Indeed, one can claim that Paul's attachment to his mother was more likely a way for him to escape any romantic entanglement with Chambers, something he clearly did not want. Yes, "if Miriam caused his mother suffering, then he hated her—and he easily hated her" (193). Still, Paul follows this clear assertion of blame by a return to an earlier concern: how this young woman made him feel unsure of himself, coming close, especially in his choice of metaphor, to speaking bluntly about his sexual misgivings: it was "as if he were uncertain of himself, insecure, an indefinite thing, as if he had not sufficient sheathing to prevent the night and the space breaking into him?" After all, this is the woman whose face, in Lawrence's most extended descriptive passage about Miriam, "scarcely ever altered from its look of brooding"—a woman like those "who went with Mary when Jesus was dead" (153).

Is this how a man describes a woman he wants to take to bed? Instead, we have Lawrence describing Miriam as a woman whose "body was not flexible and living," who "walked with a swing, rather heavily, her head bowed forward, pondering," a woman with "no looseness or abandon about her. [...] [with her whole being] gripped stiff with intensity, and her effort, overcharged, closed in on itself" (153–54).

The next chapter, "The Defeat of Miriam," deals primarily with a reworking of Lawrence's climatic "final" breaking off of his protracted adolescent relationship with Chambers, in part at his mother's urging and in part through his continued sense that something was not right with—well, no doubt—both of them. Wasn't that just the point of breaking things off, but did it have to be through such a cold letter—"May I speak of our old, worn love, this last time" (251)—the letter that Lawrence uses in the novel being a reworking of the actual letter he sent to Chambers on her twenty-first birthday in 1908?

Maybe it was alright to speak of the two kinds of love: "a spirit love" that he has given to her "this long, long time," and that other love, "embodied passion"—perhaps in plainer language that Lawrence seems to disdain when weighing in on the topic of men and women: a love based on friendship and emotional intimacy, that is, a platonic relationship, and an adult love based on physical intimacy. And his message is simple: when he looks at Jessie, what he saw was "not the kissable and embraceable part of you" (*A Personal Record* 139), reprising what we have already seen, how she is "so fine to look at, with the silken toss of hair curling over your ears." Instead, it is something we will see repeatedly in *Sons and Lovers* and many other places: this notion of the young girl, as pretty as she may be, as not something that he found sexually alluring. "What I see," he wrote in that 1908 letter, "is the deep spirit within. That I love and can go on loving all my life" (*Personal Record*)—that is, as a friend.

It was just the other part of our relationship that was in shambles. "Look, you are a nun," Lawrence writes, being cruelly blunt, at least about Chambers: "I have given you what I would give a holy nun," then adding in the novel, "as a mystic monk [would give] to a mystic nun." "In all our relations," Lawrence continues in the novel, drawing from the actual letter, "no body enters. I do not talk to you through the senses—rather through the spirit. That is why we cannot love in the common sense" (251). It is an old tune, that Jesse—Miriam in the extended letter—is just too spiritual, but now with a second melody that we have heard before: that Lawrence thinks he has been "too refined, too civilized. I think many folks are."

"So you must let me marry a woman I can kiss and embrace and make the mother of my children" (*Personal Record*), Lawrence wrote to the historical Chambers in a letter that Lawrence included almost word for word in the earliest draft of *Sons and Lovers*, the letter itself marking what Lawrence called "the first phase of Paul's love-affair."

> He was now about twenty-three years old, and, though still virgin, the sex instinct that Miriam had over-refined for so long now grew particularly strong. [...] that thickening and quickening of his blood, that peculiar concentration in the breast, as if something were alive there, a new self or a new centre of consciousness, warning him that sooner or later he would have to ask one woman or another.
>
> (252)

Poor Paul Morel, the literary character, and poor D. H. Lawrence, his creator! A man in his early twenties with a raging sex drive yet still a virgin, a man adamantly opposed to masturbation and to frequenting prostitutes, and a man who, even as he manically sought a female sexual partner in hopes of finally attaining sexual fulfillment, continued to have difficulty connecting his sexual arousal either with women's bodies or with general feelings of intimacy toward women.

The conclusion of *Sons and Lovers* portrays Lawrence's desperate times in his mid-twenties when he finally found two willing women: first, perhaps not surprisingly, with Jessie Chambers, their few intimate meetings portrayed in the aptly named chapter 11, "The Defeat of Miriam"—looked at below—and with the political activist Alice Dax, the likely model for Clara Dawes in *Sons and Lovers*, their tumultuous lovemaking reviewed at the start of the next chapter. Before examining the conclusion of Lawrence's long-standing, mostly adolescent relationship with Chambers, it is helpful to see how this ultimately stressful relationship fits into his overall maturation—a process involving the transition from an often joyous, even exuberant adolescent Chambers portrays in her memoir to the increasingly dyspeptic young adult, one frustrated in his protracted efforts to find a willing female sexual partner and then, a subject for later consideration, often just as frustrated with the three women who became his first and possibly only sexual partners.

Before looking at the tumultuous end of Lawrence's relationship with Chambers, we will briefly consider the two distinct places or situations in Lawrence's adolescence that he seems to have found especially joyous. While one might think one of these two would be Lawrence's love of literature, about which Chambers wrote so glowingly in her memoir—and Lawrence, no doubt, was a voracious reader and eager partner in these discussions with Chambers—we need to look instead at the same two places where we have already seen such apparent contentment in *Lady Chatterley's Lover*: that is, in Lawrence's extended moments of intimacy either with another male or, as we will see in the next section, with his own budding body and its place within a gentle, fertile natural world.

"But the Water Loves Me"

One of Lawrence's most telling descriptions of himself, awash with narcissistic delight in his physical development, comes in a letter from July 1908, where the 22-year-old Lawrence describes how he has just come in from the hayfield, where he had been working "for the last fortnight"; he has just had "a delicious cold bath," he tells us, and eaten "half a fruit pie," adding this only partly hyperbolic assessment that he now feels "as complacent as a god" (*Letters* 65).

What follows is a joyful and, obviously for Lawrence, somewhat unexpected reflection on the maturation of his own body. "My hands are brown, hard, and coarse; my face is gradually tanning"—the result of two weeks of hard work. "I can pick alongside a big experienced man," he adds. "Indeed I am fairly strong; I am pretty well developed; I have done a good deal of dumb-bell practice." Then, in a moment of poetic reflection, there follows an account of a maturing male body:

> Indeed, as I was rubbing myself down in the late twilight a few minutes ago, and as I passed my hands over my sides where the muscles lie suave and secret, I did love myself. I am thin, but well skimmed over with muscle; my skin is very white and unblemished; soft, and dull with a fine pubescent bloom, not shiny like my friend's.

Topped off with, "I am very fond of myself"—that is, without a tinge of the negativity Lawrence rarely can avoid in describing a woman.

It is reminiscent of one of Lawrence's early poems, "The Wild Common," which he later reworked as the opening piece in his *Collected Poems*. Its topic is the speaker's fears regarding what all the changes in nature, the "wild common," might mean for his permanence, his ultimate place in this world. The reassurance he finds comes from the awareness of his own body—what it is like as he steps into the water, feeling his soul "[run] ecstatic over the pliant folds rippling down to / my belly from the breast-lights above."

> Oh but the water loves me and folds me,
> Plays with me, sways me, lifts me and sinks me as though it were
>   living blood,
> Blood of a heaving woman who holds me,
> Owning my supple body a rare glad thing, supremely good.
>
> (Delphi 7124)

There is a similar, extended account of such delight in Lawrence's short story "Love Among the Haystacks." It is an odd story, nominally about the rivalry between two brothers in their early twenties, each of whom falls in love—the younger brother, Maurice (Lawrence's stand-in)—with an exotic European governess. Although she may have been partly modeled on Lawrence's future wife, Frieda Weekley, whom he first met in March 1912, he can only offer a guarded account of her appearance, one that notes that her blue eyes "were peculiarly lidded," making her look "piercingly, then languorously, like a wild cat," or that she had "somewhat Slavonic cheekbones, and was very much freckled" (86–87).

Instead, Lawrence reserves his lyrical power to describe the physical beauty of the male body, in this case—as we have just seen in Lawrence's letter of 1908—after a hard day's labor, and, as with Mellors and as we will see again in Chapter 8, set amidst a man's bath: "There was a trough of pure water in the hedge bottom. It was filled by a tiny spring that filtered over the brim of the trough down the lush hedge bottom of the lower field." And here we see how, for the young Lawrence, love for his own body often blends into love for a gentle, caring nature:

> All round the trough, in the upper field, the land was marshy, and there the meadow-sweet stood like clots of mist, very sickly-smelling in the twilight. The night did not darken, for the moon was in the sky, so that as the tawny colour drew off the heavens they remained pallid with a dimmed moon. The purple bell-flowers in the hedge went black, the ragged robin turned its pink to a faded white, the meadow-sweet gathered light as if it were phosphorescent, and it made the air ache with scent.
>
> (94)

Then comes the account of the bath itself: "Maurice kneeled on the slab of stone bathing his hands and arms, then his face. The water was deliriously cool"—so wondrously unconstrained and lyrical, unlike nearly any activity in Lawrence involving a woman's body:

> Laughing to himself, he squeezed his cloth into the water. He washed himself from head to foot, standing in the fresh, forsaken corner of the field, where no one could see him by daylight, so that now, in the veiled grey tinge of moonlight, he was no more noticeable than the crowded flowers.
>
> (94–95)

Lawrence here portrays Maurice as if being gently courted by the night, personified as wearing "a new look," with a "lustrous grey sheen" that Maurice did not remember ever seeing before, "nor [having] noticed how vital the lights looked, like live folk inhabiting the silvery spaces. And the tall trees, wrapped obscurely in their mantles, would not have surprised him had they begun to move in converse."

Here is a picture of a young man feeling himself at one with a gentle, even a loving world: "As he dried himself, he discovered little wanderings in the air, felt on his sides soft touches and caresses that were peculiarly delicious: sometimes they startled him, and he laughed as if he were not alone."

And, as in *Lady Chatterley's Lover*, Lawrence has saved his most lyrical writing for describing the delights of the male body, although here from a male point of view—"The flowers, the meadow-sweet particularly, haunt[ing Maurice]":

He reached to put his hand over their fleeciness. They touched his thighs. Laughing, he gathered them and dusted himself all over with their cream dust and fragrance. For a moment he hesitated in wonder at himself: but the subtle glow in the hoary and black night reassured him. Things never had looked so personal and full of beauty, he had never known the wonder in himself before.

Nor is it unusual for the young Lawrence to intertwine such a wondrous account of the male body so closely with a lush picture of nature. There is, for instance, in his first novel, *The White Peacock*, this equally rapturous celebration of September, the month of Lawrence's birth, here celebrated as a time with "no heat, no hurry, no thirst and weariness in corn harvest as there is in the hay" (58). A time when the "mornings come slowly":

Perhaps there is the regular breathing hush of the scythe—even the fretful jar of the mowing machine. But next day, in the morning, all is still again. The lying corn is wet, and when you have bound it, and lift the heavy sheaf to make the stook, the tresses of oats wreathe round each other and droop mournfully.

(59)

Or here, in the same novel, one finds his description of the Chambers farm ("Strelley Mill" in the novel) that was to play such a central role in his imagination, which again, unlike his one-on-one interactions with the Chambers daughter Jessie, is always full-throated and unabashedly positive. Then he gives us an account of an afternoon "all warm and golden," the "oat sheaves [...] whisper[ing] to each other as they freely embrace":

The long, stout stubble tinkles as the foot brushes over it; the scent of the straw is sweet. When the poor, bleached sheaves are lifted out of the hedge, a spray of nodding wild raspberries is disclosed, with belated berries ready to drop [...] Then one notices that the last bell hangs from the ragged spire of fox-glove.

And the talk is just as splendid, "of one's hopes—and the future": "of Canada, where work is strenuous, but not life; where the plains are wide, and one is not lapped in a soft valley, like an apple that falls in a secluded orchard"; as are the late afternoons, the sun turning from gold to red, "darken[ing], like a fire burning low, the sun disappears behind the bank of milky mist, purple like the pale bloom on blue plums, and we put on our coats and go home."

It is a motif we see Lawrence repeating in *Sons and Lovers*, where Paul describes his deep, abiding love for the Chambers' farm (here, the "Willey Farm"). First, the farmhouse, with its

> little pokey kitchen, where men's boots tramped, and the dog slept with one eye open for fear of being trodden on; where the lamp hung over the table at night, and everything was so silent. [...] [and the] long, low parlour, with its atmosphere of romance, its flowers, its books, its high rosewood piano. [...] was an exhilaration and a joy to him.
>
> (226–27)

Then, praise for what perhaps involved an even deeper connection for him—the surrounding fields, where he remembers going "joyfully, and spen[ding] the afternoon helping to hoe or to single turnips with his friend." It was in these fields that he "used to lie with the three brothers in the hay piled up in the barn," telling them about his office work in Nottingham.

> In return, they taught him to milk, and let him do little jobs—chopping hay or pulping turnips—just as much as he liked. At midsummer he worked all through hay-harvest with them [...] Though the lads were strong and healthy, yet they had all that over-sensitiveness and hanging-back which made them so lonely, yet also such close, delicate friends once their intimacy was won. Paul loved them dearly, and they him.
>
> (149)

In one of his early stories about his breakup with Jessie Chambers, eventually published as "The Shades of Spring," Lawrence has his stand-in admit how he

> loved the place extraordinarily, the hills ranging round, with bear-skin woods covering their giant shoulders, and small red farms like brooches clasping their garments [...] To his last day, he would dream of this place, when he felt the sun on his face, or saw the small handfuls of snow between the winter twigs, or smelt the coming of spring.
>
> (102)

"Life [...] Full of Glamour for Us Both"

"The Poem of Friendship," that key chapter from *The White Peacock* we examined in Chapter 2, also celebrates a second sort of intimacy important to the young Lawrence—the passionate, asexual intimacy with another man. The other man in that novel was George Saxton, a character based on Jessie Chambers's older brother, Alan, with their fellowship portrayed as the purest, noblest of all possible human relations. Earlier in that chapter, before the climactic swimming scene, there is a quieter moment of intimacy, during which Cyril's abiding sense of loneliness is lessened by both the beauty of nature and the tender means by which a strong friend like George can be "gentle as a woman" in protecting a sensitive soul like Lawrence's effeminate alter ego, Cyril. "There was nothing in this grey, lonely world," Cyril reflects,

> but the peewits swinging and crying, and George swinging silently at his work. The movement of active life held all my attention, and when I looked up, it was to see the motion of his limbs and his head, the rise and fall of his rhythmic body, and the rise and fall of the slow waving peewits.
>
> (219)

It began raining, with George providing a seat for his friend under a "thick hedge." A moment of shared intimacy follows, two men sitting "close together and watch[ing] the rain fall like a grey striped curtain before us, hiding the valley." What follows, the two of them watching the rain "trickle in dark streams off the mare's back, as she stood dejectedly," was for Lawrence a near-perfect moment of adolescent male bonding: "we listened to the swish of the drops falling all about; we felt the chill of the rain, and drew ourselves together in silence. He smoked his pipe, and I lit a cigarette." At such a moment, marked by such physical proximity to a strong male, Lawrence seemed to find the human intimacy he most desired, free of all the stresses associated with closeness with a woman: "The rain continued; all the little pebbles and the red earth glistened in the grey gloom. We sat together, speaking occasionally. It was at these times we formed the almost passionate attachment which later years slowly wore away."

Soon after, when the two men separate, Cyril sees "something near [his] feet, something little and dark, moving indefinitely." It is a larkie's nest—"the yellow beaks, the bulging eyelids of two tiny larks, and the blue lines of their wing quills"—and the beginning of an extended reverie that reveals the connection for the adolescent Lawrence between the narcissistic intimacy he felt for himself and that which he felt for another person. He is fixated on "the swift rise and fall of the brown fledged backs, over which waved long strands of fine down" (220).

There is a level of tenderness here that Mellors will commend himself for but which we rarely see elsewhere in the Lawrence of *Sons and Lovers*, certainly not in Paul's relations with Miriam: "The two little specks of birds lay side by side, beak to beak, their tiny bodies rising and falling in quick unison":

> I gently put down my fingers to touch them; they were warm; gratifying to find them warm, in the midst of so much cold and wet. I became curiously absorbed in them, as an eddy of wind stirred the strands of down. When one fledgling moved uneasily, shifting his soft ball, I was quite excited; but he nestled down again, with his head close to his brother's.

Lawrence's young stand-in feels anguish, but for something seemingly far removed from the sexual urges that will rack Lawrence throughout his early twenties. "In my heart of hearts," he writes, "I longed for someone to nestle against, someone who would come between me and the coldness and wetness of the surroundings. I envied the two little miracles exposed to any tread, yet so serene."

Here is a simple retelling of Aristophanes's speech in Plato's *Symposium*—about humans feeling alienated and longing to return to an earlier state of union with their other half. Thus, Lawrence's complaint of feeling "as if I were always wandering, looking for something which [these baby larks] had found even before the light broke into their shell."

With his "heavy clogs and [his] heart heavy with vague longing," Cyril begins running through a winter landscape:

> The horse-chestnuts bravely kept their white candles erect in the socket of every bough, though no sun came to light them. Drearily a cold swan swept up the water, trailing its black feet, clacking its great hollow wings, rocking the frightened water hens, and insulting the staid black-necked geese.

What did he want, Lawrence wondered, that he constantly "turned thus from one thing to another" (220)?

What follows is the already discussed swimming scene from "The Poem of Friendship," with Lawrence ending his chapter by showing us George and Cyril reluctantly parting, each going back to work—George

> to mow the island of grass he had left standing the previous evening, [Cyril] to sharpen the machine knife, to mow out the hedge-bottoms with the scythe, and to rake the swaths from the way of the machine when the unmown grass was reduced to a triangle.

It is a scene fittingly aglow with nostalgia for what even the young Lawrence—only 20 when he began its composition—may have already seen as representing a level of human intimacy he was unlikely ever again to recapture:

> The cool, moist fragrance of the morning, the intentional stillness of everything, of the tall bluish trees, of the wet, frank flowers, of the trustful moths folded and unfolded in the fallen swaths, was a perfect medium of sympathy. The horses moved with a still dignity, obeying his commands. When they were harnessed, and the machine oiled, still he was loth to mar the perfect morning, but stood looking down the valley.
>
> (223)

Or, more nakedly honest, in an earlier draft of the novel:

> It is the perfect hour for communion, subtle and sacred. When I ask him a brief question, my voice is low and full of intonation, so that he answers with a quiet "yes"; but the intonation he answers with his eyes, that have the softness of wet flowers.
>
> (386)

Here is the nub of Lawrence's golden, prelapsarian adolescence—the part that had nothing to do with either Jessie Chambers or the world-shattering angst that Lawrence invariably associated with heterosexual intercourse:

> "I shan't mow these fields any more," [George] said, and the fallen, silvered swaths flickered back his regret, and the faint scent of the limes was wistful. So much of the field was cut, so much remained to cut; then it was ended. This year the elder flowers were widespread over the corner bushes, and the pink roses fluttered high above the hedge. There were the same flowers in the grass as we had known many years; we should not know them any more.

Even George is imbued with the tenderness and poetic sensibility that Lawrence so valued, as he relates the story of his father damaging a young sycamore merely to make a walking stick:

> It seemed a cruelty. When you are gone, and we are left from here, I shall feel like that, as if my leading shoot were broken off. You see, the tree is spoiled. Yet how it went on growing. I believe I shall grow faster. I can remember the bright red stalks of the leaves as he broke them off from the bough.

Then George is off again, back to his mowing, as Cyril watches with a warm regret: "The sun caught in the uplicking scarlet sorrel flames, the butterflies woke, and I could hear the fine ring of his 'Whoa!' from the far corner. [...] It was his voice which rang the morning awake."

> Later, when the morning was hot, and the honeysuckle had ceased to breathe, and all the other scents were moving in the air about us, when all the field was down, when I had seen the last trembling ecstasy of the harebells, trembling to fall; when the thick clump of purple vetch had sunk; when the green swaths were settling, and the silver swaths were glistening and glittering as the sun came along them, in the hot ripe morning we worked together turning the hay, tipping over the yesterday's swaths with our forks, and bringing yesterday's fresh, hidden flowers into the death of sunlight.
>
> (224)

It was then, Lawrence tells us, that "we talked of the past, and speculated on the future":

> As the day grew older and less wistful, we forgot everything, and worked on, singing, and sometimes I would recite him verses as we went, and sometimes I would tell him about books. Life was full of glamour for us both.

The Climax and Its Aftermath

It was easy for Lawrence to have Paul blame either his mother or Miriam for his lack of interest in sex when all three were living in proximity; obviously, things became not as simple once they separated. "[L]ike so many young men of his own age," Lawrence tells us about Paul and himself, "[s] ex had become so complicated in him that he would have denied that he ever could want Clara or Miriam or any woman whom he *knew*" (276, emphasis in original).

In the meantime, one must ask if Lawrence could have been any more direct about his hang-up—his problem seeing a woman as the object of his sexual desire, or, as he says, Paul saw the "sex drive" as "a sort of detached thing, that did not belong to a woman." Here is a somewhat cryptic point at the center of Lawrence's convoluted notions about adult sexuality, in part adopted from his early reading of Arthur Schopenhauer—the notion that his sex drive was a universal impulse existing apart from any man's desire for any specific woman. The actual acting out of that desire with a woman thus becomes largely a matter of expediency—the sexual act between a man and a woman being what was necessary for the propagation of the species.

There is no denying a brutal component to such a philosophy and, as we shall see, no denying comparable brutality when, in his mid-twenties, Lawrence finally became determined to end his virginity.

This episode begins with Lawrence reengaging with Chambers in the fall of 1908, some nine months after breaking off their platonic relationship the previous January. During this time, Lawrence also felt alone, having left his Midlands home for a teaching position in the London suburb of Croydon. The following May, Lawrence coaxed Chambers into spending a chaste weekend at his London lodgings. During the next few months, Chambers remained a close confidante, with Lawrence sharing the progress of his writings and information about his new circle of female friends. Matters seemed to change when Lawrence renewed his efforts to convince Chambers again to become his mistress by the end of 1909 and the early months of 2010—Lawrence was then in his twenty-fifth year and still a virgin.

Nor was there much chance that things would go well, with the painful events of their lovemaking recast by Lawrence in "The Test on Miriam" chapter of *Sons and Lovers*. The chapter opens with Lawrence's claim that "after all, he was only like other men, seeking his satisfaction"—then the pivot we expect at such moments as Lawrence tries to explain away the hesitancy that always seemed to accompany thoughts of intimacy with a woman. "Oh, but there was something more in him, something deeper!" And this was his momentous insight, similar to what we have already seen in *Lady Chatterley's Lover*, that what truly mattered in intercourse was not intimacy with or somehow pleasing one's partner—here a woman— but the orgasm itself, as expressed here, the notion that "possession was a great moment in life": "All strong emotions concentrated there. Perhaps it was so. There was something divine in it" (284).

If such was the case—that there was something momentous in the orgasm itself—then maybe there may have been some higher justification for Paul's hectoring Miriam into submission: "she would submit, religiously, to the sacrifice. He should have her. And at the thought her whole body clenched itself involuntarily, hard, as if against something; but Life forced her through this gate of suffering, too, and she would submit." And if all this were just claptrap, no matter—the result would be to "give him what he wanted," which, after all, Paul argues, was likely "her deepest wish" as well.

Their initial bout of lovemaking takes place outdoors, in a "thick plantation of fir-trees and pines": "He stood against a pine-tree trunk and took her in his arms. She relinquished herself to him, but it was a sacrifice in which she felt something of horror." The reason seems clear enough—a complete lack of warmth on Lawrence's part, Mellors's vaunted tenderness notwithstanding: "This thick-voiced, oblivious man was a stranger to her" (286).

Then, fittingly, it started raining for Lawrence and Chambers and, as reenvisioned in *Sons and Lovers*, for Paul and Miriam. Lawrence also has Paul busily voicing what will eventually become Mellors's central lament about women and intercourse—their inability or unwillingness to bring themselves to orgasm in concert with their partners, as if a woman's sexual drive should be as mechanical as a man's. Paul's "heart was down, very heavy," Lawrence tells us, as he "realized that she had not been with him all the time, that her soul had stood apart, in a sort of horror." Now satiated, his other sympathetic, even tender side is free to reemerge: "Very dreary at heart, very sad, and very tender, his fingers wandered over her face pitifully." And, perhaps switching points of view here, as he will later do with Lady Chatterley, he adds how Miriam once again "loved him deeply." Why, we might ask? Because (emphasis added) "*He* was tender and beautiful."

Given that ordinary sex, such a crucial part of life, was so disappointing for Lawrence, it is easy to imagine how he quickly fell into thinking there had to be some other, deeper or darker realm of sensual experience—something possibly just out of his reach. Hence, the rhetorical question: What if "life seemed like a shadow, day a white shadow," then wouldn't "night, and death, and stillness, and inaction, [...] [seem] like *being*"? If pleasing oneself by pleasing a woman was not the object, then what was? It could only be something radically different: "To be alive, to be urgent and insistent—that was *not-to-be*. The highest of all was to melt out into the darkness and sway there, identified with the great Being." Yes, sex really could be special, but if so, its goal was not to please a partner but only to allow us "[t]o be rid of our individuality, which is our will, which is our effort—to live effortless, a kind of conscious sleep—that is very beautiful, I think; that is our after-life—our immortality" (287–88, emphasis in original).

Their second act of lovemaking—and Chambers reports during this period seeing Lawrence intimately on "fewer occasions than I could count on the fingers of one hand" (185)—started better, indeed, in the fashion of what might be called ordinary lovemaking, with the man desirous of the woman's body:

> He never forgot seeing her as she lay naked on the bed [...] First he saw only her beauty, and was blind with it. She had the most beautiful body he had ever imagined. He stood unable to move or speak, looking at her, his face half smiling with wonder.
>
> (289)

Then, as he moves forward to embrace this young woman—"Her big brown eyes [...] watching him, still and resigned and loving"—things again go off the rails. The problem? Paul's awareness that what is finally most important to Miriam is not sex but intimacy: "she lay as if she had given herself up to sacrifice: there was her body for him." Again, what he wanted was not such a shared moment but a willing, cooperative sex partner: "the look at the back of her eyes, like a creature awaiting immolation, arrested him, and all his blood fell back" (289–90).

That a woman's interest in sex might not be the same as his was a thought he "could hardly bear": "For a second, he wished he were sexless or dead." Then he did as one supposes a gay man might do when making love to a woman: "he shut his eyes again to her, and his blood beat back again." Then he made love to her:

[L]oved her to the last fibre of his being. He loved her. But he wanted, somehow, to cry. There was something he could not bear for her sake. [...] As he rode home he felt that he was finally initiated. He was a youth no longer. But why had he the dull pain in his soul? Why did the thought of death, the afterlife, seem so sweet and consoling?

Is there any better description, one might ask, of a gay man's studied efforts at loving a woman?

He spent the week with Miriam, and wore her out with his passion before it was gone. He had always, almost wilfully, to put her out of count, and act from the brute strength of his own feelings. And he could not do it often, and there remained afterwards always the sense of failure and of death. If he were really with her, he had to put aside himself and his desire. If he would have her, he had to put her aside.

(290)

That is, to have sex with her, he had to put her out of his mind.

Nor does Lawrence leave any doubt where the blame for all this lies, as explored in an early draft of the poem "Lilies in the Fire"—that he was "ashamed, you wanted me not tonight":

Your radiance dims when I draw too near, and my free
Fire enters your petals like death, you wilt dead white ...

For Lawrence, it was "a degradation deep to me" that what he envisioned as his "best / Soul['s] whitest lightning," a sure sign of "God stepping down to earth in one white stride," should be seen by his partner only as "a clogged, numb burden of flesh" (Worthen 252).

Perhaps it is only fair that we give Chambers the last word—specifically her account of how, in these few sexual encounters with Lawrence, she experienced a "tension [...] greater than I could bear": "I could not conceal from myself," Chambers continues, "a forced note in Lawrence's attitude, as if he was pushed forwards in his sensual desires—and a lack of spontaneity" (Worthen 253). They only met, Chambers adds, "under conditions both difficult and irksome," and, no surprise, always "with Lawrence's earnest injunction to me not to try to hold him" (Worthen 251).

"It was all very wonderful and glamorous here, in the old places that had seemed so ordinary." So says Lawrence's stand-in, the refined, attenuated Cyril Mersham, in Lawrence's early short story "A Modern Lover," composed in January 1910, the time of his final courtship of Chambers. At the heart of the story is Lawrence recalling the Eastwood countryside associated with the Chambers family on a problematic visit he made just that past Christmas, after some 14 months in London working as a high school teacher. What did he want, he asks, in returning to the woman (here, Muriel) and the family that had been at the heart of his happy and decidedly chaste adolescence?

And the answer for the emotionally fraught Mersham, as it no doubt was for Lawrence, is far from clear, even if there was little doubt about his principal problem: that at 24, he was determined to end his protracted virginity. He had flirted with a handful of women—"blown the low fires gently with his breath, and had leaned his face towards their glow, and had breathed in the words that rose like fumes from the revived embers"—and all for naught, plagued as he now was "with the strong drug of sufferings and ecstasies and sensations, and the dreams that ensued." In such desperate straits, dealing with women enmeshed in the "rubble of sentimentality and stupid fear," was it crazy to imagine that the one great friend of his adolescence might be coerced into helping—providing him with, in Lawrence's wonderfully euphemism, "enough of the philtre of life to stop the craving which tortured him hither and thither," and then, in language that shows how Lawrence so often connected sexual pleasure (here presumably imagined) with that joyous sense of intimacy with himself:

> enough ["of the philtre of life"] to satisfy for a while, to intoxicate him till he could laugh the crystalline laughter of the star, and bathe in the retreating flood of twilight like a naked boy in the surf, clasping the waves and beating them and answering their wild clawings with laughter sometimes, and sometimes gasps of pain.
>
> (23)

In the story, Mersham has returned to ask his former friend to have sex with him, as Lawrence did with Chambers in real life—that much, and only that much, is simple.

For starters, there is what, for Lawrence, was the ever-unresolved issue of desire. When he first sees Muriel, for instance, there is the most momentary quickening of his pulse as he takes her hand and, for an instant, "plunged overhead, as it were, [...] in her great brown eyes," only to look away immediately, only later realizing that he had not kissed her. What was it about Muriel—about Jessie and Alice Dax and, as we shall see in the next chapter, even Frieda Weekley—that made him turn away? Was it "her bowed, submissive pose, [...] the dark, small head with its black hair twining and hiding her face, that made him wince and shrink and close over his soul that had been open like a foolhardy flower to the night?" Later, as he begins their tête-à-tête in which he is going to ask Muriel to be his sexual partner, he describes her sitting with "her elbows on her knees, her chin in her hands, sucking her little finger, and withdrawing it from her lips with a little pop, looking all the while in the fire" (27)—hardly the picture of one's ideal sexual partner.

Meanwhile, Mersham "hardened his heart and turned his head from [Muriel]" to her brothers, "two well-built lads of twenty and twenty-one," who were home from the pits, their faces intriguingly covered in coal dust. Then this marvelous scopophilic description, some 18 years before Lawrence showed us Connie Chatterley's spying on the bathing Mellors: "The boys had stripped to their waists, and had knelt on the hearth-rug and washed themselves in a large tin bowl, the mother sponging and drying their backs. Now they stood wiping themselves, the firelight bright and rosy on their fine torsos, their heavy arms swelling and sinking with life. They seemed to cherish the firelight on their bodies. Benjamin, the younger, leaned his breast to the warmth, and threw back his head, showing his teeth in a voluptuous little smile"— with Mersham "watch[ing] them, as he had watched the peewits and the sunset" (25).

Then one last telling moment in the story, by far its most erotically charged moment, obviously not with Muriel, who listens sympathetically to his plea for sex without agreeing to it, but with Muriel's new boyfriend, Tom Vickers, a man, like George Saxton from *The White Peacock*, short in stature but muscular—with "fine limbs, the solid, large thighs, and the thick wrists"—a man of "handsome, healthy animalism, and good intelligence." Mersham accompanies Vickers to the barn where he has stored his bike, which now has a flat tire. Vickers, ever the strong, silent mate, holds out his hand to guide Mersham past a low beam. Mersham "knew the position of the beam to an inch, however dark the barn, but he allowed Vickers to guide him past it." Why? Because, as we saw with Cyril in "The

Poem of Friendship," he "rather enjoyed being taken into Tom's protection" (37).

Next, Vickers strikes a match, "bowing over the ruddy core of light and illuminating himself like some beautiful lantern in the midst of the high darkness of the barn." What follows is another scopophilic description of such precision that one wonders how anyone, Lawrence included, could have ever doubted the sincerity of his homoerotic desire:

> For some moments [Vickers] bent over his bicycle-lamp, trimming and adjusting the wick, and his face, gathering all the light on its ruddy beauty, seemed luminous and wonderful. Mersham could see the down on his cheeks above the razor-line, and the full lips in shadow beneath the moustache, and the brush of the eyebrows between the light.

And, just in case there were any doubts, Lawrence gives us Mersham's thought: "After all [...] he's very beautiful; she's a fool to give him up."

The conclusion of this scene, Vickers "shut[ting] the lamp with a snap, and carefully crush[ing] the match under his foot," requires no commentary:

> Then he took the pump from the bicycle, and crouched on his heels in the dimness, inflating the tyre. The swift, unerring, untiring stroke of the pump, the light balance and the fine elastic adjustment of the man's body to his movements pleased Mersham.

The story itself ends as one might expect, with Mersham failing either to get Muriel's agreement to become his sexual partner or even to kiss her goodbye as they were about to part. Nor can it be a surprise that what follows is a reverie—that beautiful snapshot of nature that Lawrence always seems to prefer to intimacy with a woman. Here, he gives us a picture of "the water in a little brook under the hedge [...] running, chuckling with extraordinary loudness": "away on Nethermere they heard the sad, haunting cry of the wild-fowl from the North. The stars still twinkled intensely." Mersham can think of nothing to say, with Muriel now little more than a part of the setting—"the pale blotch of her face upturned from the low meadow beyond the fence": "The thorn boughs tangled above her, drooping behind her like the roof of a hut. Beyond was the great width of the darkness" (41).

The parting lacks even a glimmer of passion, with Mersham "unable to gather his energy to say anything vital." As he turns to leave, he sees "her white uplifted face vanish, and her dark form bend under the boughs of the tree, and go out into the great darkness. She did not say good-bye."

Happy Days—A Coda

It may seem odd to continue discussing Lawrence's adolescence in the summer of 1908 when he was close to 23, but this is the period covered in the later chapters of *Sons and Lovers*, dealing with all his difficulties, mainly sexual, with Jessie Chambers, as well as the period he was working on the early drafts of what was to become his first novel, *The White Peacock*, published in 1911. In other words, these were the halcyon days of Lawrence's late adolescence, the time before having to confront the many unresolved complexities of heterosexual lovemaking (the subject of the next chapter)—when, as we have just seen, he still could unabashedly extol the joys of his own body, the natural world, especially that surrounding the Chambers' farm, and of the male companionship that he found there, primarily with Alan Chambers—the experiences that taken together were likely the jewels of his adolescence. However, we can find this same zest for life in Lawrence's own voice in two magnificent letters from 1908 that he wrote to a woman confidante, Blanche Jennings, whom, oddly enough, he met only once in person.

These letters exhibit the two key elements of the youthful Lawrence free of adolescent angst: his love of nature and his close contact with men who struck Lawrence as at ease in nature. The first of these two letters, dated June 25, 1908, opens with a spectacular reverie celebrating, in Shakespearean fashion, the pleasures of a summer's day, with Lawrence having "just gathered some gooseberries for a pudding, and picked them out here on our little mat of grass, sitting in the united shade of an elder and a lilac bush" (56).

Lawrence's immediate problem is asking indulgence to continue writing in pencil—he's too lazy to go inside to get a proper pen—while "lounging here on the grass, where the still warm air is full of the scent of pinks, spicy and sweet, and a stack of big red lilies a few yards away impresses me with a sense of hot, bright sunshine." Nor is Lawrence done with describing the summer flowers—"vivid potentillas just mov[ing] in a little breeze that brings hot breath of hay across the permanent spice of pinks." Then, from "the field at the bottom of the garden," Lawrence hears

the 'chack" and jingle of a horse-rake; the horse is neighing; there, they come into sight between the high larkspur and the currant bushes!; the man sits like a charioteer; his bare arm glistens in the sun as he stretches forward to pull up the tines; they have gone again.

"It is a true mid-summer day," he continues, in a reverie, one with no other purpose than to share his delight in the world, starting with the "languorous grey mist over the distance; Shipley woods, and Heanor with its solid church are hidden today": "The haze just falls on Eastwood; the church is blue, and seems fast asleep, the very chimes are languid. Only the bees are busy, nuzzling into some wide white flowers;—and I am busy too, of course" (57).

He admits his picture may sound too idyllic. Still, why bother "hunt[ing] out the ugly side of the picture," he asks rhetorically, "when nature has given you an eye for the pretty, and a soul for flowers, and for lounging in the lozenge lighted shade of a lilac tree"? All without a whiff of the anxiety and disappointment that we have seen and will continue to see in Lawrence's accounts of lovemaking, at least those from a male point of view.

Then, a month later (July 30), there is the letter previously cited in which Lawrence expresses such delight in his body and even his skin— "very white and unblemished; soft, and dull with a fine pubescent bloom." He continues with another issue in Lawrence's long-term psychic development—namely, how his general lack of interest in boys' games and sensitive nature had led to his having more female friends while in school.

"You tell me I have no male friends," he adds, before describing how he had been just working in the field with "the original of my George [from *The White Peacock*]"—that is, Jessie's older brother, Alan. "I am very fond of my friend, and he of me," Lawrence adds. "Sometimes, often," he continues, touching on a central motif related to *tenderness* from *Lady Chatterley's Lover*, "he is as gentle as a woman towards me." Indeed, Lawrence adds, all his male friends are "on the whole, soft-mannered towards me." Then Lawrence goes into a lengthy analysis of that lifelong concern—the difficulty of male friendship, or what he refers to here as the achievement of David and Jonathan, describing it "as impossible [to him] as magnificent love between a woman and me" (65–66). (Seventeen years later, Lawrence would write a play, *David*, based on this relationship— briefly discussed in Chapter 6 below.)

There is little doubt what Lawrence is seeking in a male friend—a kind of natural affinity predicated on "the breadth of [another's] understanding [...] that delicate response from the chords of feeling which is involuntary." Again, anticipating Mellors, Lawrence relies on a long-standing stereotype to make his point—that women are too emotional, their "soul" not "so distinctly divided and active in part as a man's." "Set a woman's soul vibrating in response to your own," he continues, "and it is her whole soul which trembles with a strong, soft note of uncertain quality." Lawrence wants something quieter ("more satisfactory") that exudes calm and strength, much as Mellors did for Connie. "But a man will respond, if he be a friend, to the very chord you strike, with clear and satisfying timbre, responding with a part, not the whole, of his soul."

Yet, as Connie also realizes, most men are "stubborn and unwieldy instrument[s]," lacking, as they do, the tenderness she credits to Mellors. For the mass of men are not tender or sensitive—

> [e]ver so many chords are slack, and won't sound; most of the subtle semi-notes are missing; you may call from [them] the notes of the scale of C, but hardly more; the deep bottom tones, and the shrill, sharp notes at the top which verge on madness, they are all missing.

Lawrence, alas, sees a sensitive young man like himself—he was 22 when he wrote this letter and likely still a virgin—as trapped: Turn to a woman instead, he continues; "[s]et up her response, and the whole range of her chords of feeling vibrates with incoherent frenzy." The result is the sort of resignation to a sort of solitary life we eventually see Mellors opt for at the end of *Lady Chatterley's Lover*: "So to make a Jonathan for me"—to "complete the key board," in his extended metaphor—"it would take the natures of ten men such as I know."

And here we have an encapsulation of the *hidden* Lawrence at the heart of this study—a man ideally attuned to his female correspondent in a chatty, intimate way. Consider, for instance, the wonderfully gentle way—dare we call it a *tender* way?—that Lawrence describes the empty chatter of women, that "murmur of her whole soul answering at once, when there is no call for such an answer": "like bees in a great lime tree, hidden altogether, so that the tree seems to be speaking and saving nothing."

We see a man fully at ease with women as friends, sharing with this one correspondent his concern over the difficulty of establishing that perfect male friendship—nor is turning to a woman, Lawrence continues, an adequate substitute. The problem here is that the initial sexual attraction men and women have for each other is way too shallow: "Most people marry with their souls vibrating to the note of sexual love—and the sex notes may run into beautiful aesthetics, poetry and pictures, and romance." But this is far from enough, at least for Lawrence. And again, we are close to the heart of our thesis, the "hidden" Lawrence baring his soul: a 22-year-old male, still a virgin, disparaging a relationship between men and women—but clearly with his situation in mind, what he needs in a partner to make him happy—because of the need to reach some other sort of harmony with that other person. Here he uses a double negative to blunt the force of his notion of sexual incompatibility, anticipating Mellors's final resolution of his relationship with a woman:

> I am not sure whether the chords of sex, and the fine chords of noble feeling do not inevitably produce a discord; in other words, whether

one could possibly marry and hold as a wife a woman before whom one's soul sounded its deepest notes.

(66–67)

The letter ends with another hymn to the joys of male fellowship—how "[f]rom morning till night I have worked in the fields, when the willows have glittered like hammered steel in the morning, till evening when the yellow atmosphere seemed thick and palpable with dense sunshine at evening." It is there in the Chambers' fields, Lawrence continues, that

you might have found me crawling from side to side on the horse rake, bending, then a jingle as the tines fell behind the winrow [...] [or] heard the whirr of the file as I sharpened the bristling machine-knife under the hornbeam.

Again, we see Lawrence blending intimacy with himself and with other men, adding that

you could have seen me high on the load, or higher on the stack, like a long mushroom in my felt hat, sweating, with my shirt neck open. In the evening, as we moved, we four men, turning the silvered swaths, we sang the songs we learned at school, and then my beloved Schumann, and Giordani.

And Lawrence's coda to this near-perfect letter—one last glimpse of the exuberant adolescent: "The sun is gay on the nasturtiums and marigolds. A gypsy woman has come. She wants a few marigolds. 'I dew so love 'em in broth'" (69).

Works Cited

Chambers, Jessie. *D. H. Lawrence: A Personal Record*. 2nd Edition. Ed. J. D. Chambers. Frank Cass, 1965.

Lawrence, D. H. *Complete Works*. Delphi Classics, 2015.

———. *Lady Chatterley's Lover*. The Orioli edition, privately printed in Italy in 1928.

———. *Letters of D. H. Lawrence*. Vol. 1: September 1901 – May 1913. Ed. James T. Boulton. Cambridge UP, 1979.

———. "Love Among the Haystacks." In *Love Among the Haystacks and Other Stories*. Ed. John Worthen. Grafton Books, 1988, 78–110.

———. "A Modern Lover." In *Love Among the Haystacks and Other Stories*. Ed. John Worthen. Grafton Books, 1988: 22–41.

———. *The Rainbow*. Ed. Mark Kinkead-Weekes. Penguin Books, 1995.

———. "Shades of Spring." In *The Prussian Officer and Other Stories*. Ed. John Worthen. Penguin Books, 1995: 98–112.

———. *Sons and Lovers* (CE). Eds. Helen Baron and Carl Baron. Cambridge UP, 1992.

———. *Sons and Lovers*. Viking P, 1971.

———. *A Study of Thomas Hardy and Other Essays*. Ed. Bruce Steele. Cambridge UP, 2002.

———. *The White Peacock*. Ed. Andrew Robertson. Cambridge UP, 2002.

Worthen, John. *D. H. Lawrence: The Early Years 1885–1912*. Cambridge UP, 1991.

4 The Other Three Women

"Clara Dawes"—Lawrence's First Adult Relationship

Lawrence does not end *Sons and Lovers*, his coming-of-age novel, with Paul Morel's protracted sexual liaison with the great friend of his adolescence— the complicated affair we saw recounted in our last chapter and reflecting events that occurred in the first half of 1910, months before Lawrence's twenty-fifth birthday. Instead, he carries his story forward with Paul's affair with the older, married Clara Dawes, a relationship based on the only other sexual partner we know Lawrence had before meeting Frieda Weekley in March 1912. This affair, likely begun in August 1911, a year after he had ended physical relations with Chambers, was with Alice Dax, an activist in the suffrage movement and, like Frieda, a married woman some half-dozen years Lawrence's senior.

With Alice Dax—and much about their affair remains conjecture based on the fictional rendering of Clara Dawes—Lawrence finally seems to have found the willing sexual partner he long felt he needed. In *Sons and Lovers*, it is a volume of poetry—an unexpected birthday gift to Paul, with Clara's inscription referencing her own "isolation"—which brings the lovers together. "Paul flushed hot," Lawrence notes, "suddenly intensely moved": "He was filled with the warmth of her. In the glow he could almost feel her as if she were present—her arms, her shoulders, her bosom, see them, feel them, almost contain them" (273). The incident here may be a nod to a widely circulated story about the impromptu nature of Lawrence's first sexual encounter with Dax, which supposedly began as a routine social visit until Dax, seeing the young Lawrence despondent over his inability to complete a poem, "took him upstairs and gave him sex" (Worthen 364).

This unconfirmed anecdote, supposedly circulated by Dax, captures the open, "adult" nature of this second sexual relationship for Lawrence and just how different it seemed, at least at the outset, from his tortured

DOI: 10.4324/9781003495093-4

involvement with Chambers. The grand romantic moment of Paul and Clara's relationship came on the night he took her to the theater, with Clara dressed in "a sort of semi-evening dress that left her arms and neck and part of her breast bare." Here, for once, we see Lawrence favorably impressed with a woman, albeit perhaps as much with her clothes as her features:

> Her hair was done fashionably. The dress, a simple thing of green crape, suited her. [...] He could see her figure inside the frock, as if that were wrapped closely round her. The firmness and the softness of her upright body could almost be felt as he looked at her.
>
> (330–31)

Still, there is no denying Paul's erotic arousal as he sits in the theater "beside her beautiful naked arm, watching the strong throat rise from the strong chest, watching the breasts under the green stuff, the curve of her limbs in the tight dress." Indeed, what seems to have triggered Paul's arousal was the contrast between his arousal and Clara's utter composure—"as she balanced her head and stared straight in front of her, pouting, wistful, immobile [...] A kind of eternal look about her, as if she were a wistful sphinx."

Paul misses his train that evening and has to stay the night at Clara's, who was then living with her mother. Later that night, Paul makes his way up to her room, but not before, in a scene restored in the Cambridge edition, discovering a pair of Clara's stockings left on a chair and "stealthily" putting them on himself—an act of self-arousal, anticipating through a change of clothes the full-scale swapping of gender identities we have already suggested was the norm for Lawrence in *Lady Chatterley's Lover*.

Regardless, the lovemaking that follows is surprisingly positive from a male's point of view, unlike anything in *Lady Chatterley's Lover*, with a single paragraph cut from the original publication especially compelling. In it, Lawrence describes how Paul's "blood began to run free" as he loosened her gown:

> Looking at her, he had to bite his lip, and the tears of pain came to his eyes, she was so beautiful, and so desirable. The first kiss on her breast made him pant with fear. The great dread, the great humility, and the awful desire, were nearly too much. Her breasts were heavy.
>
> (CE 383)

—this last note, possibly a reference to the matronly Frieda, with whom he was already living when he composed this scene.

Paul's passion here is visceral:

> He held one in each hand, like big fruits in their cups, and kissed them, fearfully. He was afraid to look at her. His hands went travelling over her, soft, delicate, discriminate, fearful, full of adoration. Suddenly he saw her knees, and he dropped, kissing them passionately.

Nor should we be surprised that Lawrence would end this excised paragraph by shifting the focus to Clara: "She quivered. And then again, with his fingers on her sides, she quivered."

Lawrence continues this focus on Clara in the novel's next scene back at work—Paul's proximity to Clara having become "a cruelty to her." In this scene, Paul somehow gets magically transformed from the sniffling momma's boy we have seen until this precise moment to the sort of male erotic ideal we have already seen in *Lady Chatterley's Lover*. Clara, Lawrence writes, "knew exactly how his breast was shapen under the waistcoat, and she wanted to touch it," and, as with Connie Chatterley, we see Lawrence focusing all the desire in the woman, or, more accurately, in her as directed toward the male. What she wanted, Lawrence tells us, was "to break through the sham of it, smash the trivial coating of business which covered him with hardness, get at the man again; but she was afraid" (351).

When their lovemaking continues, the focus shifts back to Paul. Only now, Lawrence no longer shows us the secure lover from their night at the theater but someone closer to Miriam's tortured lover from earlier in the novel—a man with urgent sexual needs but, as with the young Lawrence, someone unsure how those needs fit into his life's trajectory. " 'Don't ask me anything about the future,' [Paul] said miserably," adding, "I don't know anything. Be with me now, will you, no matter what it is—" (352).

Clara responds, holding him passionately, with Lawrence noting how she "could not bear the suffering in his voice." Meanwhile, Paul continues to act more in the manner of Chambers's account of Lawrence's strange, other-worldly nature during the few times they made love—Chambers noting, for instance, how "the whole question of sex had for him the fascination of horror" (153). Only now, Lawrence is the one who gives voice to this odd behavior, with Clara, not Chambers, the one growing "afraid in her soul":

> He might have anything of her—anything; but she did not want to *know*. She felt she could not bear it. [...] She stood clasping him and caressing him, and he was something unknown to her—something almost uncanny. She wanted to soothe him into forgetfulness.
>
> (353, emphasis in original)

What follows is a fleshed-out account of the young Paul, a stand-in for Lawrence, in the middle of his first adult sexual relationship. And what it shows us is likely a near-perfect distillation of what heterosexual love-making likely meant for Lawrence at the time—as a "struggle [going] down in his soul" until he lost awareness of Clara, until she "was not there for him, only a woman, warm, something he loved and almost worshipped, there in the dark." This is a view of lovemaking whose sole purpose is to provide him with a partner, another person willing to submit to his desires. "The naked hunger and inevitability of his loving her, something strong and blind and ruthless in its primitiveness, made the hour almost terrible to her." Here, finally, was a partner who "knew how stark and alone he was."

Next comes a marvelous account of their lovemaking, beginning with "peewits [...] screaming in the field" and Lawrence's sense that surely Clara was equally mesmerized by the profound loneliness they shared—what he could tell by looking into her eyes, "dark and shining and strange, life wild at the source staring into his life, stranger to him, yet meeting him; and he put his face down on her throat, afraid." What sort of person could it be that could provide him with such relief?

A strong, strange, wild life, that breathed with his in the darkness through this hour. It was all so much bigger than themselves that he was hushed. They had met, and included in their meeting the thrust of the manifold grass-stems, the cry of the peewit, the wheel of the stars.
(353)

Then, in the morning, "considerable peace," initially with Paul happy, "almost as if he had known the baptism of fire in passion, and it left him at rest." But also with more confusion, not unlike what a gay man might experience trying to make sense of his strange, mixed experience of heterosexual intercourse—the recognition that his relief "was not Clara": "It was something that happened because of her, but it was not her. They were scarcely any nearer each other. It was as if they had been blind agents of a great force" (354).

It is a position Lawrence expands as Paul and Clara vacation together at a beach in Lincolnshire, with their lovemaking, once started, "strong enough to carry with it everything—reason, soul, blood—in a great sweep, like the Trent carries bodily its back-swirls and intertwinings, noiselessly." In the sex act, he became "not a man with a mind, but a great instinct. His hands were like creatures, living; his limbs, his body, were all life and consciousness, subject to no will of his, but living in themselves" (363).

Here, we see Lawrence's ability to describe the power of sex, tracing the source of arousal not to the woman beside him but to the life force pulsating through nature—"the vigorous, wintry stars [...] strong also with life." Paul and the stars, not Clara,

> struck with the same pulse of fire, and the same joy of strength which held the bracken-frond stiff near his eyes held his own body firm. It was as if he, and the stars, and the dark herbage, and Clara were licked up in an immense tongue of flame, which tore onwards and upwards.
>
> (364)

This is typical of lovemaking in Lawrence narrated from the male point of view—the lover seemingly unconcerned either with pleasing his partner or even being pleased by her, and thus all so different from the ecstatic lovemaking scenes we have seen in *Lady Chatterley's Lover*. What we see here instead are echoes of what the young Lawrence had first learned from reading Schopenhauer—this notion of sex as a primal force pulsing through all living things, essentially independent of an individual's actual desire for another person:

> Everything rushed along in living beside him; everything was still, perfect in itself, along with him. This wonderful stillness in each thing in itself, while it was being borne along in a very ecstasy of living, seemed the highest point of bliss.

All perfect, at least for that one particular moment, but what if the woman failed to experience her orgasm simultaneously with his? Wouldn't lovemaking then lose its spontaneity and the whole experience take on a mechanical quality, not unlike masturbation? "Gradually," Lawrence opines, it was as if "some mechanical effort spoilt their loving, or when they had splendid moments, they had them separately, and not so satisfactorily"—with the result that the Lawrence of *Sons and Lovers* is quickly back to Mellors's general complaint against women as sexual partners.

Meanwhile, *Sons and Lovers* quickly comes to a close—with the death of Paul's mother and his odd realization, considered in greater detail in the next section, that maybe he is less interested in Clara than in her husband and putative rival, Baxter Dawes—indeed, enough interest for Paul to help effect their reconciliation, much as Lawrence may have done with Alice Dax, who soon reconciled with her husband after this brief affair, eventually becoming pregnant with her second child.

Regardless, soon it would be March 1912, when the 26-year-old Lawrence—already the author of two novels, *The White Peacock* (published in January 1911) and *The Trespasser* (to be published that May)—would visit the Nottingham home of one of his professors, Ernest Weekley. There, he would meet the professor's wife and mother of their three children, the woman with whom, in nine weeks, he would travel to Europe, not returning to England for some 25 months. By then, Lawrence would be the celebrated author of the coming-of-age novel *Sons and Lovers* (published in May 1913) and, by the month of his return in June 1914, at last, Frieda Weekley's husband.

Frieda Weekley—First Impressions

Lawrence met his future wife—Emma Maria Frieda Johanna Weekly (née von Richthofen, born 1879)—on a Sunday in March 1912, on a visit to his former professor to discuss the possibility of a teaching position in Germany. During this visit, he had a lively discussion with the professor's wife, displaying some of his iconoclastic positions against women's suffrage. Frieda's unconventional response was enough to trigger in Lawrence the sense that here was another independent spirit, possibly his equal—and, in terms of pedigree and personal experience with the latest European thinkers, clearly his superior.

Here, he sensed, was a woman with none of the sexual inhibitions that had so plagued his relations with all women his age, starting with Jessie Chambers and including Louie Burrows, his fiancée for 14 months before he broke off their engagement just a few weeks before. While Lawrence may have found his other older lover, Alice Dax, somewhat parochial, partly because of her involvement in local Nottingham politics, Frieda struck him as a different sort of woman—sophisticated, worldly, and freethinking. Soon after this meeting, Lawrence sent her a one-sentence letter: "You are the most wonderful woman in all England" (376), a phrase he would repeat in the months ahead and one that encapsulates the essence of Frieda's appeal to him—as a complete psychic entity, more a free spirit or moral force than an alluring sexual object like the shirtless Mellors whom Connie Chatterley had spied washing.

There is no record of Lawrence saying anything else about Frieda for over a month until he alerts his editor, Edward Garnett, in mid-April that he soon hopes to introduce him to Mrs. Weekley. She is "ripping," he tells Garnett, "the finest woman I've ever met," before reviewing her pedigree as "the daughter of Baron von Richthofen, of the ancient and famous house of Richthofen." Then, again falling back on her psychic essence and not her appearance, he noted how she was "perfectly unconventional, but really good—in the best sense. I'll bet you've never met anybody like her, by a long chalk. [...] Oh but she is the woman of a lifetime" (384).

To see Lawrence's rendering of his first impression of Frieda in the more robust voice of the novelist, one must go to his unfinished novel, *Mr. Noon*, a work whose second half closely tracks his first months with Frieda. In the novel, their first meeting is moved from Nottingham to Germany, with the details likely as Lawrence remembered them—as Gilbert Noon, his stand-in, "sat facing a young and lovely, glowing woman": "The woman was glowing with zest and animation, her grey-green eyes laughed and lighted, she laughed with her wide mouth and showed all her beautiful teeth." The woman, Johanna, is no longer presented as a moral force—much of the text for *Mr. Noon* was written during the winter of 1920–21, nearly nine years after their meeting—nor can Lawrence's description here, as with so many of his other favorable portraits of women, be called anything other than decorous, reflecting the stock details from a woman's magazine:

> Her hair was soft and brownish and took glints, her throat, as it rose from the fine texture of her blouse, that was dark blue and red frail stuff transparent over white, rose like a lovely little column, so soft and warm and curd-white. She was full-bosomed and full of life, gleaming with life, like a flower in the sun, and like a cat that looks round in the sunshine and finds it good.

Lawrence seems unable to get beyond a similar superficiality in dealing with his stand-in, Gilbert, reducing his response—nominally about the great love of his life—to a matter of "being smitten," only this time more so:

> Now he was struck all of a heap, so much so that he did not even know he was smitten at all, but only watched and listened, was all eyes and ears and soul-attentiveness, with no saving afterthought to steady him.

Alas, one has to look elsewhere to see anything of substance about Lawrence's first interactions with Frieda. One place is Frieda's memoir, in which she retells the anecdote about what first elicited her love for Lawrence. It was an early spring outing with her two small girls soon after their first meeting. As they approached a small brook, Lawrence deftly folded paper into boats and set them afloat downstream with matches aflame. "Then," Frieda adds, "he put daisies in the brook, and they floated down with their upturned faces. Crouched by the brook, playing there with the children, Lawrence forgot about me completely" (5).

Here we see the puckish, childlike element in Lawrence—he was praised throughout his life as an incomparable mimic—reminiscent of a scene in *Sons and Lovers* where the adolescent Paul bewitches his older brother's fiancée, the three of them lying in a meadow, with "a beautiful quivering screen of poplars" on one side: "Hawthorn was dropping from the hedges; penny daisies and ragged robin were in the field, like laughter." Then, while the older brother dozed and his fiancée played with his hair, Lawrence shows us Paul gathering daisies, deftly weaving them "in her jet-black hair—big spangles of white and yellow, and just a pink touch of ragged robin" (128–29).

What woman searching for a sensitive soul as a lover—perhaps one capable of evoking a lost innocence in her own life—wouldn't be entranced by such a young man? Or, as Frieda would write about this day trip with Lawrence and her two girls—echoing that key term we see repeatedly in describing Lawrence's erotic life—"Suddenly I knew I loved him. He had touched a new tenderness in me" (*Not I* 5).

"After that," she adds, "things happened quickly"—but perhaps not nearly as quickly as modern readers might think, accustomed to seeing Lawrence as the breaker of Victorian sexual properties and modern prophet of sexual liberation. There is, for instance, that time soon after that first meeting when Lawrence returned to Frieda's while her husband was away. When she implored him to spend the night, Lawrence's response, perhaps reflecting either his mother's chapel-going morality or his misgivings about intercourse, was, "No, I will not stay in your husband's house while he is away, but you must tell him the truth and we will go away together, because I love you."

And leave they did on May 3, less than two months after their first meeting, although not as some modern readers might imagine or even as Frieda herself likely thought, as an actual elopement. Instead, at least for Frieda, it was more about bringing Lawrence along for fun on her scheduled trip to visit her family in Germany. After all, she had already had a series of lovers, including at least one after her marriage to Weekley. Meanwhile, the onset of their lovemaking, what Lawrence would call their "honeymoon," was still on hold for another three weeks.

After their arrival in Germany in early May 1912, the lovers were almost immediately separated, with Lawrence mistaken for an English spy and forced to leave Metz. Regarding Frieda, Lawrence's plan from the outset was to win her as his wife, even to the point of forcing Frieda's hand by writing directly to Weekley. What stands out here is how Lawrence's argument relies less on any claim of their mutual love, which he barely mentions, than on his sense of Frieda's standing as a moral being—specifically, his fear of her "being stunted and not allowed to grow" in her current marriage, and hence his determination that "she must live her own life." Then, an even broader ethical plea: "All women in their natures are like giantesses. They will break through everything and go on with their own lives" (392).

A day or two later, he again writes Garnett, now playing up Frieda's family, especially how Frieda and her two sisters are such independent spirits: "the sort of woman one reverences." Here was the sort of woman that most intrigued Lawrence at the time—an independent spirit ready to offer him sexual satisfaction, free of the emotional demands that so hampered his relationship with Jessie Chambers. "Lord, what a family," he concludes. "I've never seen anything like it" (395).

On May 10, Frieda took her mother and one sister to visit Lawrence; the next day, he takes an arduous train journey with four connections, his last being the village of Hennef, "a nice place [...] nearly like England," and here, exhausted but momentarily refreshed, his heart opens up: "I know I only love you," he writes on a postcard to her. "The rest is nothing at all. And the promise of life with you is all richness. Now I know." Later, Lawrence would celebrate this moment in the exquisite lyric "Bei Hennef," announcing that only in this peaceful twilight, beside "the soft 'Sh!' of the river / That will last forever," was he able to see his condition fully, putting aside all that pained him these recent troublesome years:

You are the call and I am the answer,
You are the wish, and I the fulfillment,
You are the night, and I the day.
        What else—it is perfect enough,
        It is perfectly complete,
        You and I.

Perfect, possibly, but then, the disquieting note of the concluding line: "Strange, how we suffer in spite of this!" (203).

Nor is this disquiet dispelled a few days later (May 14), when, fretting over their pending sexual union, he writes to Frieda about how he is handling the suspense, noting that "we can wait even a bit religiously for one another." How, he continues, "[m]y next coming to you is solemn, intrinsically—I am solemn over it—not sad, oh no—but it is my marriage, after all, and a great thing—not a thing to be snatched and clumsily handled." The reference to "marriage" here, of course, is literally to the consummation of their relationship, what Lawrence would elsewhere refer to as his "honeymoon," and something Lawrence had no interest in rushing into. Instead, his intention was only to come to Frieda when matters were settled "safely, and firmly": "So we must wait and watch for the hour. Henceforth, dignity in our movements and our arrangements— no shuffling and underhandedness" (401).

Such is Lawrence at 26—the man who will eventually become world-famous advocating more open sexual relations between men and women— here at the outset of his "married" life, sounding less like the priest of love than the good son of a proper, chapel-going mother. "I love you—and I am in earnest about it," he writes to Frieda. "I'm not going to risk fret and harassment, which would spoil our intimacy, because of hasty forcing of affairs" (402). Nor should Frieda take his caution as a sign that "I love you less": "The best man in me loves you. And I dread anything dragging our love down." Then, the peroration, almost as if Lawrence remembered lines from his mother's Congregational chapel: "Be definite, my dear; be detailed, be business-like. In our marriage, let us be business-like. The love is there—then let the common-sense match it."

On May 15, Lawrence raised two new concerns—finances and pregnancy: "I want you to have children to me—I don't care how soon. [...] But you see, we must have a more or less stable foundation if we are going to run the risk of the responsibility of children." How radically Lawrence had changed in just two years, from the 24-year-old virgin who hectored Chambers into sleeping with him to now in Germany casting himself in the role of the reluctant maiden: "Can't you feel how certainly I love you and how certainly we shall be married. Only let us wait just a short time, to get strong again." Or, if not a maiden, then like a chaste knight: "I seem to want a certain time to prepare myself—a sort of vigil with myself. Because it is a great thing for me to marry you, not a quick, passionate coming together" (403).

It is all fine-sounding, nominally in service of established morality but possibly also expressing a genuine fear: "I know in my heart 'here's my marriage.' It feels rather terrible—because it is a great thing in my life—it is my life—I am a bit awe-inspired—I want to get used to it."

Is it possible that Lawrence's sexual experiences over the last two years made him question the place heterosexual intercourse could ever occupy in his life? "If you think it is fear and indecision," he continues, "you wrong me. It is you who would hurry who are undecided. It's the very strength and inevitability of the oncoming thing that makes me wait, to get in harmony with it." How odd a plea from the man who, only two years earlier, had been so critical of Chambers for being unwilling to have sex with him, or unable to enjoy it without a greater sense of emotional intimacy! Now, it seems the tables are turned, and Lawrence is speaking of their impending lovemaking as a once-in-a-lifetime commitment to marriage— "a far greater thing than ever I knew." "Give me till next week-end, at least," he adds. "If you love me, you will understand. If I seem merely frightened and reluctant to you,—you must forgive me."

And what about the frenetic sex drive from only two years ago—what then he referred to as "one's passion" and "sex drive"—how strange it feels, Lawrence adds, seeing it no longer as "a sort of wandering thing, but steady, and calm." Where once there was youthful passion, now there is a kind of resignation: "I think, when one loves, one's very sex passion becomes calm, a steady sort of force, instead of a storm. Passion, that nearly drives one mad, is far away from real love." Is this—or is this not— casuistry from someone who is overjoyed to be "in love," even if such a state entailed a distinct cessation of arousal? Lawrence now sends Frieda a copy of his poem, "Snap-Dragon"—a lover's complaint that he had addressed to his former fiancée for her unwillingness to provide him with physical satisfaction. His point being that he "would never write that to you"—that is, it is not sexual relief he seeks in this new relationship. "I shall love you all my life. That also is a new idea to me. But I believe it."

Then, on May 16, Lawrence begins by mentioning the malaise he has been experiencing as the consummation of their relationship (what he continues to refer to as their "marriage") approaches. He is "always well," he notes, before adding that "last week made me feel queer—in my soul mostly—and I want to get that well before I start the new enterprise of living with you. Does it seem strange to you?" he asks, referring to what seems to be panic. "Give me till tomorrow or Saturday week, will you? I think it is better for us both." But Lawrence, hounded by doubt, repeats his rhetorical question: "Does it seem unloving and unnatural to you?"

What follows is the start of an honest answer—"Perhaps it is a bit of the monk in me"—before finding safer ground: "No, it is not. It is simply a desire to start with you, having a strong, healthy soul. [...] Tell me you understand, and you think it is—at least perhaps, best. A good deal depends on the start" (404).

Next is an unexpected twist: Frieda alerts Lawrence that she is being aggressively pursued by a German officer, with Lawrence, in turn, seemingly eager to grant her permission to consummate this arrangement. "If you want Henning, or anybody, have him," Lawrence writes, comparing her actions to taking a drug: "[H]e's not much else to you. But sometimes one needs a dose of morphia"—adding hyperbolically, "I've had many a one."

And, when the deed is done, as presumably confessed in one of Frieda's missing letters, Lawrence is quick to dismiss her actions as similar to those of the wet nurse in a Maupassant short story who, while riding in a train, allowed a hungry young man to nurse at her uncomfortably bloated breasts, her single action providing much-needed relief for both of the parties. Perhaps what is most interesting is that here we see—even before the start of Lawrence's "married" life, when he had only made love to two women—the same dismissal of heterosexuality so prominent in the Mellors complaints throughout *Lady Chatterley's Lover*.

Finally, on Tuesday, May 21, Lawrence writes Garnett again, recounting the confusion surrounding Frieda's confession to Weekley about two previous lovers, with Weekley wrongly assuming that Lawrence was one of them.

And how does Lawrence end this letter, written only four days before his scheduled "honeymoon"—the sexual consummation of his relationship with the woman of his dreams, some ten weeks after their first meeting? He does it with another one of his distinctive reveries—not about

Frieda nor women generally nor even the sexual pleasure that awaits him, but about what would remain such an integral part of Lawrence's psyche, his delight in depicting the wondrous world around him. Here, it is his delight in the "little hole" of a town in Germany in which he was staying, a place that for him would always be "a land of exile—and slow, slow cattle drawing the wagons":

> Those slow, buff oxen, with their immense heads that seem always asleep, nearly drive me mad as they step tinkling down the street. After them, I could hug the dog in the milk-cart, that lifts his paw quickly and daintily over the shaft, and sits down panting.

Frieda Weekley—The "Honeymoon"

"The night was a failure / but why not—?" So begins Lawrence's candid account of his "honeymoon" night in the poem "First Morning" (Delphi 7208):

> In the darkness
> with the pale dawn seething at the window
> through the black frame
> I could not be free,
> not free myself from the past, those others—
> and our love was a confusion,
> there was a horror,
> you recoiled away from me.

In *Mr. Noon*, Lawrence offers a similar account, albeit in the mock-heroic tone typical in that work, of "that famous first night of theirs"—what was "not a success for either of them": "The passion did not get free in either, and therefore neither of them felt satisfied or assuaged or fulfilled."

Yet in both the poem and the novel, things were fine in the morning, graced as they were by his delight in the natural world:

> And see so near at our feet in the meadow
> Myriads of dandelion pappus
> Bubbles ravelled in the dark green grass
> Held still beneath the sunshine—

"Everything starts from us," the poem concludes: "We are the source."

In *Mr. Noon*, the lovers are "rather happy," we are told, in what might well be the mantra of Lawrence's entire marriage, "just being together": "The very fact that the attempt at passion had failed for the moment kindled a deeper gratification in companionship." Then he adds this odd simile, reinforcing what might be deemed the moral nature of their relationship—two beings happy in each other's presence: "They were delighted like two children at being together" (131).

We likewise find this feeling of general well-being in Lawrence's letters in the following weeks. Here he is in early June, writing to Sallie Hopkins, an old friend from Eastwood who may have been playing the role of a surrogate parent, explaining how he had finally met up with Frieda and "stayed in Munich a night." The main section of the letter shows Lawrence at his happiest and most lyrical, as we have seen before, extolling his intimacy with nature. "In the morning we used to have breakfast under the thick horse-chestnut trees," he writes, "and the red and white flowers fell on us":

> The garden was on a ledge, high over the river, above the weir, where the timber rafts floated down. The Loisach—that's the river—is pale jade green, because it comes from glaciers. It is fearfully cold and swift. [...] Across from the inn, across a square full of horsechestnut trees, was the church and the convent, so peaceful, all whitewashed, except for the minaret of the church, which has a black hat. [...] There are flowers so many they would make you cry for joy—alpine flowers.—By the river, great hosts of globe flowers, that we call bachelor's buttons—pale gold great bubbles—then primulas, like mauve cowslips, somewhat—and queer marsh violets, and orchids, and lots of bell-flowers, like large, tangled, dark-purple harebells, and stuff like larkspur, very rich, and lucerne, so pink, and in the woods, lilies of the valley—oh, flowers, great wild mad profusion of them, everywhere.
>
> (413)

Frieda is barely mentioned, except for the note that he had to stop suddenly while writing this letter because she had "banged her head on the cupboard."

Then he gives us another exquisite reverie we had seen before, only now shared with a loving partner:

> So we stood and looked out. Over the hills was a great lid of black cloud, and the mountains nearest went up and down in a solid blue-black. Through, was a wonderful gold space, with a tangle of pale, wonderful mountains, peaks pale gold with snow and farther and farther away—such a silent, glowing confusion brilliant with snow. Now the thunder is going at it, and the rain is here.
>
> (414)

This marvelous letter ends with Lawrence's direct exclamation: "I love Frieda so much I don't like to talk about it. I never knew what love was before"—possibly referring to his relief in his newfound intimacy with a woman, echoing something of the emotional closeness Chambers had also wanted. "The world is wonderful," he continues, "and beautiful and good beyond one's wildest imagination. Never, never, never could one conceive what love is, beforehand, never. Life can be great—quite god-like. It can be so. God be thanked I have proved it."

Two weeks later (June 15), we see a sharper, less pleasant edge to Lawrence's protestations about his marital bliss, this time to Arthur McLeod, his closest colleague from his time teaching at Croydon and a lifelong bachelor whom Lawrence, possibly obtuse regarding his friend's romantic interests, appears all too ready to bludgeon into getting married himself. Being in love, Lawrence insists, is "the greatest thing that can happen to a man. I tell you, find a woman you can fall in love with. *Do* it. *Let* yourself fall in love, if you haven't done so already. You are wasting your life" (emphasis in original).

Lawrence, who will write voluminously about a man's need to keep himself separate from a woman's dominance, here seems more like an uxorious cheerleader. "Nowadays," he continues,

> men haven't the courage and the strength to love. You must know that you're committing slow suicide. Do for the lord's sake find some woman you can respect and love, and love her, and let her love you. Decide to do it. As you go on, you die. Now decide to live.
>
> (418)

This change of heart in Lawrence seems genuine, even if temporary, and possibly brought on by the relief, emotional as well as sexual, that he seems to have experienced in those first weeks with Frieda. It is a mood Lawrence captures in the lyric "Frohnleichnam" (209–10), the title referring to the solemn German celebration of Corpus Christi, literally "joyous body." Here, Lawrence shows us Frieda "[g]listening with all the moment and all your beauty," while the poet is solely intent on lovemaking: "At last I can throw away world without end, and meet you / Unsheathed and naked and narrow and white":

> Shameless and callous I love you;
> Out of indifference I love you;
> Out of mockery we dance together,
> Out of the sunshine into the shadow,
> Passing across the shadow into the sunlight,
> Out of sunlight to shadow.

As we dance
Your eyes take all of me in as a communication;
As we dance
I see you, ah, in full!
Only to dance together in triumph of being together
Two white ones, sharp, vindicated,
Shining and touching,
Is heaven of our own, sheer with repudiation.

Meanwhile, in *Mr. Noon*, Lawrence portrays Johanna as "hovering in the doorway of her room [...] . [a] bright, roused look [...] on her face." At last, we see Lawrence straining to capture the allure of making love to a woman. "She lifted her eyelids with a strange flare of invitation, like a bird lifting its wings. And for the first time the passion broke like lightning out of Gilbert's blood: for the first time in his life." Perhaps Lawrence is sincere in this unpublished novel about Johanna's appeal to Gilbert. Still, in the spirit of Mellors, his account of their subsequent lovemaking that night is decidedly pedestrian:

> He went into her room with her and shut the door. The sultriness and lethargy of his soul had broken into a storm of desire for her, a storm which shook and swept him at varying intervals all his life long.
>
> (136)

To mask his difficulty in describing lovemaking lyrically in *Mr. Noon*, Lawrence uses two sleights of hand. First, he regularly opts for satire, falling into a mock-heroic tone we have already mentioned, as in this apostrophe to "wonderful desire: violent, genuine desire":

> Oh storms of acute sex passion, which shatter the soul, and re-make it, as summer is made up out of the debacle of thunder! Oh cataclysm of fulminous desire in the soul: oh new uprising from the cataclysm. This is a trick of resurrection worth two.
>
> (137)

Second, he focuses on that one part of lovemaking he also emphasized in describing Paul's interactions with Clara Dawes—that is, the mystery of the male orgasm, although again often in a mock-heroic vein:

> Oh thunder-god, who sends the white passion of pure, sensual desire upon us, breaking through the sultry rottenness of our old blood like jagged lightning, and switching us into a new dynamic reaction, hail! Oh thunder-god, god of the dangerous bolts.

Still, how different, how strident, how censorious Lawrence becomes—to return to his letter to his Croydon colleague—when he is no longer describing the beauty of the physical world. Here, in a nutshell, are our two Lawrences. One, the lyrical or *hidden* Lawrence who pens this perfect picture of the mountain village of Beuerberg, with its "great church, white-washed outside, with a white minaret and a black small bulb—half renaissance, half moorish—brought back from the Turkish wars, a reminiscence—but inside, baroque, gilded, pictures, gaudy, wild, savagely religious." And that other, public Lawrence, the scold eager to lecture his bachelor friend about his recent, hard-won romantic success, almost as if he had survived a trial by fire:

> Lord, it's a great thing to have met a woman like Frieda. I could stand on my head for joy, to think I have found her. We've been together for three weeks. And I love her more every morning, and every night. Where it'll end, I don't know. She's got a great, generous soul—and a splendid woman to look at.
>
> (418)

After their "honeymoon" night at the end of May, Lawrence and Frieda spent the next two months together in a small town outside of Munich. In early July, he wrote his editor and friend Edward Garnett about their daily ritual of swimming in the Isar, noting how Frieda "swims finely, and looks fearfully voluptuous, rolling in the pale green water" (425). Later that month, when they are joined by Garnett's 20-year-old son, David (Bunny), Lawrence offers the senior Garnett a far more fulsome account of his son swimming in the same stream—adding how he "simply smashes his way through the water, while F. sits on the bank bursting with admiration, and I am green with envy"; or later, how Bunny performs some Russian dances he has recently learned, "with great orange and yellow and red and dark green scarves of F's, and his legs and arms bare [...] Such a prancing whirl of legs and arms and raving colours you never saw [...] Oh the delightful Bunny" (429)!

In *Mr. Noon*, Lawrence tones down his enthusiasm for Bunny ("Terry") only slightly, praising his thoroughness as an outdoorsman—swimming "in a fierce river, [...] clamber[ing] over mountains, [...] collect[ing] flowers and press[ing] them in a blotting-paper book," then describing the outings the two of them took with all the relish of Charlotte Brontë's portrait of winter:

> Down they clambered to black depths between the cliffs—they got on to a bushy island in mid-stream—they roasted pieces of veal on sticks before a fire, far away down there in the gloom. Then Terry flung himself into a water-fall pool.
>
> (255)

Soon, the three travelers are joined by another handsome youth, Bunny's friend Harold Hobson ("Stanley"); in the novel, Stanley is presented both as a mommy's boy in a funk over a recent romantic breakup, and as a dare-devil, jumping on the parapet of a nearby bridge, running there "riskily and funnily, like a boy, or like a dog." Lawrence's account of Stanley evokes the same scopophilic impulse we saw in the bathing scenes from his first novel, *The White Peacock*, and his last, *Lady Chatterley's Lover*. This young man's "black hair," Lawrence notices, "was brushed straight back, he had a beautiful profile, pale, with an arched nose and a well-shaped brow," and with another reference to "his delicate ankles in their purple socks show[ing] as he ran backwards and forwards there in the air." He was petulant for sure, reluctant to confront adult responsibilities, yet, as Lawrence can't help noting, "there was a charm, a wilful, spoilt charm about [him]" (257).

Nor was his charm lost on Frieda's stand-in, Johanna, who commented on how "any woman might love him" (258). When the two young men depart, Lawrence's stand-in remarks how he "particularly" missed Stanley: "He missed him almost acutely—missed the sort of heightening of life that the American youth had brought, the thrill, the excitation." Stanley, Lawrence continues,

> sent little thrills through the air, as electricity thrills through water. And this acted as a stimulant, almost like a drug on the nerves of the pair of finches. And now it was taken away, they felt an emptiness, a wanting.
> (271)

Gilbert's regret here has an odd quality, as Johanna is about to inform him how she and Stanley had made love only days before, at the time Gilbert was on a botany outing with Terry (Bunny)—the account in *Mr. Noon* seems to be an accurate picture of Frieda's second act of infidelity in just their first few months together, this time without prior approval. Johanna's confession "was such a surprise to [Gilbert]," Lawrence writes, likely rec-reating what he remembered from that time, that "he did not know what to feel, or if he felt anything at all"—the whole thing "such a complete and unexpected statement that it had not really any meaning for him." Soon after, Gilbert throws his arms around his new wife, telling her how we all "do things we don't know we're doing"; he then "kissed her and clung to her passionately in a sudden passion of self-annihilation" (276).

It is hardly surprising that Frieda's stand-in, Johanna, is unnerved by Gilbert's odd lack of anger, feeling "rather caught-out by his passionate spiritual forgiveness: put in a false position than ever" (277). It is as if Lawrence is here portraying Johanna as a woman who never quite grasped the different, knotted nature of her husband's erotic psyche—noting, for instance, how she failed to see how Gilbert's response may have had less to do with his forgiving heart than a shared sexual interest in Johanna's young lover—a possibility, one wonders, that neither Lawrence's two stand-ins, Johanna or Gilbert, nor their originals, Frieda or Lawrence, may have fully grasped. Lawrence gives us a hint, however, of another explanation, if only in a single sentence, noting that on that same night as his Johanna's confession, "he loved her"—that is, the woman who had just confessed to cuckolding him—"with a wild self-abandon."

Once one starts to look, the presence of this "other man" turns out to be a recurring fixture in the erotic lives of several of Lawrence's fictional stand-ins. For instance, the rugged outdoorsman, George Sexton, at the center of *The White Peacock*, is not just the character who elicits the narrator's intensely lyrical writing in the erotically charged "The Poem of Friendship"; he is also the brother of the woman whom Lawrence's effeminate stand-in, Cyril, is nominally courting throughout that novel—the young woman and her brother, based on Jessie Chambers and her older brother, Alan.

Likewise, in *Sons and Lovers*, Lawrence provides a far more detailed, erotically charged description of Clara Dawes's husband, Baxter, than he does of Clara herself. It is Baxter who, if not the rugged outdoorsman so admired in George Sexton for his purity, is still something of a man's man: "a big, well-set man, also striking to look at, and handsome," and, oddly, with "a peculiar similarity between himself and his wife":

He had the same white skin, with a clear, golden tinge. His hair was of soft brown, his moustache was golden. And he had a similar defiance in his bearing and manner. But then came the difference. His eyes, dark brown and quick-shifting, were dissolute. They protruded very slightly, and his eyelids hung over them in a way that was half hate. His mouth, too, was sensual. His whole manner was of cowed defiance.

(185)

Nor have many readers of *Sons and Lovers* failed to notice the unexpected erotic tension Lawrence builds into Paul's fight with Baxter, anticipating the better-known wrestling scene from *Women in Love* (looked at in Chapter 6). Here, Lawrence tells us, Paul felt "his whole body unsheath itself like a claw," eventually submitting to this overwhelming male force in a manner not unlike Connie's erotic submission in *Lady Chatterley's Lover*. Now it is Paul who hangs on

to the bigger man like a wild cat, till at last Dawes fell with a crash, losing his presence of mind. [...] His body, hard and wonderful in itself,

cleaved against the struggling body of the other man; not a muscle in
him relaxed.

(366)

Only after this struggle does Paul begin working assiduously to bring the
estranged couple back together.

Likewise, a similarly odd moment in *Mr. Noon* involves the extended
and wholly unnecessary passage Lawrence includes praising Johanna's
former husband, Everard (based on Frieda's husband and Lawrence's
former teacher, the noted etymologist Ernest Weekley). At the center of
this passage is Lawrence's perplexity (speaking through Gilbert) over
what for most men might be the relatively simple matter of male arousal,
referred to here as "the Priapic mysteries"—that is, Gilbert opines,
things that

> can't be learned with the head, nor dictated from the mind, nor
> practised by deliberate intent. You can no more bring about, delib-
> erately, a splendid passional sexual storm between yourself and your
> woman than you can bring about a thunderstorm in the air.
>
> (190)

Lawrence's point here is straightforward—that, without desire, sexual
performance is neither easy nor especially enjoyable. "All the little tricks, all
the intensifications of will remain no more than tricks and will-pressure,"
he explains, before emphasizing the necessity of a man's "releas[ing] from
mental control the deep springs of passion: and after that there has got
to be the leap to polarised adjustment with the woman." Not everyone
would agree with Lawrence here that a man's sexual desire for a woman
should be considered one of the universe's "deep mysteries" or that for
most men it takes "a long time [...] to release the profound desires from
all mental control."

What Lawrence casts as theoretical speculation, admittedly through the
fictional character of Gilbert Noon, seems more like a confession of his
wonder that men like Johanna's husband, as well as the George Saxtons and
the Baxter Daweses of the world, seem capable of satisfying their female
partners in ways he cannot. "To tell the truth," he continues, "Johanna
had had far more sensual satisfaction out of her husband, Everard, than
out of her other lovers"—presumably, himself included. He was a "dark-
eyed, handsome man, rather stiff and marquis-like, learned and a bit sar-
castic," a man who "loved his Johanna violently" (191).

How does he do it, Lawrence wonders. Where does this "terrible passion
for Johanna" come from? How could "kneel[ing] before her [...] [and]

kiss[ing] her feet in a frenzy of craving sensual desire"—likely something Frieda had confessed to him—possibly arouse this man, arouse any man? What a mystery that any man should be so aroused by a woman—that, of all people, Everard (or Weekley) should be by the very woman who so seldom aroused him!

This Everard was then a man who seemed to have solved the Priapic mysteries in what strikes Lawrence as the strangest of fashions—not merely by fulfilling his conjugal duty, as Lawrence must have felt he was often doing, but by desiring a woman in the flesh, by actually "ask[ing] for it, [...] crav[ing] for it as if in some way it were a sin." Here, Lawrence realizes, is the "terrific, the magnificent black sin of sensual marriage: the gorgeous legal sin, which one was proud of, but which one kept dark: which one hated to think of in the open day, but which one lusted for by night"—in Weekley's case, his erotic fantasy that transformed his wife into "an eternal white virgin whom he was almost violating" (192).

Here, in other words, was a level of erotic arousal for a woman at which Lawrence could only marvel, even while acknowledging how Johanna claimed to have tired of her former husband's ribald imagination, preferring instead her new lover's ability to "look on the naked woman of his desire without starting to grovel" (194). Perhaps this is a reworking of a sentiment that Frieda expressed to him that summer of 1912: that she genuinely preferred a lover intent on doing his duty, even if ignorant of the Priapic mysteries, instead of one muddled as Everard had been by "profound desire." Still, one must wonder if any writer has cast a more blistering self-critique of his own love life!

Everard could enjoy deep, sensual pleasure with his wife, as she could enjoy it with the young Stanley. Meanwhile, only once in the months following their late May "honeymoon," when the couple reached Riva in early September, was Lawrence finally able to write lyrically about Gilbert's sensual pleasure, about how "something seemed to come loose in [his] soul, quite suddenly"—how it "broke like a dry rock that breaks and gushes into life" (290). Nor was it likely an accident that the spark for this rare night of passion involved incidental contact with the one lower erotic zone shared by men and women. "Quite suddenly, in the night one night he touched Johanna as she lay asleep with her back to him, touching him, and something broke alive in his soul that had been dead before."

Perhaps of greater interest is how Lawrence's account of Gilbert's passion, much like his account of Connie's in *Lady Chatterley's Lover*, is almost entirely focused on the pleasure enjoyed by just one partner—a version of lovemaking that likens Gilbert's sudden erotic arousal to the exuberance of a youthful Lawrence celebrating in the wonders of his own body:

> Ach richness—unspeakable and untellable richness. Ach bliss—deep, sensual, silken bliss! It was as if the old sky cracked, curled, and peeled away, leaving a great new sky, a great new pellucid empyrean that had never been breathed before. Exquisite deep possibilities of life, magnificent life which had not been life before. Loveliness which made his arms live with delight, and made his knees seem to blossom with unfolded delight. Now all his life he had been accustomed to know his arms and knees as mere limbs and joints for use.
>
> (290)

"Now suddenly," the passage continues, "like bare branches that burst into blossom they seemed to be quivering with flowers of exquisite appreciation, exquisite, exquisite appreciation."

An appreciation of what, we might ask, with Lawrence only at the end of matters getting around to mentioning Gilbert's partner—that "exquisite appreciation of her." Thus, his surprise that, after his previous experience of intercourse with two other women and a few months of lovemaking with Johanna (Frieda), he had finally discovered something that he "had never known" before—namely, "that one could enjoy the most exquisite appreciation of the warm, silken woman, not in one's mind or breast, but deep in one's limbs and loins."

As is often the case, what is likely to trigger Lawrence's lyrical voice is less an account of lovemaking than that of a man alone in the natural world. Here, in *Mr. Noon*, for instance, there is the brilliant account of Gilbert's botany outing with Terry (Bunny), the two of them "clamber[ing] up amongst [...] a jagged mass of great broken rocks that had wedged and ceased to slip." Gilbert, we are told, found it all "rather terrifying, as the silent, icy twilight drew on, to be jumping one's way across these jagged massive avalanches." Gilbert found something "terrific about this upper world": "Things which looked small and near were rather far, and when one reached them, they were big, great masses where one expected stones, jagged valley where one saw just a hollow groove" (263).

Gilbert "climbed alone rather high," suddenly realizing "how tiny he was—no bigger than a fly": "Such terrible, such raw, such stupendous masses of the rock-element heaved and confused. Such terrible order in it all." Lawrence then describes Gilbert looking "at the inaccessible, dread-holy peaks of snow and black rock beyond the precipice—and the vast slopes opposite, the vast slope on which he was overwhelmed, the fir-trees just below like a hairy fringe."

It was a moment not unlike those we will see in Chapter 5, with one of Lawrence's stand-ins agape at the masculine power one can find in other characters or, as here, in the natural world. Thus, Lawrence is content to show us an ecstatic Gilbert

> scrambling between fierce rocks which had looked to him like stones, now he felt all the suspended mass of unutterably fierce rocks round him, he knew it was not human, not life-size. It was all bigger than life-size, much bigger, and fearful.

Alone now and afraid, Lawrence "wanted to get back, back to the level of the cranberries and the grass, back to the path, to the house."

Once back to safety, he found himself alone, looking out at "the flush of evening on the peaks," a moment that led to another lyrical reverie, this one focused on that critical scopophilic element of the viewer's isolation or hidden status—"Strange and icy the heart became—without human emotion—up here: abstracted, in the eternal loneliness":

> The eternal and everlasting loneliness. And the beauty of it, and the richness of it. The everlasting isolation in loneliness, while the sun comes and goes, and night falls and rises. The heart in its magnificent isolation like a peak in heaven, forever. The beauty, the beauty of fate, which decrees that in our supremacy we are single and alone, like peaks that finish off in their perfect isolation in the ether. The ultimate perfection of being quite alone.
>
> (264)

How ironic that Gilbert was experiencing such delight looking at the world at the same moment we later learn that Johanna was making love with Stanley! Is it any wonder that Gilbert, or Lawrence—an artist intent on so brilliantly chronicling his place in the natural world—should have been so unperturbed by what must have struck him as his partner's decidedly humdrum activity?

Nor is it surprising that Lawrence would have Gilbert downplay whatever pleasure Johanna might have received from her lovemaking in favor of his being alone with nature. The closing chapters of *Mr. Noon* also contain three additional vignettes exhibiting this same scopophilic delight in Lawrence's stand-in that will play a prevalent role in our next chapter.

In the first, we see Gilbert observing a column of soldiers approaching their lodging. Initially, he shows disgust for the artillery pieces—"What is more horrible than the neutral grey of war-implements"—but is fascinated by one soldier, "a young, strong, handsome fellow," who has stopped for water. Gilbert watches him "crouch over the tub and put his face in the water and drink"—this soldier with "a strong body, under the blue cloth, and the back of his neck [...] ruddy and handsome." When the order came to move on, Gilbert tells us, all "the riders with their strong, heavy-muscled legs swung into the saddle" (209) before noting the "hitch and strain of harness" that marked "that strange pace of artillery, straining forward, as if with haste, and yet without swiftness."

Here is the start of another reverie, one with an unmistakable erotic tinge, as Gilbert watched "the last horse-flanks disappear round the corner of the white, low-roofed farm—and then he stared in silence across the shallow, sun-shimmering valley." "Stared with regret," Lawrence adds—"a deep regret": "He forgot the woman at his side—and love, and happiness. And his heart burned to be with the men, the strange, dark, heavy soldier, so young and strong with life, reckless and sensual." This was the world he wanted—"not only life with a woman," but this other thing: "The thrill of soldiery went heavily through his blood: the glamour of the dark, positive fighting spirit."

Lawrence then describes the simple meal of eggs, asparagus, and cheese they shared and how a "great silence seemed to have come over him": "the deep longing, and the far off desire to be with men, with men alone, active, reckless, dangerous, on the brink of death: to be away from woman, beyond her, on the borders." It was a longing for a "womanless life" that Lawrence describes as "so deep" as to be "all indefinite and as yet unconscious, or semi-conscious," while Johanna, like Frieda, the daughter of a military commander, can only remember all the complaints of the soldiers she overheard growing up—"that horrible, vile discipline, and the agonies they suffer."

The second vignette occurs the next day as they set off walking and discover two raftsmen working their long poles, "blonde, ruddy men with hard muscles": "mountain woodsmen [...] like hawks, with their keen, unseeing faces and their bare, fierce knees under the little, wide leather breeches, like football-breeches." And again, Gilbert is overcome with "nostalgia for the man's life": "life apart from the woman—life without domesticity or marital implication—the single life of men active together" (210).

And the final vignette from the fall of their honeymoon travels—as Gilbert watches farmhands working in a row, mowing the tall corn with their scythes. He could stand all day on his balcony, Lawrence tells us, "watching them work in the misty morning, watching them come in at noon-day, when the farm-bell rang, watching the dusk gather over them":

And always, he wished he were one with them—even with the laborers who worked and whetted their scythes and sat down to rest under the shade of the standing corn. To be at one with men in a physical activity. Why could he not?

And here we remember that intimacy Lawrence once shared with Alan Cumming and celebrated in "The Poem of Friendship," as he now laments how his talent as a writer rendered him a mere observer of men—forever "a separate, unmixing specimen": "At the bottom of his heart he set an immense value on friendship—eternal, manly friendship" (228).

In retrospect, it is hardly surprising that the moment of greatest intimacy between Gilbert and Johanna was not in their lovemaking. Except for that one "accidental" encounter when they reached Riva, there is no ardent lovemaking in *Mr. Noon*. In "Manifesto" (Delphi 7264–67), a poem in his collection reflecting his early months with Frieda, with the apt title, *Look! We Have Come Through*, Lawrence speaks disparagingly of the male sex drive—what he can only see as a "hunger for the woman"—calling it "so deep a Moloch, ruthless and strong," that is, "like the unutterable name of the dread Lord, / not to be spoken aloud":

Yet there it is, the hunger which comes upon us,
which we must learn to satisfy with pure, real satisfaction;
or perish, there is no alternative.

"No alternative," that is, other than sex with a woman, however difficult that may be.

Nor are women as much the problem as the ardent, unpleasant nature of the male sex drive itself, which inevitably leaves one "in the dark, [...] tortured, ravening, unfree / Ashamed, and shameful, and vicious." It is what leaves him "so terrified of strong hunger," a "terror" he labels "the root of all cruelty." The result is the speaker "mad with voracious desire," unable to do more than look "sideways, furtively" at the woman standing before him who, even then, desired him.

No, the only real intimacy with Johanna came for Gilbert, not in love-making, but as it might have for Lawrence himself—his wife at his side, an active presence in one of his marvelous reveries. One such moment comes immediately after Gilbert's rant about the inevitable antagonism between men and women; only now, instead of conflict, we find Gilbert and Johanna "crowded into one of the beds, under one of the great feather overbolsters, which rode upon them like a cumulous cloud." The night was pitch black, with "a wild, strange scent in the air, a strange thrill." The couple ends up holding themselves "fast together like children in the darkness," spending much of the night "capturing the cumulous cloud, which showed a disposition to float away and leave some portion either of her or of him exposed to the cool air" (199).

And then in the morning, "a dream of beauty," with the man and woman standing "at their window in the early morning and look[ing] out in bliss": "The mountains in the distance sparkled blue with snow and ice. The foot-hills were green-golden, and the wonderful meadows, a sea of blue and yellow flowers, surged nearer in the pure, transcendent light." Here is the "hidden" Lawrence in full glory, neither a master lover nor an exceptionally reliable guide to the tension between the sexes, but instead one of the world's great writers, here intent on capturing the "magic" of that morning:

> A few great trees by the road, and two farm-houses with enormous sweeping roofs, white gables and black balconies! And then a pond, and a bridge downhill, and most lovely birch-trees standing translucent and gleaming along the wet, white way between the river-meadows. And everything crystal-pure, having the magic of snow-Alpine perfection. The crystal, paradisal calm of everything on such a morning is such as only the great snow-radiant north can offer: the sheer heavenliness that is in gentian flowers and the curve-horned chamois.

There is a serenity here that, perhaps for an artist like Lawrence, might equal the sexual gratification with which he seemed to be in a near-lifelong struggle. And it is here, as they arrive in Italy in the fall of 1912—the start of what will be for them a lifetime of travels—that we can leave our "honeymoon" couple. It is where they will remain on and off for the next two years before returning to England in the summer of 1914. There, following Frieda's divorce, they will marry that July, beginning 16 years of married life, with this odd and perhaps not unexpected twist, reported by one set of biographers—that after 1916 "almost no one records the Lawrences holding hands, kissing, hugging, or showing affection" (Squires and Talbot 208).

Rosalind Baynes—Lawrence's Final Partner?

In the early fall of 1920, eight years after his "honeymoon" trip through Italy, Lawrence found himself alone for a few weeks in Florence, where he reunited with a family friend, Rosalind Baynes, a 29-year-old acclaimed beauty and mother of three, who was in the process of obtaining a divorce. She had rented a spacious thirteenth-century villa but offered it to Lawrence when she discovered its windows had recently been blown out by a nearby blast. Soon after, they met for supper on what was Lawrence's thirty-fifth birthday, at which time, as Baynes recorded in her diary, Lawrence brought up the question of her current loveless state. In the spirit of Lawrence's first lover, Baynes responded that, naturally, "there must be more to it than a few pretty words and then off to bed." Lawrence partially conceded, "Yes there must be more to it than that," before insisting that "God save us from the so-called Love—that most indecent kind of egoism and self-spreading." Still, Baynes recorded Lawrence speaking euphemistically about love "as a force outside and getting us. It is a force, a god" (Kinkead-Weekes 602).

Baynes was smitten, perhaps as Frieda had been eight years before and likely Alice Dax before that—"Firenze and her lights twirled around and I felt off the world"—but with Baynes still perplexed at how Lawrence could talk so openly about love yet still be so fastidious about sex. Lawrence's answer here was in line with so much of his writing on love— which was to suggest something mystical, always an "understanding of the god *together*" (emphasis in original).

Baynes sensed nothing intimate was going to happen that night ("though I longed to dash into his arms," she writes), nor the next day when Lawrence returned, even though "I tidied everything in my room to make it sweet for him"—but remained hopeful for the third day, and then after lunch and a memorable afternoon spent walking the nearby hills, gathering food for their supper. Only then, Baynes tells us (and hers is our only direct testimony), as they were sitting in the dark, "our hands held together in union." Then what for Baynes was her perfect ending: "And so to bed"—just like that, accomplishing what only one other woman since Alice Dax some nine years before had accomplished, coaxing this most reluctant of lovers into active lovemaking.

Although we have no record of Lawrence commenting directly on that night or any subsequent nights with Baynes over his remaining days in Florence, one could hardly expect a writer so conditioned to drawing heavily on his own experiences to stay silent here, and two of his responses seem most pertinent here. First are the six fruit poems that open the volume *Birds, Beasts, and Flowers*—marked as written in San Gervasio, the location of Baynes' villa—with the suggestion that the unusual richness of the imagery found in these poems, including "Figs," reflects a newfound attitude toward sensuality in Lawrence. "For fruits are all of them female," including the fig, a poem used in Ken Russell's film version of *Women in Love*: "Involved, / Inturned, / The Flowering all inward and womb-fibrilled; / And but one orifice" (Delphi 7348–49).

But imagery can be a two-way street, and in "Medlars and Sorb-Apples" (Delphi 7346–47), a poem finally in praise of male isolation—the subject of Lawrence's other response to his Florentine lovemaking—we find rotted apples contrasted with white gods, possibly a reference to the male statues of Florence's Piazza della Signoria:

> Gods nude as blanched nut-kernels,
> Strangely, half-sinisterly flesh-fragrant
> As if with sweat,
> And drenched with mystery.

Indeed, Lawrence saved his extended response to Florence's testosterone-filled Piazza della Signoria for his novel *Aaron's Rod*. There, he shows us his stand-in, Aaron Sisson, "[standing] still and look[ing] round him in real surprise, and real joy." Against the feminine sexual suggestions of ripe fruit, here Lawrence gives us something entirely different and far more forceful: the "dark, sheer front of the Palazzo Vecchio [going] up like a cliff, to the battlements, and the slim tower soar[ing] dark and hawk-like, crested, high above": "And at the foot of the cliff stood the great naked David, white and stripped in the wet, white against the dark, warm-dark cliff of the building—and near, the heavy naked men of Bandinelli" (his *Hercules and Cacus*), the back of one of those statues, "a great naked man of marble, with a heavy back and strong naked flanks over which the water was trickling. And then to come immediately upon the David"—a cousin to the bathing Mellors—"so much whiter, glistening skin-white in the wet, standing a little forward, and shrinking."

Sexual intimacy with a woman might well have its attractions—and, as described in the next section, Lawrence does describe three nights of lovemaking with a married woman in *Aaron's Rod*—but it is here in the Piazza della Signoria that Lawrence's protagonist, Aaron Sisson, like Lawrence himself while in Florence, on the lam from his wife, finally has a sense of "having arrived—of having reached a perfect centre of the human world" (212).

Of course, the lovemaking with the married Marchesa certainly has its own interests, in part signaling what for Aaron proved to be the startling return of sexual desire, or, as Lawrence writes, "For such a long time his desire for woman had withheld itself, hard and resistant. All his deep, desirous blood had been locked, he had wanted nobody, and nothing." Then, perhaps as happened with Lawrence in his time with Baynes, "now came his desire back," although expressed pointedly with hardly a reference to the object of his desire. Praise, instead, for the return of desire itself, "strong, fierce as iron": "Like the strength of an eagle with the lightning in its talons. Something to glory in, something overweening, the powerful male passion, arrogant, royal, Jove's thunderbolt" (258).

The first night of lovemaking seems to have gone well, at least in terms of Aaron's performance; all we learn about the Marchesa, however, is that she was surprisingly childlike—"In the dark sightlessness of passion [...] seem[ing] almost like a clinging child in his arms." What it wasn't was the no-nonsense sex that Lawrence had told Baynes he wanted—two people worshiping the same god—with the result that Aaron was spooked. As she put "her "frail and childish arms" around him, "her tangle of hair over his face," even then, "he felt her deadly," wanting, above all else, "to be gone. [...] to get out of her arms and her clinging and her tangle of hair and her curiosity and her strange and hateful power" (262). There is no assurance that Aaron's experience here reflects Lawrence's with Baynes, but what is incontrovertible is how unpleasant Aaron found this intimacy, wiping his face and mouth as he left to remove the scent of her bedding. "To be alone in the night! For this he was unspeakably thankful" (264).

Some of Aaron's specific interactions with the Marchesa have the ring of memoir, as if based on Lawrence's experience with Baynes that possibly occurred just months before Lawrence drafted his novel. One such instance is Aaron's indecision after their first night of lovemaking: the tension between his desire "never to see her again" balanced against a feeling of indebtedness in Lawrence's for having accepted the use of Baynes' villa—Aaron, presumably like Lawrence, once again the dutiful son. A second is Aaron's thought of using his married state as grounds for ending this affair, in some ways similar to how the youthful Paul Morel had used his mother to keep Jessie Chambers at arm's length. So what, Aaron reasons, if his relationship with his wife is no longer physical? It is still his marriage: "Well, I am a husband, if I am anything. And I shall never be a lover again, not while I live. No, not to anybody. I haven't it in me."

Despite these good intentions, Aaron agrees to a second night of lovemaking, leading to a third memoir-like moment, this time with Lawrence focusing on the intensity of Aaron's orgasm: how

his passion [was] drawn from him as if a long, live nerve were drawn out from his body, a long live thread of electric fire, a long, living nerve finely extracted from him, from the very roots of his soul. A long fine discharge of pure, bluish fire, from the core of his soul. It was an excruciating, but also an intensely gratifying sensation.

(272)

This florid account of Aaron's pleasure might not rival Connie Chatterley's; it also differs in celebrating the phallic pleasure of the active, not the receptive partner. "As his passion broke from him to her," Lawrence continues, "he felt the long live hot fire-thread drawn downwards through him, terribly down his legs and through his heels, leaving his heels feeling bruised, and himself feeling vacant. It was like a discharge of lightning, but longer, more terrible."

Then, there is the fourth and longest memoir-like segment, and what we have seen repeatedly in Lawrence: Aaron's deeply embedded, profound regret—one might call it gay or at least male panic—over the level of reciprocity, intimacy, trust, and, yes, even tenderness that this woman seems to expect from him at such a moment. It starts with the sense of his now being trapped in their post-coital intimacy, having to stay the rest of the night while this other person—not a man ready to move on with his life once the sex act was completed—but this person of the other sex who "seemed to love clinging to him and curling strangely on his breast."

Yet this was a woman he knew so well in other situations as a fully functioning adult: "How could she now in a sort of little ecstasy curl herself and nestle herself on his, Aaron's breast, tangling his face all over with her hair." He had had his orgasm—and what an orgasm it was; if only she were like him, that should have been enough. Instead, he "verily believed that this was what she really wanted of him: to curl herself on his naked breast, to make herself small, small, to feel his arms around her, and his slow, still breathing lifting her," even while his only thought was that he was done.

What was going on in this woman's psyche, Lawrence asks, as if clueless, that she should think his mere male presence, detached as it were from his actual thoughts at the moment, could provide this level of emotional comfort to her. Why was she lying beside him now, as if gratified? He had no idea; he "only knew it had nothing to do with him: and that, save out of complaisance, he did not want it."

Baynes recorded Lawrence telling her how sex was "a force, a god," with Lawrence noting how Aaron felt the force of "phallic immortality" (272) and no doubt hoping that the Marchesa had been placed in touch with her god as well. Sex indeed could be earth-shattering; it was the putative, tender aftermath that was so debilitating—with the Marchesa "us[ing] him to curl herself up against, and again to nestle deeper into."

Nor can there be much doubt that Lawrence is using his stand-in to voice his persistent displeasure with such intimacy: "His soul stood apart and decided. At the bottom of his soul he disliked her. Or if not her, then her whole motive. Her whole life-mode"—that is, as he first made so clear with Jessie Chambers and later with Alice Dax, here we see Lawrence reiterating his dislike of a woman's inability to experience physical pleasure without the afterglow of emotional intimacy. On this matter, Lawrence— "neither God nor victim: neither greater nor less than himself"—remained forever resolute: "His soul, in its isolation as she lay on his breast, chose it so, with the soul's inevitability. So, there was no temptation."

Then, with daylight, a fifth and final memoir-like note, for once, a comic detail—Aaron's "difficulty in unfastening the various locks and bars and catches of the massive door downstairs," in the process his beginning "in irritation and anger, to feel he was a prisoner, that he was locked in": "But suddenly the ponderous door came loose, and he was out in the street. The door shut heavily behind him, with a shudder. He was out in the morning streets of Florence" (274). Aaron Sisson, free at last, and if the novel draws on an actual short romantic entanglement with Rosalind Baynes, then Lawrence was free as well, free from his fourth and—likely to his relief—his final female sexual partner.

Works Cited

Chambers, Jessie. *D. H. Lawrence: A Personal Record*. 2nd Edition. Ed. J. D. Chambers. Frank Cass, 1965.

Kinkead-Weekes, Mark. *D. H. Lawrence, Triumph to Exile, 1912–1922*. Cambridge UP, 1996.

Lawrence, D. H. *Aaron's Rod*. Ed. Mara Kalnins. Penguins Books, 1995.

———. *Complete Works*. Delphi Classics, 2015.

———. *Letters of D. H. Lawrence*. Vol. 1: September 1901 – May 1913. Ed. James T. Boulton. Cambridge UP, 1979.

———. *Mr. Noon*. Ed. Lindeth Vasey. Cambridge UP, 1984.

———. *Sons and Lovers* (CE). Eds. Helen Baron and Carl Baron. Cambridge UP, 1992.

———. *Sons and Lovers*. Viking P, 1971.

Lawrence, Frieda. *"Not I, But the Wind... ."* Viking P, 1934.

Squires, Michael and Lynn K. Talbot. *Living at the Edge: A Biography of D.H. Lawrence and Frieda Von Richthofen*. U Wisconsin P, 2002.

Worthen, John. *D. H. Lawrence: The Early Years 1885–1912*. Cambridge UP, 1991.

5 Greiffenhagen's Shepherd

A Passionate Embrace

In 2015, an image of a woman's dress went viral on the Internet—millions viewed and commented on whether they saw a blue dress trimmed in black or a white dress trimmed in gold. Here was a single image subject to two competing interpretations that, like those aroused by Ludwig Wittgenstein's famous duck-rabbit, were not readily reconcilable. People who saw the dress as blue and black had difficulty seeing it as white and gold, and vice versa. One wonders if D. H. Lawrence faced a similar dilemma in his early twenties when he became fascinated by Maurice Greiffenhagen's painting *An Idyll* (1891)—so fascinated that he made at least four copies of it to send to friends, all while working on his first novel, *The White Peacock*, a work in which the painting, as discussed below, figures prominently.

At the center of Greiffenhagen's pastoral image is a passionate embrace between a tall, well-lit young woman, her arms hanging loosely at her side, with a coy, hard-to-read expression on her face—one not quite fear or enjoyment—and a male shepherd, a Pan-like figure, clothed in animal fur and, much like Mellors when spotted that day by Connie, naked from the waist up. There is no disputing what is in the painting—a satyr-like male embracing a demure young woman—just as there is no disputing the 2015 image of a striped dress. Our question, of course, is what Lawrence saw in this painting—a man looking at a woman or a woman being looked at by a man.

One approach is to see the Greiffenhagen painting as another variation of John Berger's well-known dictum about the primary male and female roles in Western art: "Men look at women. Women watch themselves being looked at" (47). Men would thus see the shepherd looking at the young woman and wanting to embrace her, thus identifying with his arousal—a scene a feminist critic Laura Mulvey, drawing upon Berger's work, would

DOI: 10.4324/9781003495093-5

see as another "surveyed female," or as she writes, "In a world ordered by sexual unbalance, pleasure in looking has been split between active/male and passive/female."

Mulvey then describes what she sees as the traditional or dominant male view of such a scene, with the "determining male gaze project[ing] its fantasy unto the female figure, which is styled accordingly" (436)—that is, seeing the female in the middle of Greiffenhagen's *Idyll* as the scopophilic object and, in the traditional view, a male like Lawrence sharing the shepherd's pleasure in observing the woman on display.

And this is also how Lawrence seems to feel about the painting, at least in his most direct comment. "As for Greiffenhagen's Idyll," the 23-year-old Lawrence writes in a letter from December 1908, "it moves me almost as much as if I were fallen in love myself"—presumably with Lawrence seeing himself as the shepherd embracing a young woman. "Under its intoxication," he continues,

> I have flirted madly this Christmas; [...] it is largely the effect of your *Idyll* that has made me kiss a certain girl till she hid her head in my shoulder; but what a beautiful soft throat, and a round smooth chin, she has; and what bright eyes, looking up! Mon Dieu, I am really half in love!
>
> (*Letters* 103)

Here, Lawrence sounds like Berger's or Mulvey's typical male viewer, with the female envisioned as prey. But why, we might ask, only "half in love"? And how to explain the sudden change in tone when Lawrence notes his fear of being unable to love "with the splendid uninterrupted passion of the Idyll"? Might Lawrence's problem be related to what we have seen in previous chapters—namely, his sense that, in matters of the heart, he is often, as he notes, "too conscious, and vaguely troubled"?

"Where there is no 'abandon' in a love," he continues, "it is dangerous," with "abandon" here presumably referring to being able to lose oneself in the moment, having the nerve to break the barriers of convention as an integral component of sexual pleasure—although, as Lawrence notes, "mother declares the reverse," his mother, the arch-enforcer of traditional sexual mores in his youth.

Such seems to be the point that the youthful Lawrence makes in questioning whether "in love, or at least in lovemaking, [...] the woman is always passive, like the girl in the Idyll—enjoying the man's demonstration, a wee bit frit [scared]—not active?" (103).

Lawrence then makes clear his discomfort at seeing the Greiffenhagen painting strictly from the shepherd's viewpoint, a lusty man ogling this immobile, uncertain young woman. If he has to be the man in the scene, Lawrence adds, he would prefer a more assertive woman: "a little devil—a Carmen—I like not things passive."

The "girls I have known are mostly so"—that is, passive—Lawrence continues; "men always declare them so, and like them so." Lawrence's subsequent attachment to the sexually experienced, worldly Frieda Weekley two years later merely confirms his preference for a different sort of woman. However, far more crucial here is the recognition of how Lawrence repeatedly found himself gravitating toward that other role in *An Idyll*—that is, imagining himself as the young person (nominally, the woman) at the center of the painting, especially when the other figure was like Greiffenhagen's shepherd—a virile, partially clothed outdoorsman.

As noted, at the time of this letter discussing *An Idyll*, Lawrence was busy at work on his first novel, *The White Peacock*, where the attraction between his two young lovers is played out through a discussion of Greiffenhagen's painting. The young woman, the narrator's sister Lettie, is described as "tall and supple," not unlike Lawrence himself; nor is it insignificant that Lawrence gives her elements of his background, including his sense of how "my mother hated my father before I was born" (28). Meanwhile, Lettie's shepherd, George Saxton, the first of Lawrence's rugged outdoorsmen—modeled on the great male friend of Lawrence's youth, Jessie Chambers' older brother, Alan—is described as "no taller than she, and looked shorter, being strongly built." The contrast between the two is clear: Lettie, "elegant in her movements"; George, with "a grace of his own," but not indoors, not "as he sat stiffly on a horse-hair chair" (24) or as he is offered elegant pastries ("tantafflins"), and instead requests a simple piece of cheese.

After the meal, Lettie continues teasing George about his discomfort, even as she entertains him at the piano, at one point asking, "with a flash of raillery," if he likes her playing any better than the meal. Then, as he looks at her without responding—this deeply quiet man, "his features [...] too often in a heavy repose"—we see the full arc of Lawrence's career as a novelist: "when he looked up and smiled unexpectedly," Lawrence notes, "he flooded her with an access of tenderness" (26).

Lettie continues her teasing, anticipating the discussion of Greiffenhagen's *Idyll* by noting how different men look at her: "Some look at my hair, some watch the rise and fall of my breathing, some look at my neck, and a few,—not you among them,—look me in the eyes for my thoughts" (27). George, whom she fittingly calls a "primitive man," sees her as quite different—"a fine specimen, strong." Then, as she goes through some books of prints, George stops her when he sees the Greiffenhagen. For the bashful George, it is a moment to press his case: "'Wouldn't it be fine?' he exclaimed, looking at her with glowing eyes, his teeth showing white in a smile that was not amusement. [...] 'That—a girl like that—half afraid—and passion'" (29)! In other words, a girl with the spirit of a Carmen, like the one Lawrence mentioned in his letter.

Greiffenhagen's painting, we learn, is also a favorite of Lettie's, although she is reluctant to admit it here, continuing instead to tease George: "She may well be half afraid, when the barbarian comes out in his glory, skins and all." Her implication is clear: she is too sophisticated to be attracted to such a man. "Make love to the next girl you meet, and by the time the poppies redden the field, she'll hang in your arms. She'll have need to be more than half afraid, won't she?"

George tries to protest that he is being misconstrued. While he is fumbling to find the right words, Lettie continues her attack, calling him "Precious Sir Galahad"—suggesting his lack of physical passion—while "stroking his cheek with her finger": "Are you studying just how to play the part?" she asks.

By now, George is aroused, "breathlessly quivering under the new sensation of heavy, unappeased fire in his breast, and in the muscles of his arms," but unable to find the right words. Instead, he can only look up at her, "his eyes wide and vivid with a declaration that made her shrink back as if flame had leaped towards her face." The power dynamic has now shifted to George—his physical presence giving him the power to arouse his partner. For a moment, they exchange glances before turning away:

> It was a torture to each of them to look thus nakedly at the other, a dazzled, shrinking pain that they forced themselves to undergo for a moment, that they might the moment after tremble with a fierce sensation that filled their veins with fluid, fiery electricity.
>
> (30)

George, struck silent by his rising passion, is hardly Greiffenhagen's bold shepherd. "There was a painful perplexity in his brow," Lawrence tells us, "a sense of something hurting, something he could not understand." Lettie, meanwhile, remains the center of Lawrence's focus, as in the painting, the study of a woman confused over her arousal. To break this uncomfortable moment and to avoid confronting her newly awakened desire—one, we are suggesting, likely shared by the young Lawrence—Lettie begins chattering in French, "speaking high and harshly." Eventually, they are both speechless; then a simple "Good-bye" from Lettie, "[h]er voice [...] full of insurgent tenderness"—again, tenderness as the one emotion that Lawrence offers instead of passion: "He looked at her again, his eyes flickering. Then he took her hand. She pressed his fingers, holding them a little while" (31).

Throughout this first novel, Lawrence struggled over how best to handle his two lovers, the genteel Lettie, so close to Lawrence's temperament, and the rugged George, Cyril's idol in the already discussed "Poem of Friendship." In an early draft of the novel, he has them marry before eventually consigning each to an unhappy marriage in his final draft.

Later in the novel, after Lettie has cast her fate with a wealthy and otherwise ill-suited partner, Lawrence affords his two young lovers a final escape to Greiffenhagen's "high and warm" wood, this time with Lawrence providing the brilliant scene-painting—starting with how they "left the tall, flower-tangled paths to go in among the bluebells, breaking through the close-pressed flowers and ferns till they came to an oak which had fallen across the hazels, where they sat half screened." There they are surrounded by bees that "swung down in a blunder of extravagance among the purple flowers"—"The sound of their hearty, wanton humming came clear upon the solemn boom of the wind overhead." "If you were a faun," Lettie tells George, "I would put guelder roses round your hair, and make you look Bacchanalian" (214).

But the subjunctive mood here says it all: The lovers' meeting is anticlimactic precisely because George has now become more of a puddle than a masculine ideal. "No, Lettie; don't go," he pleads. "What should I do with my life? Nobody would love you like I do—and what should I do with my love for you" (215)?

Biographer John Worthen speculates Lawrence did not begin his first copy of *An Idyll* until the night of his mother's death, in December 1910—what Worthen takes as a sign of Lawrence's finally being ready to assert his independence from his mother's strict sense of moral propriety. Worthen also suggests that this was the moment Lawrence began reassessing his father's role in his life, a process possibly connected to the question with which we started this chapter—how Lawrence finally came around to viewing the Greiffenhagen painting from the woman's point of view, that is, from the point of view of someone who felt strangely drawn to the erotic presence of a powerful outdoorsman.

Demon Lovers—Men and Other Beasts

The thesis of the present study aligns with the counterintuitive approach to Greiffenhagen's *Idyll*—the claim that Lawrence saw it as depicting a demure woman discreetly eyeing a powerful man. Equally central is the claim that depicting such scenes in his writings, starting with the two scenes recounted below, fully unlocked the powers of Lawrence's lyrical genius.

The first of these scenes is from the opening chapter of Lawrence's most praised novel, *Women in Love*, with the 25-year-old Gudrun, one of the two women of the title, playing the role of Greiffenhagen's maiden. Regarding Gudrun's appearance, Lawrence, not surprisingly, has little to say, offering only a single sentence in which he notes that she "was very beautiful, passive, soft-skinned, soft-limbed." This he follows with a slightly more fulsome account of her clothes, noting that she "wore a dress of dark-blue silky stuff, with ruches of blue and green linen lace in the neck and sleeves; and [that] she had emerald-green stockings." Then, two more sentences about what seems more important to Lawrence than Gudrun's or any woman's appearance, her character: "Her look of confidence and diffidence contrasted with Ursula's sensitive expectancy. The provincial people, intimidated by Gudrun's perfect *sang-froid* and exclusive bareness of manner, said of her: 'She is a smart woman' " (2).

However, before this first chapter is half over, she runs into one of Lawrence's most fully realized shepherds, Gerald Crich. Here, too, there is only a single sentence of direct description—that he "was of a fair, sun-tanned type, rather above middle height, well-made, and almost exaggeratedly well-dressed"—before a lengthy, charged account of the destabilizing impact this male presence has on Gudrun:

> But about him also was the strange, guarded look, the unconscious glisten, as if he did not belong to the same creation as the people about him. [...] There was something northern about him that magnetised her. In his clear northern flesh and his fair hair was a glisten like sunshine refracted through crystals of ice. And he looked so new, unbroached, pure as an arctic thing.
>
> (8–9)

Lawrence's depiction of Gerald can be seen as a reworking of Greiffenhagen's shepherd, one that plays up both his rugged beauty and his danger: "His gleaming beauty, maleness, like a young, good-humoured, smiling wolf," as well as "the significant, sinister stillness in his bearing, the lurking danger of his unsubdued temper." At least for a moment, however, the sides are hardly in balance, with the shepherd now, as if by an act of synecdoche, identified with the skin he is wearing: " 'His totem is the wolf,' [Gudrun] repeated to herself. 'His mother is an old, unbroken wolf.' "

What follows then is a lengthy account of Gudrun's shock of recognition—"a keen paroxysm, a transport, as if she had made some incredible discovery, known to nobody else on earth"—akin to Lady Chatterley's reaction when she happened upon the bathing Mellors: "A strange transport took possession of her, all her veins were in a paroxysm of violent sensation." She was both surprised, even frightened, by the intensity of her response and yet tortured with desire to see him again, a nostalgia, a necessity to see him again, to make sure it was not all a mistake, that she was not deluding herself, that she really felt this strange and overwhelming sensation on his account, this knowledge of him in her essence, this powerful apprehension of him.

She even questions whether she is "singled out for him in some way," as if transported directly into Greiffenhagen's *Idyll*, highlighted by "some pale gold, arctic light that envelopes only us two." "And she could not believe it, she remained in a muse, scarcely conscious of what was going on around."

The pattern could hardly be more straightforward: the Greiffenhagen woman as the subject through whose consciousness we view the world; the shepherd, the primary object in her line of vision. Such is the pattern that we can see perhaps even more clearly in our second example—this one involving the Irish widow, Kate Leslie, the protagonist in Lawrence's Mexican novel, *The Plumed Serpent*, written right before *Lady Chatterley's Lover*.

In this passage, Kate contemplates marrying her shepherd—Don Cipriano, a Mexican general involved with the violent reestablishment of ancient Aztec rites. He is short, unlike Gerald Crich, but, like him, a man possessing an oversized, often menacing aura.

The extended passage on what Kate senses in her lover—what Lawrence calls "the mystery of the primeval world"—can be read as an over-the-top gloss on Greiffenhagen's painting. In it, we can see Kate's growing awareness, "in all its shadowy, furious magnificence," of Cipriano as the menacing shepherd, a force in this "shadowy world where men were visionless, and winds of fury rose up from the earth":

> Once you entered his mystery the scale of all things changed, and he became a living male power, undefined, and unconfined. The smallness, the limitations ceased to exist. In his black, glinting eyes the power was limitless, and it was as if, from him, from his body of blood could rise up that pillar of cloud which swayed and swung, like a rearing serpent or a rising tree, till it swept the zenith, and all the earth below was dark and prone, and consummated.
>
> (310)

Lawrence's description has an intensely erotic dimension, what can almost be seen as a quasi-crazed, black arts version of Connie's wholesome vision of Mellors bathing:

Those small hands, that little natural tuft of black goats' beard hanging light from his chin, the tilt of his brows and the slight slant of his eyes, the domed Indian head with its thick black hair, they were like symbols to her, of another mystery, the mystery of the twilit, primitive world, where shapes that are small suddenly loom up huge, gigantic on the shadow, and a face like Cipriano's is the face at once of a god and a devil, the undying Pan face. The bygone mystery, that has indeed gone by, but has not passed away. Never shall pass away.

(311)

It is difficult not to quote this passage in full—perhaps Lawrence's most complete description of the devilish god Pan he first saw in Greiffenhagen's painting: Cipriano sitting "in silence, casting the old, twilit Pan-power over her," as Kate "felt herself submitting, succumbing." Each one—the man and the woman, or, more accurately, the beloved male and his shy, beseeching lover—playing the role laid out by Greiffenhagen: "He was once more the old dominant male, shadowy, intangible, looming suddenly tall, and covering the sky, making a darkness that was himself and nothing but himself, the Pan male. And she was swooned prone beneath, perfect in her proneness."

It was the ancient phallic mystery, the ancient god-devil of the male Pan. Cipriano unyielding forever, in the ancient twilight, keeping the ancient twilight around him. She understood now his power with his soldiers. He had the old gift of demon-power.

He would never woo; she saw this. When the power of his blood rose in him, the dark aura streamed from him like a cloud pregnant with power, like thunder, and rose like a whirlwind that rises suddenly in the twilight and raises a great pliant column, swaying and leaning with power, clear between heaven and earth.

Nor is there any need to switch the pronouns here to the first person to see Lawrence's intense personal investment in this erotic fantasy:

Ah! and what a mystery of prone submission, on her part, this huge erection would imply! Submission absolute, like the earth under the sky. Beneath an over-arching absolute.

Ah! what a marriage! How terrible! and how complete! With the finality of death, and yet more than death. The arms of the twilit Pan. And the awful, half-intelligible voice from the cloud. She could conceive now her marriage with Cipriano; the supreme passivity, like the earth below the twilight, consummate in living lifelessness, the sheer solid mystery of passivity. Ah, what an abandon, what an abandon, what an abandon!—of so many things she wanted to abandon.

(311)

Nowhere in his voluminous writings, it must be noted, is there anything near as complete an account of Greiffenhagen's *Idyll* from the shepherd's point of view; rarely does Lawrence show us a man lusting after a woman. Instead, here is what Lawrence repeatedly offers us:

> Cipriano put his hand, with its strange soft warmth and weight, upon her knee, and her soul melted like fused metal. "En poco tiempo, verdad?" he said to her, looking into her eyes with the old, black, glinting look, of power about to consummate itself. "In a little while, no?"
> She looked back at him, wordless. Language had abandoned her, and she leaned silent and helpless in the vast, unspoken twilight of the Pan world. Her self had abandoned her, and all her day was gone. Only she said to herself:
>
> ("My demon lover!" 312)

Indeed, one almost feels a little callous in pulling back the curtains here, seeing Kate Leslie's fervid response as part of Lawrence's long fascination with Greiffenhagen's *Idyll* going back some 15 years:

> Her world could end in many ways, and this was one of them. Back to the twilight of the ancient Pan world, where the soul of woman was dumb, to be forever unspoken.
> The car had stopped, they had come to Jamiltepec. He looked at her again, as reluctantly he opened the door. And as he stepped out, she realized again his uniform, his small figure in uniform. She had lost it entirely. She had only known his face, the face of the supreme god-demon; with the arching brows and slightly slanting eyes, and the loose, light tuft of a goat-beard. The Master. The everlasting Pan.

We can see a more controlled reworking of the Greiffenhagen painting in Lawrence's 1925 novella, *St. Mawr*. The point of view is again that of a female protagonist, the unhappily married Lou Carrington. She is an American living in England who has become exhausted with the super-ficialities of modern life and hopes to escape to her shepherd's dark forest by buying the horse, St. Mawr, an animal capable of arousing dark, erotic feelings in her—"as if that mysterious fire of the horse's body had split some rock in her":

The wild, brilliant, alert head of St. Mawr seemed to look at her out of another world. It was as if she had had a vision, as if the walls of her own world had suddenly melted away, leaving her in a great darkness, in the midst of which the large, brilliant eyes of that horse looked at her with demonish question, while his naked ears stood up like daggers from the naked lines of his inhuman head, and his great body glowed red with power.

(31)

"What was it?" Lawrence asks, and the answer is obvious—Greiffenhagen's shepherd:

Almost like a god looking at her terribly out of the everlasting dark, she had felt the eyes of that horse; great, glowing, fearsome eyes, arched with a question and containing a white blade of light like a threat. What was his non-human question, and his uncanny threat? She didn't know. He was some splendid demon, and she must worship him.

One can make a case for taking Lawrence literally here, seeing *St. Mawr* and *The Plumed Serpent* as explorations into the psychic worlds of two women, Lou Carrington and Kate Leslie, and, indeed, some women may identify with the submissive fantasies Lawrence ascribes to his two female protagonists. Others may find it more helpful, however, to see Lawrence's interest in these two works less in his female protagonists, less in the full range of emotions and challenges that constitute a woman's life, than in the repressed, erotic attraction that any sensitive soul, female or male, might feel in the presence of the larger-than-life shepherd that haunts Greiffenhagen's *Idyll*.

For Lawrence to express such feelings through a male character would risk exposing a deep strain of homoerotic desire, one with masochistic overtones. It was a strain, alas, of which we as readers can never be confident Lawrence himself was fully aware, much less ready to acknowledge— rarely able to present directly and, as depicted repeatedly in this study, regularly only via a series of subtle transformations, often involving female protagonists (the subject of Chapter 7, "Hiding in Plain Sight").

We close this section on Greiffenhagen's shepherd by looking at Lawrence celebrating a vision of Pan in his own voice—albeit here in praise for the nonhuman figure of a tree, specifically the "big pine tree" that he describes as "ris[ing] like a guardian spirit" in front of his New Mexico cabin: "Long, long ago the Indians blazed it. And the lightning, or the storm, has cut off its crest. Yet its column was always there, alive and changeless, alive and changing. [...] with its own aura of life." This tree is, for Lawrence, a life force, "gather[ing] up earth-power from the dark bowels of the earth, and a roaming sky-glitter from above." It is that powerful, unmoving male force, "all unto itself, [...] enormous, slow but unyielding with life, bristling with acquisitive energy, obscurely radiating some of its great strength."

> It vibrates its presence onto my soul, and I am with Pan. I think no man could live near a pine tree and remain suave and supple and compliant. Something fierce and bristling is communicated. The piny sweetness is rousing and defiant, like turpentine, the noise of the needles is keen with æons of sharpness. In the valleys of wind from the western desert, the tree hisses and resists. It does not lean eastward at all. It resists with a vast force of resistance, from within itself, and its column is a ribbed, magnificent assertion.
>
> ("Pan in America" 209–10)

His Fearsome Father

It is hardly a coincidence that the most compelling passage Lawrence ever wrote about the fear his father evoked in his childhood, as reenvisioned in *Sons and Lovers*, should also involve a tree, the "huge old ash-tree" next to the family's house on Walker Street—the one "on the brow of the hill, commanding a view of the valley," to which his family moved when Lawrence was an impressionable six-year-old. "The west wind, sweeping from Derbyshire, caught the houses with full force," causing the ash-tree to shriek. Paul's father in the novel, closely modeled on Arthur Lawrence, loved the effect—"It's music [that] sends me to sleep"—while the insecure Paul "hated it," associated its "demoniacal noise" with insecure feelings "of night, of vastness, and of terror," that is, with the very male power that as a sensitive, sickly child he sensed were so sorely lacking in his own life: the "terror [that] came in from the shrieking of the tree and the anguish of the home discord" (59).

Here is Greiffenhagen's shepherd, a would-be Pan, on a rampage, with the young Paul, as if in a nightmare, "wak[ing] up, after he had been asleep a long time, aware of thuds downstairs"—the thuds, the marks of untrammeled male power: "Instantly he was wide awake," listening in fear to "the booming shouts of his father, come home nearly drunk," his mother's protests ineffectual:

> then the bang, bang of his father's fist on the table, and the nasty snarling shout as the man's voice got higher. And then the whole was drowned in a piercing medley of shrieks and cries from the great, wind-swept ash-tree.
>
> (60)

It is the terrifying moment that the 20-year-old Lawrence captured in his short poem "Discord in Childhood" (Delphi 7126), as "the lash of the tree" that "Shrieked and slashed the wind, as a ship's / Weird rigging in a storm shrieks hideously." The cause of distress in the poem is the same as in the novel—the father, specifically "the dreadful sound" of his "thick lash booming and bruising, until it drowned / The other voice in a silence of blood."

This one section of *Sons and Lovers* shows Lawrence at his most unforgiving of his father—all the fright of Greiffenhagen's leering shepherd, seemingly with almost none of his underlying attraction. Instead, we get this picture of the young Lawrence and his siblings "lay[ing] in suspense, waiting for a lull in the wind to hear what their father was doing," wondering if he "might hit their mother again. [...] lay[ing] with their hearts in the grip of an intense anguish":

The wind came through the tree fiercer and fiercer. All the chords of the great harp hummed, whistled, and shrieked. And then came the horror of the sudden silence, silence everywhere, outside and downstairs. What was it? Was it a silence of blood? What had he done?

Harm to their mother was, of course, their one great fear, a fear only relieved when it was clear the father had finally gone to bed for the night and that Paul and his siblings "could go to sleep in peace" (60).

"Paul hated his father," Lawrence wrote about his young self, a boy with "a fervent private religion": " 'Make him stop drinking,' he prayed every night. 'Lord, let my father die,' he prayed very often." And yet, even here, there was a sign of possible redemption: " 'Let him not be killed at pit,' he prayed when, after tea, the father did not come home from work."

While Freud's analysis of the different ways a boy's fears of being beaten by his father can get contorted may strike some as too simplistic or too reductive, his brief article "A Child Is Being Beaten" is rife with suggestions for how in some boys the fundamental Oedipal conflict in which the boy sees his father as a rival for his mother's affection becomes inverted, resulting in what Freud describes elsewhere as the boy "behav[ing] like a girl and display[ing] an affectionate feminine attitude to his father and a corresponding jealousy and hostility towards his mother" ("The Ego and the Id" 641).

In such a state, a boy is less likely to see himself as a future father and thus his mother's or any woman's potential lover. Instead, Freud suggests, emotions somehow get inverted, much as we have seen with Lawrence and the Greiffenhagen painting, with the son now seeing the world from the mother's or a woman's point of view, and hence with the father no longer seen as a rival but instead the very object of his desire—an inversion that occurs despite, or even because of, the father's grandeur and fury, or with desire and fear within the boy inextricably intertwined, possibly for a lifetime. Or, as Freud writes, "This being beaten"—or, just as likely, as seems to be the case with Paul Morel and Lawrence, the fear or the heightened sensation associated with the fear of being beaten—"is now a meeting place between the sense of guilt and sexual love": "It is not only the punishment for the forbidden genital relation, but also the regressive substitute for it, and from this latter source it derives the libidinous excitement which is from this time forward attached to it" (108).

The feminist psychoanalyst JJessica Benjamin amplifies Freud's notion, oddly enough, in her analysis of women's illicit desires in *The Bonds of Love*, where she locates "the prototype of ideal love—a love in which the person seeks to find in the other an ideal image of himself"—in this case, in what she calls the "identificatory, homoerotic bond between toddler son and father" (107). At the core of this idealized relationship, she sees a means by which a highly imaginative boy like the young Lawrence can overcome his sense of helplessness—and Lawrence we know was a sickly child, one who later at school avoided most boy games—by "comfort[ing] himself with the belief in parental omnipotence": "In this parental power," Benjamin continues, "he will seek to recognize the power of his own desire"—to love and to be loved—"and he will elaborate it in the internally constructed ideal [of the all-powerful father]." It is this idealized and eroticized image of the masculine father whom Benjamin sees as the model for a son's negotiating the "rapprochement between independence and helplessness," those two conflicting components of Lawrence's adult psyche: a disposition that blended a fiery independent streak that resisted any forms of dependence along with the dreamy helplessness of Greiffenhagen's maidens. And, of course, it is such dreamy helplessness that best describes Connie Chatterley's ultimate erotic fulfillment as depicted in Chapter 2—a fulfillment that began, we remember, when Lawrence's sensitive, tender stand-in found herself aghast spying upon her half-clothed shepherd.

A friend of Lawrence's later years recounts Lawrence suddenly expressing regret that "he had not done justice to his father in *Sons and Lovers* and felt like rewriting it"—likely thinking back on the ash-tree sequence and the earlier sequence when his inebriated father had locked his pregnant mother out of the house for most of a night. What had triggered this regret in 1922, the friend recounts, was Lawrence watching a worker in Ceylon deftly "arranging a screen on the verandah." Lawrence saw this man as a more ingratiating, less threatening instance of Greiffenhagen's shepherd—someone "alert; with sure, graceful movement and fine head; his dark eyes flashing; his features regular; the beard clipped in an elegant line," and, in the end, Lawrence noting how "he resembled [my] father—the same clean-cut and exuberant spirit, a true pagan" (Nehls 126).

Still, 12 years earlier, even before writing *Sons and Lovers*, in a letter from December 1910, as his mother was dying, there were already signs of ambivalence in his attitude toward his father. Yes, there is the assertion of a kind of intense Oedipal perfection in his bond with his mother—the claim that "[w]e have loved each other, almost with a husband and wife love, as well as filial and maternal"—coupled with the same apparent dislike of his father: the admission that "I was born hating my father: as early as ever I can remember, I shivered with horror when he touched me." Yet, even in this letter, he describes his mother using what will soon become derogatory terms for Lawrence—labeling her "a clever, ironical delicately moulded woman, of good, old burgher descent." He described his "shepherd" father, meanwhile, as "dark, ruddy, with a fine laugh"—a man with a "sanguine temperament, warm and hearty" (190).

Nor is Walter Morel, Lawrence's fictional father in *Sons and Lovers*, without his redeeming moments; indeed, immediately after the scene where he locks his pregnant wife out of the house, Lawrence offers this expanded view of his father's gentle, solitary breakfast, starting with the first of the morning's sounds—"the bang, bang of the poker against the raker, as Morel smashed the remainder of the coal to make the kettle, which was filled and left on the hob, finally boil" (27). What follows is a loving picture, in the spirit of Vincent Van Gogh's early Borinage paintings of peasants—"His cup and knife and fork, all he wanted except just the food, [...] laid ready on the table on a newspaper."

Here was "an hour of joy" in a room made snug by his "pack[ing] the bottom of the doors with rugs to shut out the draught, [and] pil[ing] a big fire": "He toasted his bacon on a fork and caught the drops of fat on his bread; then he put the rasher on his thick slice of bread, and cut off chunks with a clasp-knife, poured his tea into his saucer." He ate with his "clasp-knife," Lawrence tells us, "loath[ing] a fork [...] [as] a modern introduction which has still scarcely reached common people."

> Then, in solitude, he ate and drank, often sitting, in cold weather, on a little stool with his back to the warm chimney-piece, his food on the fender, his cup on the hearth. And then he read the last night's newspaper—what of it he could—spelling it over laboriously. He preferred to keep the blinds down and the candle lit even when it was daylight; it was the habit of the mine.

After his father prepared his lunch—"two thick slices of bread-and-butter" and tea without sugar—he would take a cup to Lawrence's mother. About her, Lawrence only offers this modest account—noting how she "had a winsome face when her hair was loose"—before continuing with his loving portrait of his father, now depicted as a gentle variation of Greiffenhagen's shepherd: Here was a man who "tied a scarf round his neck, put on his great, heavy boots, his coat, with the big pocket that carried his snap-bag and his bottle of tea, and went forth into the fresh morning air." Then we learn how he would regularly give himself an extra half-hour to explore the neighboring fields, in the summer hunting for mushrooms, "straying through the thick wet grass in his pit-boots, looking for the lurking, white-fleshed things," carefully placing any he found in his coat pocket. "So he appeared at the pit-top, often with a stalk from the hedge between his teeth, which he chewed all day to keep his mouth moist, down the mine, feeling quite as happy as when he was in the field" (28).

Then there are the details of how his parents met: his always proper mother, in the mode of Greiffenhagen's demure maiden—refined, middle-class, "well set-up, erect, and very smart"—and his strange, alluring father, already portrayed as a shepherd, with his "wavy black hair that shone again," Lawrence writes, "and a vigorous black beard that had never been shaved": "His cheeks were ruddy, and his red, moist mouth was notice-able because he laughed so often and so heartily. He had that rare thing, a rich, ringing laugh" (9).

The young Walter Morel, modeled on Lawrence's father, Arthur, was struck by his future wife's genteel pronunciation ("a purity of English which thrilled him to hear"); she, conversely, was struck by his tempera-ment—"soft, non-intellectual, warm, a kind of gambolling" so unlike the carping, critical bent of her father. Then there was his future father's dan-cing and that "certain subtle exultation like glamour in his movement, and his face the flower of his body, ruddy, with tumbled black hair, and laughing alike whatever partner he bowed above" (10). Although his mother had been raised "puritan, like her father, high-minded, and really stern," Lawrence was already ready to depict her in the mode of Connie Chatterley, as a woman ready to praise her man as "rather wonderful, never having met anyone like him":

> the dusky, golden softness of this man's sensuous flame of life, that flowed off his flesh like the flame from a candle, not baffled and gripped into incandescence by thought and spirit as her life was, seemed to her something wonderful, beyond her.

It can hardly be an accident that Lawrence placed this one incident—the erotic appeal that a man dancing might have for an otherwise respectable woman—at the center of one of his earliest stories, "The White Stocking." The woman, Elsie Whiston, although seemingly happily married, is none-theless the recipient of a series of inappropriate Valentine's gifts from her former employer, Sam Adams. One gift, a pair of pearl earrings, was wrapped in a white stocking she brought to a Christmas party hosted by Adams, "mistakenly" thinking it was her handkerchief.

On the surface, the story is about how a married couple can withstand a bump in the road—in this case, these inappropriate gifts from Adams. However, what seems to interest the young Lawrence far more than a couple's travails—and the one area where his writing glows—is in recreating the erotic appeal a man dancing can have for the respectable, married Elsie, a stand-in for his mother but an early instance of the lyrically adept *hidden* Lawrence as well.

At his party, Adams cues the bandleader at just the right moment, turning to Elsie "with a curious caress in his voice that seemed to lap the outside of her body in a warm glow, delicious. She gave herself to it. She liked it." And why not? Adams was "an excellent dancer," a graceful embodiment of Greiffenhagen's shepherd,

> seem[ing] to draw her close in to him by some male warmth of attraction, so that she became all soft and pliant to him, flowing to his form, whilst he united her with him and they lapsed along in one movement.

Again, Lawrence's focus is on the woman's rapture, with Elsie "carried in a kind of strong, warm flood, her feet moved of themselves, and only the music threw her away from him, threw her back to him, to his clasp, in his strong form moving against her, rhythmically, deliriously" (75).

And then a second dance, "an intoxication to her"—with Lawrence again giving us another picture of a maiden with her shepherd: "After the first few steps, she felt herself slipping away from herself," unsure if she had ever agreed to this pleasure.

> She lay in the arm of the steady, close man with whom she was dancing, and she seemed to swim away out of contact with the room, into him. She had passed into another, denser element of him, an essential privacy.
>
> (76)

Then a drowning metaphor of being "under sea, with a flow of ghostly, dumb movements," so similar to what Lawrence will use some 14 years later to describe Lady Chatterley's lovemaking: "But she herself was held real against her partner, and it seemed she was connected with him, as if the movements of his body and limbs were her own movements, yet not her own movements—and oh, delicious!"

And what of Elsie's shepherd, the man who "bore her round the room in the dance"—a distant figure, like so many of Lawrence's eroticized men, here "given up, oblivious, concentrated, into the dance"? He may have appeared aloof—"[h]is eye [...] unseeing"—but how different "his large, voluptuous body" with its "subtle activity." "His fingers seem[ing] to search into her flesh," and again with Elsie's swoons anticipating Connie's: "Every moment, and every moment, [feeling] she would give way utterly, and sink molten: the fusion point was coming when she would fuse down into perfect unconsciousness at his feet and knees."

For the proper Elsie—a character nominally based on Lawrence's mother, who may have been the source of the plot element involving Elsie's mistaking a stocking for her handkerchief at a dance—the whole experience was "exquisite," with her partner able "to sustain all her body with his limbs, his body, and his warmth seemed to come closer into her, nearer, till it would fuse right through her, and she would be as liquid to him, as an intoxication only" (77). Here, Elsie has that ecstatic experience, which we will see repeatedly with all of our female protagonists in Chapter 7, the result of feeling controlled by, even submerged in, a robust, distant male. "When it was over," Lawrence continues, Elsie "was dazed, and was scarcely breathing." She waited as they stood in the middle of the room for the touch of "his lips on her bare shoulder," only to realize that "they were not alone." Lawrence's comment on this realization: "It was cruel."

There are also two additional loving accounts of Paul's father in *Sons and Lovers*. Both highlight what Lawrence remembered about his father that day in Ceylon—how he was "a good workman, dexterous" (63). In the first account, he is mending household items, "run[ning] with a piece of red-hot iron into the scullery, crying: 'Out of my road—out of my road!' " Then follows this beautiful account of how his father "hammered the soft, red-glowing stuff on his iron goose, and made the shape he wanted. Or he sat absorbed for a moment, soldering." Paul and his siblings

> watched with joy as the metal sank suddenly molten, and was shoved about against the nose of the soldering-iron, while the room was full of a scent of burnt resin and hot tin, and Morel was silent and intent for a minute.

Then he would mend his boots, always singing "because of the jolly sound of hammering," staying happy as "he sat putting great patches on his moleskin pit trousers, which he would often do, considering them too dirty, and the stuff too hard, for his wife to mend."

The second account features Paul's father making fuses for the mine, a process that began with carefully cleaning wheat-straws "till each one gleamed like a stalk of gold." Paul assisted in this task, as he "loved to see the black grains trickle down a crack in his palm, into the mouth of the straw, peppering jollily downwards till the straw was full." "Look dad!" Paul would cry out. " 'That's right, my beauty,' replied Morel, who was peculiarly lavish of endearments to his second son" (64). Then, their father would tell funny tales about life in the mines, especially about the horses, and the evening would quickly end as he went to bed early, before the children. Still, his presence now provided a calm in their lives on such nights, as they "lay and talked softly awhile," until they were taken by light "suddenly sprawling over the ceiling from the lamps that swung in the hands of the colliers tramping by outside, going to take the nine o'clock shift" (90). As this passage concludes, we can most clearly see this imaginative bond between male strength and physical intimacy that figures so prominently in Lawrence's life and his writing:

> They listened to the voices of the men, imagined them dipping down into the dark valley. Sometimes they went to the window and watched the three or four lamps growing tinier and tinier swaying down the fields in the darkness. Then it was a joy to rush back to bed and cuddle closely in the warmth.
>
> (65)

"Under the Colliery Railway"—Being Kissed by a Miner

Gerald Crich, as noted, is the Pan figure lurking throughout *Women in Love* and arousing the erotic interest of the younger Brangwen sister, Gudrun. Later in the novel, Gerald insists on walking Gudrun home the night his mine-owner father lies dying at home. It is nighttime, and Gerald, Lawrence's would-be shepherd, is preoccupied—"Blind to her, thinking only of himself"—as he draws his maiden, Gudrun, close: "Her heart fainted, feeling herself taken. But then, his arm was so strong, she quailed under its powerful close grasp. She died a little death, and was drawn against him as they walked down the stormy darkness." It was in Gerald's strength that Gudrun could balance herself, "perfectly in opposition to himself," finding him "liberated and perfect, strong, heroic"—"The exultation in his voice [...] like a sweetish, poisonous drug to her." Here, too, we see the same conjoining of fear and attraction: "Did she then mean so much to him! She sipped the poison" (321).

Lawrence does give us an account of Gudrun's impact on Gerald: "She nestled against him. He felt her all soft and warm, she was the rich, lovely substance of his being." It is just that when he focuses on what Gerald sees in Gudrun, the writing rarely rises above the pedestrian: "The warmth and motion of her walk suffused through him wonderfully"; as with the Greiffenhagen painting, Lawrence's interest is almost entirely with the maiden's response to the shepherd, here the man who "was so strong, so sustaining, [that] he could not be opposed." Imagine the passage in first person, from Gudrun's point of view—as we did earlier with Lady Chatterley—and the writing takes on an eerily dreamlike quality, with the speaker, possibly Lawrence, imagining some hidden part of his persona "drift[ing] along in a wonderful interfusion of physical motion, down the dark, blowy hillside" (321).

They continue "their strange walk," coming to a location that Gudrun (and Lawrence) knew well—"the square arch where the road passed under the colliery railway," the spot where a young boy from town may have liked to stand so that he could "hear the train rumble thundering over the logs overhead," the spot he also knew as the place "under this dark and lonely bridge [where] the young colliers stood in the darkness with their sweethearts, in rainy weather" (322). Gerald and Gudrun have arrived at the very spot where Lawrence, as a young boy, may have "listened to the voices of the [miners], imagined them dipping down into the dark valley." Here, this same young boy, now a novelist, identifies with Gudrun, another young maiden, eager to stand "with *her* sweetheart"—her miner—"and be kissed under the bridge in the invisible darkness" (emphasis in original).

Thus it was that "under the bridge, they came to a standstill, and he lifted her upon his breast"—this comingling of memory and desire once again produced one of Lawrence's most wondrous love scenes, and, as with *Lady Chatterley's Lover*, all narrated from the woman's point of view. It is "[h]is body [that] vibrated taut and powerful as he closed upon her and crushed her, breathless and dazed and destroyed, crushed her upon his breast":

> Ah, it was terrible, and perfect. Under this bridge, the colliers pressed their lovers to their breast. And now, under the bridge, the master of them all pressed her to himself! And how much more powerful and terrible was his embrace than theirs, how much more concentrated and supreme his love was, than theirs in the same sort! She felt she would swoon, die, under the vibrating, inhuman tension of his arms and his body—she would pass away.
>
> (322–23)

Here is our maiden—and, vicariously, one imagines, our author—"almost unconscious," luxuriating in memories of long unfulfilled, youthful desires:

> So the colliers' lovers would stand with their backs to the walls, holding their sweethearts and kissing them as she was being kissed. Ah, but would their kisses be fine and powerful as the kisses of the firm-mouthed

master? Even the keen, short-cut moustache—the colliers would not have that.

And the colliers' sweethearts would, like herself, hang their heads back limp over their shoulder, and look out from the dark archway, at the close patch of yellow lights on the unseen hill in the distance, or at the vague form of trees, and at the buildings of the colliery wood-yard, in the other direction.

(323)

Then, the now familiar sense of immersion, with "[h]is arms [...] fast around her," Gerald "gathering her into himself, her warmth, her softness, her adorable weight, drinking in the suffusion of her physical being, avidly." It is as if she is to disappear completely: "He lifted her, and seemed to pour her into himself, like wine into a cup."

How does one stop quoting such masterful prose capturing what feels like the very fulfillment of Greiffenhagen's maiden, as Gudrun "relaxed, and seemed to melt, to flow into him, as if she were some infinitely warm and precious suffusion filling into his veins, like an intoxicant"?

Her arms were round his neck, he kissed her and held her perfectly suspended, she was all slack and flowing into him, and he was the firm, strong cup that receives the wine of her life. So she lay cast upon him, stranded, lifted up against him, melting and melting under his kisses, melting into his limbs and bones, as if he were soft iron becoming surcharged with her electric life.

Till she seemed to swoon, gradually her mind went, and she passed away, everything in her was melted down and fluid, and she lay still, become contained by him, sleeping in him as lightning sleeps in a pure, soft stone. So she was passed away and gone in him, and he was perfected.

(323–24)

Nor is there any letting up in the aftermath of Gudrun's sexual fulfillment. As she opened her eyes, "it seemed to her strange that the world still existed, that she was standing under the bridge, resting her head on Gerald's breast. Gerald—who was he?" And the answer, for both Lawrence and his heroine, was the same: "He was the exquisite adventure, the desirable unknown to her."

And then this wondrous tribute to the perfection of a certain sort of male beauty—homage paid to another Pan commingling fear and attraction—as Gudrun looks up in the darkness and sees "his face above her, his shapely, male face": "There seemed a faint, white light emitt[ing] from him, a white aura, as if he were visitor from the unseen." It is then that Gudrun "reached up, like Eve reaching to the apples on the tree of knowledge":

> and she kissed him, though her passion was a transcendent fear of the thing he was, touching his face with her infinitely delicate, encroaching wondering fingers. Her fingers went over the mould of his face, over his features. How perfect and foreign he was—ah, how dangerous! Her soul thrilled with complete knowledge. This was the glistening, forbidden apple, this face of a man. She kissed him, putting her fingers over his face, his eyes, his nostrils, over his brows and his ears, to his neck, to know him, to gather him in by touch. He was so firm, and shapely, with such satisfying, inconceivable shapeliness, strange, yet unutterably clear. He was such an unutterable enemy, yet glistening with uncanny white fire. She wanted to touch him and touch him and touch him, till she had him all in her hands, till she had strained him into her knowledge. Ah, if she could have the precious knowledge of him, she would be filled, and nothing could deprive her of this. For he was so unsure, so risky in the common world of day.
>
> (324)

Gudrun's one thought—"You are so *beautiful*"—is followed by the misgivings we regularly see in Lawrence, associated with heterosexual intimacy: "For the time, her soul was destroyed with the exquisite shock of his invisible fluid lightning. She knew. And this knowledge was a death from which she must recover."

In our next chapter, we will look at the famous wrestling scene from this novel, the one involving Gerald and Lawrence's stand-in, Rupert Birkin, and the place some readers may go to view Lawrence's most direct expression of homosexual desire. These same readers are thus likely content to take Lawrence at his word here, seeing this scene under the train tracks, told as it is primarily from a woman's point of view, as mainly about a woman's desire, in this case, the desire of the fictional Gudrun Brangwen, a character some think was loosely modeled on Lawrence's friend the writer Katherine Mansfield.

Such readers may be reluctant to see Lawrence's desires directly at work here, reluctant to see Lawrence as the one so eager for extended intimacy with the man of her dreams: "Ah much, much, many days harvesting for her large, yet perfectly subtle and intelligent hands upon the field of his living, radio-active body. Ah, her hands were eager, greedy for knowledge" (324–25). That was for some future time: "Too much" now and Lawrence's alter ego would be shattered, the "fine vial of her soul" breaking from having been "too quickly" filled. "Enough now—enough for the time being. There were all the after days when her hands, like birds, could feed upon the fields of his mystical plastic form—till then enough."

Or, as the prophetic Lawrence adds here, a man whose intense, rich erotic life was so deeply a product of the imagination—"For to desire is better than to possess, the finality of the end was dreaded as deeply as it was desired." Let Gudrun, the gentle maiden, and Gerald, her fearsome shepherd, remain frozen together, as if in Greiffenhagen's *Idyll*.

Works Cited

Benjamin, Jessica. *The Bonds of Love: Psychoanalysis, Feminism, and the Problem of Domination*. Pantheon Books, 1988.

Berger, John. *Ways of Seeing*. British Broadcasting Corporation, 1972.

Freud, Sigmund. "A Child Is Being Beaten." In *Sexuality and the Psychology of Love*. Basic Books, 1997: 97–122.

———. "The Ego and the Id." In *The Freud Reader*. Ed. Peter Gay. W.W. Norton, 1989: 628–58.

Lawrence, D. H. *Complete Works*. Delphi Classics, 2015.

———. *Letters of D. H. Lawrence*. Vol. 1: September 1901 – May 1913. Ed. James T. Boulton. Cambridge UP, 1979.

———. "Pan in America." In *The Bad Side of Books*. Ed. Geoff Dyer. New York Review of Books, 2019: 206–17.

———. *The Plumed Serpent*. Ed. L. D. Clark. Cambridge UP, 2002.

———. *Sons and Lovers*. Viking P, 1971.

———. *St. Mawr*. In *St. Mawr and Other Stories*. Ed. Brian Finney. Cambridge UP, 2002: 19–155.

———. *The White Peacock*. Ed. Andrew Robertson. Cambridge UP, 2002.

———. "The White Stocking." In *Selected Short Stories*. Ed. Brian Finney. Penguin Books, 1982: 67–87.

———. *Women in Love*. Heinemann, 1971.

Mulvey, Laura. "Visual Pleasure and Narrative Cinema" (1975). In *Feminisms Redux: An Anthology of Literary Theory and Criticism*. Eds. Robyn R. Warhol and Diane Price Herndl. Rutgers UP, 2009: 432–42.

Nehls, Edward. *D.H. Lawrence: A Composite Biography, Vol 2: 1919–1925*. U Wisconsin P, 1958.

6 Man-to-Man

Wrestling with Desire—*Women in Love*

In his widely cited article on Lawrence and homosexuality, biographer Jeffrey Meyers points to four well-known scenes involving male-to-male touching in Lawrence's novels. In Chapter 2, we looked at the most lyrical of these four, the bathing scene from Lawrence's first novel, *The White Peacock*, which, as noted, was that rare scene in Lawrence to arouse the interest of gay readers in his lifetime. Two of the other three scenes involve little pretense of erotic arousal and can be commented on briefly here.

The first is the initiation scene from Lawrence's Mexican novel, *The Plumed Serpent*, featuring the leader of the revolution, Don Ramón Carrasco, and his second-in-command, the same Don Cipriano we saw in the last chapter, eliciting such an intense response from the 40-year-old Irish widow, Kate Leslie. In this initiation scene, Kate is only a disinterested third party, resulting in some surprisingly flat writing by Lawrence, such as his description of Don Ramón holding "his arms close round Cipriano's waist, pressing his black head against his side," or Cipriano "feel[ing] as if his mind, his head were melting away in the darkness" (368). Nor does Lawrence's faint attempt at poetic imagery—for instance, describing Cipriano as "a man without a head, moving like a dark wind over the face of the dark waters"—add much erotic tension. Instead, we are left with this pale rendering of one man touching another—of Cipriano, "rigid and motionless," as "Ramón clasped the two knees with his hands, till they were warm, and he felt them dark and asleep like two living stones, or two eggs" (369). Ramón then binds Cipriano's knees, grasping his ankles "as one might grasp the base of a young tree, as it emerges from the earth": "Crouching on the earth, he gripped them in an intense grip, resting his head on the feet." And the grand result? "The moments passed, and both men were unconscious."

The other scene is from *Aaron's Rod*, a work briefly discussed in Chapter 4 regarding Lawrence and Rosalind Baynes. It is also a work

DOI: 10.4324/9781003495093-6

in which Lawrence oddly opts to use two separate male stand-ins. The first and more significant is the eponymous Aaron Sisson, who has left his Midlands home—his wife, children, and clerical job in a coal mine—to see if he could live, as Mellors tries to do at the conclusion of *Lady Chatterley's Lover*, without an assortment of traditional commitments, including that greatest of all bugaboos, heterosexual intimacy. In London, he falls seriously ill after allowing himself to be seduced by a young artist and is nursed back to health by Lawrence's other stand-in, the writer Rawdon Lilly.

One oddity of the scene involves Lawrence displaying his meticulous housekeeping skills, showing us, for instance, Lilly happy to "put on the kettle, and quietly set cups and plates on a tray," managing the "clean and cosy and pleasant" room he was tidying up for his seriously ill friend. "[A]s efficient and inobtrusive a housewife as any woman" is Lawrence's summation: "While the kettle boiled, he sat darning the socks which he had removed from Aaron's feet when the flautist arrived, and which he had washed." Altogether, Lawrence shows us the full range of domestic chores for which he was known among his contemporaries, although it is unclear if, like Lilly, Lawrence also "preferred that no outsider should see him doing these things" (98).

Lilly's touching of his friend is nominally therapeutic and hence an extension of his housekeeping chores, beginning the assertion that he will rub his friend with oil "as mothers do their babies whose bowels don't work." In what follows, we see Lilly "uncover[ing] the blond lower body of his patient, and [...] rub[bing] the abdomen with oil, using a slow, rhythmic, circulating motion, a sort of massage." He continued rubbing "finely and steadily [...] over the whole of the lower body, mindless, as if in a sort of incantation." When done, Lilly covered up his friend and "sat down in fatigue to look at his patient" (96). Scholars might argue about the exact nature of this restorative massage, including the degree of anal contact it might have entailed. What is beyond dispute, however, is the uninspired descriptive writing. One key is that the scene lacks the scopophilic dimension we find with other protagonists; here, instead, all we ever learn about Aaron—the recipient of Lilly's caress—is that he was "a good-looking man, fair, and pleasant, about thirty-two years old."

The most intense erotic writing in *Aaron's Rod* is neither in this scene of male-to-male touching nor in that involving Aaron's heterosexual love-making with the Marchesa discussed in Chapter 4, but, perhaps unexpectedly, in Aaron's rapturous response to the male statues adorning Florence's Piazza della Signoria. There, for instance, we find this description of Michelangelo's *David*—"the adolescent, the white, self-conscious, physical adolescent: enormous, in keeping with the stark, grim, enormous palace, which is dark and bare as he is white and bare"—or, with an even sharper erotic edge, the account of "heavy naked men" of Bandinelli's *Hercules and Cacus*. Aaron was shocked, Lawrence adds, by this "great naked man of marble, with a heavy back and strong naked flanks over which the water was trickling" (211).

Lawrence saw each statue—Michelangelo's and Bandinelli's—as perfect in its own way. David, "standing forward stripped and exposed and eternally half-shrinking, half-wishing to expose himself." He represents young manhood—"the white, self-conscious, physical adolescent: enormous, in keeping with the stark, grim, enormous palace, which is dark and bare as he is white and bare." Behind the son stands the figure that arouses more significant interest in Lawrence—"the big, lumpy Bandinelli men," figures with rugged masculinity lacking in either Michelangelo's David or Cellini's equally celebrated Perseus. Indeed, compared to Bandinelli's father, Lawrence notes, "Cellini's dark hero looked female, with his plump hips and his waist, female and rather insignificant: graceful, and rather vulgar" (212).

The two Bandinelli figures "may be ugly," Lawrence concludes, but they possess "their own lumpy reality." They belong there as well, and not just belong but dominate, much as fathers are apt to do in a son's imagination: "And this morning in the rain, standing unbroken, with the water trickling down their flanks and along the inner side of their great thighs, they were real enough, representing the undaunted physical nature of the heavier Florentines."

The flatness of writing that characterizes these first two scenes of men touching is not an issue with our third scene, the well-known wrestling sequence from the "Gladiatorial" chapter in *Women in Love*. Here, the focus is on Rupert Birkin, a young man like Lawrence in his early years of marriage, trying to balance an ongoing heterosexual relationship with his homoerotic attraction for Gerald Crich, the manliest of our shepherds from Chapter 5. The narration here begins as from a neutral third party, similar to the initiation scene from *The Plumed Serpent*, but with an added erotic edge from the start, evident in the simple observation that the two men were "very dissimilar"—with Birkin, like Lawrence, "tall and narrow, his bones [...] very thin and fine," and Gerald, "much heavier and more plastic" (262).

Nor is it possible to miss Lawrence's attachment to Birkin and his admiration for his more powerful adversary: "[Gerald's] bones were strong and round, his limbs were rounded, all his contours were beautifully and fully moulded. He seemed to stand with a proper, rich weight on the face of the earth" The two men, according to Lawrence, form a perfect pair: Gerald, the erotic ideal, with his "rich, frictional kind of strength, rather mechanical, but sudden and invincible," and Birkin, the fervent observer, "abstract as to be almost intangible": "He impinged invisibly upon the other man, scarcely seeming to touch him, like a garment."

As the wrestling begins, Birkin is quickly on the attack, the weaker man here egging on the stronger—"piercing in a tense fine grip that seemed to penetrate into the very quick of Gerald's being." Eventually, Gerald responds, and "a real struggle" ensues, with both men "seem[ing] to drive their white flesh deeper and deeper against each other, as if they would break into a oneness." Birkin shows "an uncanny force, weigh[ing Gerald] like a spell put upon him," only to have Gerald "heave free, with white, heaving, dazzling movements."

Initially, it may seem odd that Birkin, the weaker man, is the aggressor until we remember how the weaker Paul Morel was also the attacker against the stronger Baxter Dawes in *Sons and Lovers* and how, regularly in Lawrence, the more muscular male figure remains distant and aloof. Soon enough, however, Birkin and Gerald find themselves "entwined," with Birkin able "to penetrate into Gerald's more solid, more diffuse bulk, to interfuse his body through the body of the other, as if to bring it subtly into subjection."

Birkin's interest here seems to go beyond a mere physical confrontation to seeking a kind of Neoplatonic unity with Gerald. "It was as if Birkin's whole physical intelligence," Lawrence continues, "interpenetrated into Gerald's body, as if his fine, sublimated energy entered into the flesh of the fuller man, like some potency, casting a fine net, a prison, through the muscles into the very depths of Gerald's physical being" (262).

The result is Lawrence's portrayal of two men—"rapturously, intent and mindless at last"—taking on the appearance of lovers:

> two essential white figures working into a tighter closer oneness of struggle, with a strange, octopus-like knotting and flashing of limbs in the subdued light of the room; a tense white knot of flesh gripped in silence between the walls of old brown books.
>
> (263)

What exactly, one wants to ask, was Lawrence imagining here—this picture of these two men, "now and again [giving off] a sharp gasp of breath, or a sound like a sigh, then the rapid thudding of movement on the thickly-carpeted floor, then the strange sound of flesh escaping under flesh"?

> Often, in the white interlaced knot of violent living being that swayed silently, there was no head to be seen, only the swift, tight limbs, the solid white backs, the physical junction of two bodies clinched into oneness. Then would appear the gleaming, ruffled head of Gerald, as

the struggle changed, then for a moment the dun-coloured, shadow-like head of the other man would lift up from the conflict, the eyes wide and dreadful and sightless.

The aftermath of such intense activity—wrestling or lovemaking—which Lawrence either knew from his married life or just imagined, has Lawrence's stand-in, Birkin, carried away, not unlike how we saw Connie Chatterley in her three grand love scenes. Lawrence tells us that Birkin was exhausted, scarcely able to breathe, while the "earth seemed to tilt and sway, [...] a complete darkness [...] coming over his mind." Unsure of what had just happened, Birkin

> slid forward quite unconscious, over Gerald, and Gerald did not notice. Then he was half-conscious again, aware only of the strange tilting and sliding of the world. The world was sliding, everything was sliding off into the darkness. And he was sliding, endlessly, endlessly away.
>
> (263)

When Birkin awakens, he is surprised to discover that "he had fallen prostrate upon Gerald's body." And here Lawrence gives us a paean to male intimacy almost indistinguishable from actual male-to-male sodomy, here with Birkin "leaning with all his weight on the soft body of the other man":

> It startled him, because he thought he had withdrawn. He recovered himself, and sat up. But he was still vague and unestablished. He put out his hand to steady himself. It touched the hand of Gerald, that was lying out on the floor. And Gerald's hand closed warm and sudden over Birkin's, they remained exhausted and breathless, the one hand clasped closely over the other. It was Birkin whose hand, in swift response, had closed in a strong, warm clasp over the hand of the other. Gerald's clasp had been sudden and momentaneous.
>
> (264)

At the heart of this powerful passage is the idealization of a kind of male bonding, a notion that seems to lie at the core of Lawrence's psychosexual nature, something at once deeply important to him, part of his self-identity, and yet it seems independent of any actual intimacies in his life. If he never touched another man sexually but instead married a woman and remained faithful to her ... well, what then?

Part of the answer to this question lies in the prologue that Lawrence wrote for *Women in Love*, a novel many have noted might have been more accurately titled *Men in Love* or even *One Man's Love*. The prologue, written in 1916 but suppressed when the novel was published four years later and not published until 1963, is a tract nominally celebrating a kind of platonic lovers' bond between Birkin and Gerald, but one in which Lawrence gave unusually free rein to "Birkin's" homoerotic desires, tracing his acquaintance with Gerald back to a week's holiday mountain-climbing in the Tyrol and a certain feeling for each other that both men immediately felt—"that sudden connection which sometimes springs up between men who are very different in temper," what Lawrence calls "a subterranean kindling in each man": "Each looked towards the other, and knew the trembling nearness." And when this holiday was over and it was time for leave-taking, there remained "the absolute recognition that had passed between them then, the knowledge that was in their eyes as they met at the moment of parting. They knew they loved each other, that each would die for the other" (489–90).

Like so much of Lawrence's writing, the prologue has a distinctly confessional quality, especially as a response to the implicit complaint of an "incapacity to love" according to expectations, that is, to love a woman passionately—the same difficulty we have seen addressed repeatedly with Lawrence, here worded as Birkin's "incapacity to desire any woman, positively, with body and soul, this was a real torture, a deep torture indeed." Lawrence's response to this complaint continues, almost as a gloss on the desperate state of mind we will see in "The Woman Who Rode Away" in Chapter 7:

> never to be moved by a power greater than oneself, but always to be within one's own control, deliberate, having the choice, this was horrifying, more deadly than death. Yet how was one to escape? How could a man escape from being deliberate and unloving, except a greater power, an impersonal, imperative love should take hold of him?
>
> (497)

And then, one of the most honest moments in Lawrence—the recognition, long in coming, that even as he "was always drawn to women," even from childhood, "feeling more at home with a woman than with a man, yet," he continues, "it was for men that he felt the hot, flushing, roused attraction which a man is supposed to feel for the other sex." While his actual sexual life was "normal"—he was "always terribly intimate with at least one woman, and practically never intimate with a man"—it was "the male physique [that] had a fascination for him, and for the female physique he felt only a fondness, a sort of sacred love, as for a sister" (501–02).

How can anyone read such a confession and not recognize the central proposition of this study, put forth initially in Chapter 2 in analyzing the odd shape of *Lady Chatterley's Lover*, that in writing about men as erotic ideals, even from a woman's perspective, Lawrence is almost always expressing his desire?

Lawrence is hardly finished, however, continuing in an even more direct manner. "In the street," he adds, "it was the men who roused him by their flesh and their manly, vigorous movement, quite apart from all the individual character"—"individual character" here perhaps referring to their moral worth. What turned on Birkin was purely their sensual qualities, essentially their manliness; at the same time, women interested him as companions: "whilst he studied the women as sisters, knowing their meaning and their intents"—basically as beings with whom he shared a common emotional life. As summed up by Birkin,

> It was the men's physique which held the passion and the mystery to him. The women he seemed to be kin to, he looked for the soul in them. The soul of a woman and the physique of a man, these were the two things he watched for, in the street.

Yet such a situation, alas, Lawrence claims, was "a new torture to him"—that a woman's face did not move him "in the same manner, with the same sense of handsome desirability, as the face of a man" (502)?

One wants to ask how this literary genius, capable of seeing so deeply into the darkest corners of the human soul, could also appear so blind when looking into his own heart.

"Why was a man's beauty, the beauté male, so vivid and intoxicating a thing to him," Lawrence's proclamation continues, admittedly in Birkin's voice, "whilst female beauty was something quite unsubstantial, consisting all of look and gesture and revelation of intuitive intelligence?" Lawrence found women beautiful "purely because of their expression"; then the crucial point, that "it was plastic form that fascinated him in men"—that which can be touched—"the contour and movement of the flesh itself."

Later in the prologue comes this fascinating moment when Lawrence describes Birkin's having to give up on long-standing male acquaintances, "even those to whom he had been attached passionately, like David to Jonathan" (503). These were men "whose presence he had waited for cravingly, the touch of whose shoulder suffused him with a vibration of physical love." So be it, he says, but "every now and again, would come over him the same passionate desire to have near him some man he saw, to exchange intimacy, to unburden himself of love to this new beloved"— that is, a sort of intimacy with a man off the street, possibly leading to what Lawrence seems to have desired going back to Jessie Chambers—sex without the burden of any emotional attachment.

This confession continues by noting how any man might trigger his response: "a policeman who suddenly looked up at him, as he inquired the way, or a soldier who sat next to him in a railway carriage." Here we see Lawrence echoing sentiments and language straight out of gay hookup culture:

> How vividly, months afterwards, he would recall the soldier who had sat pressed up close to him on a journey from Charing Cross to Westerham; the shapely, motionless body, the large, dumb, coarsely-beautiful hands that rested helpless upon the strong knees, the dark brown eyes, vulnerable in the erect body.
>
> (503)

Then, an exquisitely rendered sentiment close in spirit to Thomas Mann's Gustav von Aschenbach—*Death in Venice*, a work Lawrence reviewed in 1913:

> Or a young man in flannels on the sands at Margate, flaxen and ruddy, like a Viking of twenty-three, with clean, rounded contours, pure as the contours of snow, playing with some young children, building a castle in sand, intent and abstract, like a seagull or a keen white bear.
>
> (503)

Understanding how Lawrence could here write so openly, even beautifully, about gay desire as "Birkin" while, under his own name, comfortably labeling Mann's masterpiece "absolutely, almost intentionally, unwholesome"—and Mann himself "sick, body and soul" (33)—takes us to the very heart of this study: what it is like to unmask the *hidden* Lawrence, to see him using an array of characters, often female, to give full voice to his most expressive erotic desires.

Nor is it just Birkin and *Women in Love* that Lawrence seems to have in mind when discussing his connection with gay hookup culture. There is also this easy-to-miss incident in the predecessor to that novel, *The Rainbow*, involving Will Brangwen, another of Lawrence's personas. Like Lawrence, Will was struggling to adapt to the ongoing strains of a recent marriage, feeling "shackled and in darkness of torment." One remedy involved his going out alone to Nottingham on Saturdays, to the football match, and then to a music hall—"all the time," as in Lawrence's confessional prologue, "watching, in readiness." Even at the music hall, we learn, "He never cared to drink. But with his hard, golden-brown eyes, so keen seeing with their tiny black pupils, he watched all the people, everything that happened, and he waited" (210).

Then, one Saturday night, he finds next to him not one of Greiffenhagen's manly shepherds but a beguiling youth, nominally a woman but described entirely in terms of her boyishness—that is, "rather small, common, with a fresh complexion," someone whose "lips pressed outwards in a kind of blind appeal." "A gleam lit up in [Will]" as he wondered how he might attract this person's attention and thus finally begin living that other life, what he calls "the unadmitted life of his desire." Why not now, he wonders? "His own life was barren, not enough." What he wanted was this "other," and not in the abstract but in the flesh, with this boyish creature next to him—so small, "almost like a child, and pretty," one whose "childishness whetted him keenly."

Outside the music hall, Will eventually reaches out and wraps his arm around this "sensual object of his attention," his hand sliding across one particular curve—a moment that for Will was like a revelation:

> like a new creation to him, a reality, an absolute, an existing tangible beauty of the absolute. It was like a star. Everything in him was absorbed in the sensual delight of this one small, firm curve [...] that his hand, and his whole being, had lighted upon.
>
> (213)

When this "absolute beauty he [had] touched" abruptly puts an end to his advances, Will heads home intent on his marital partner, only now on new terms—something his wife recognizes right away, noting how he has "come home very strange." This strangeness, of course, was his unusual arousal—"profoundly, violently, even before he touched her." Nor is Lawrence interested in hiding the cause: his aborted adventure with "the little creature in Nottingham had but been but leading up to this" (218).

The result was the sort of pure sexual gratification that Lawrence so craved—sexual interaction with none of the emotional sensitivities presumably built into traditional male and female roles. Instead, Will and his wife "abandoned in one motion the moral position, each was seeking gratification pure and simple": "Strange his wife was to him. It was as if he were a perfect stranger, as if she were infinitely and essentially strange to him, the other half of the world, the dark half of the moon." For Will, it was "a duel: no love, no words" and, as we have seen, always preferred by Lawrence, "no kisses even"; instead, only that which might be exchanged between any two adults, "the maddening perception of beauty consummate, absolute through touch."

"But still the thing terrified him," Lawrence continues—this experience of pure sexual gratification, presumably with an imaginary partner and playing a nontraditional, inverted role. Here was a different sort of sexual experience, one that was "[a]wful and threatening"—"dangerous to a degree, even whilst he gave himself to it." While there is no clear allusion to sodomy, this was a sexual encounter associated with "pure darkness": "All the shameful things of the body revealed themselves to him now with a sort of sinister, tropical beauty."

There is little reason to alter more than one gendered referent, with Will lost in erotic delight with a barely mentioned partner, one with no identifiable female qualities. However, the reference to "[a]ll the shameful, natural and unnatural acts of sensual voluptuousness" that he and his partner "partook of together" suggests male-to-female anal contact—acts that had "their heavy beauty and their delight": "Shame, what was it? It was part of extreme delight. It was that part of delight of which man is usually afraid. Why afraid? The secret, shameful things are most terribly beautiful" (220).

Nor is any change in gender necessary for the coda to this scene: "They accepted shame, and were one with it in their most unlicensed pleasures. It was incorporated. It was a bud that blossomed into beauty and heavy, fundamental gratification"—a type of gratification, one suspects, that Lawrence saw intimately connected to the Latin root for *bottom*.

"*Noli Me Tangere*"—Curtailed Desire in Three Stories

Given the confessional nature of Lawrence's unpublished prologue to *Women in Love*, it is easy to see how he might have been more comfortable describing the pyrotechnics of male-to-male touching than their softer intimacies—a situation reflected in the novel's wrestling scene, which so appealed to the British director Ken Russell in his 1970 film version of Lawrence's novel. This same tension between these two sorts of male touching—one based on physical competition between men or traditional bonhomie, and the other on male tenderness—lies at the heart of three of Lawrence's most memorable short stories considered next: "The Old Adam" (1911), "The Blind Man" (1920), and "The Prussian Officer" (1914).

In "The Old Adam," which predates *Sons and Lovers*, Lawrence uses a stand-in, Edward Severn, based upon his "quite chaste" (78) life as a teacher in London. As the story opens, the 27-year-old Severn, tall and thin like Lawrence, is living as a lodger in the Thomas house and, like so many of Lawrence's young men, is unsure how to make sense of his erotic desires. On the one hand, he was eager for sex, with "a pain in his chest that made him pant, and an involuntary tension in his arms, as if he must press someone to his breast"; on the other, he did not seem especially interested in women, including Mrs. Thomas, his landlord's wife, with whom he has a suggestive tête-à-tête early in the story. Indeed, the notion that Mrs. Thomas was this "someone" he might want to caress was an "idea that would have shocked him too much had he formed it."

Lawrence's muddled explanation here is that his "passion had run on sub-consciously, till now it had come to such a pitch it must drag his conscious soul into allegiance."

Nor was it just Severn who had no interest. About this seductress, Lawrence could only manage a five-word description—that she was "a good-looking woman, well made"—fewer words than he devotes to describing the lamp she is sitting next to, the one with a shade "of red silk lined with yellow" (77).

What interests Severn far more than his landlady—and likely what also interested the young Lawrence—is apparent in the magnificent vignette with which the story opens, featuring Severn in the family garden with the Thomas daughter: "a little girl of three, dressed in white. [...] very bonny, very quick and intent in her movements; she reminded him of a fieldmouse which plays alone in the corn, for sheer joy" (72). She beckons him to join her, "flinging herself at his legs, grasping the flannel of his trousers, and tugging at him wildly." In Lawrence's playful response, we can see the lighthearted figure who so attracted Frieda when he first played with her two small girls along that brook.

The daughter he describes as "a wild little Mænad," who "flew shrieking like a revelling bird down the garden, glancing back to see if he were coming." The good-hearted Severn "went swiftly after her," and "in the obscure garden," we see Lawrence at his most lyrical in describing their fun:

> the two white figures dart[ing] through the flowering plants, the baby, with her full silk skirts, scudding like a ruffled bird, the man, lithe and fleet, snatching her up and smothering his face in hers. And all the time her piercing voice reechoed from his low calls of warning and of triumph as he hunted her. Often she was really frightened of him; then she clung fast round his neck, and he laughed and mocked her in a low, stirring voice, whilst she protested.
>
> (72)

Here again is Lawrence, the exuberant adolescent from Chapter 3—although possibly 25 when he began this story—barely able to contain his enthusiasm for this "beautiful girl," this

> bacchanal with her wild, dull-gold hair tossing about like a loose chaplet, her hazel eyes shining daringly, her small, spaced teeth glistening in little passions of laughter within her red, small mouth. [...] such a little bright wave of wilfulness, so abandoned to her impulses, so white and smooth as she lay at rest, so startling as she flashed her naked limbs about.
>
> (74)

It is unclear if, as Lawrence insists, she was "growing too old for a young man to undress"; what is not in doubt is that the story is principally about Severn's recognition that he is the one growing too old to be satisfied with such child's play—something that becomes apparent when Thomas, his landlord, returns late from the office. Here is a potential rival, like Baxter Dawes in *Sons and Lovers*, if only Severn were as interested in Mrs. Thomas as he was in her husband—"a thickly-built man of forty, good-looking," someone who had "grown round-shouldered with thrusting forward his chin in order to look the aggressive, strong-jawed man" (79).

An argument soon ensues between the two men—Severn, the urbane supporter of women's suffrage, and the rugged Thomas, an opponent. Still, before Severn can turn in for the evening, the servant Kate asks him if he would mind assisting Thomas in bringing her heavy trunk down a narrow set of stairs. "It was surprising," Lawrence notes, "how friendly the two men were, as soon as they had something to do together, or when Mrs. Thomas was absent," their common task transforming them into comrades: "Thomas, the elder, the thick-set, playing the protector's part, though always deferential to the younger, whimsical man" (81–82).

Nor is it a surprise that a physical confrontation between these two would-be friends was in the offing. Coming down the stairs, Severn, "feeling particularly reckless," has a "subconscious instinct" to take a risk with his rival beneath him, even though Lawrence assures us he would not "knowingly have hurt a hair of his landlord's head." Just then, Severn slips, "quite accidentally," we are told, with Severn "glissad[ing] down the stairs" and Thomas being "flung backwards across the landing, and his head went thud against the banister post" (83).

When Severn attempts to laugh off the incident, Thomas is incensed, "straightway [...] fetch[ing] the young man two heavy blows, upon the jaw and ear." Nor was the match even, with Thomas, a man's man, "a footballer and a boxer in his youth, [who] had been brought up among the roughs of Swansea." In contrast, Severn, a man with Lawrence's build and temperament, had studied "in a religious college in France" and had never having been "struck in the face before."

Thomas was ready to continue throwing punches, but Severn, with "no instinct of fisticuffs," flung himself at his adversary—the result, a fight not unlike the one between Paul Morel and Baxter Dawes in *Sons and Lovers* or Birkin and Gerald in *Women in Love*. As in those instances, it is Lawrence's stand-in who is immediately on the attack, "[flinging] himself again forward, and then, catching Thomas's collar, brought him down with a crash," his "exquisite hands [...] [digging] in the other's thick throat, the linen collar having been torn open."

Lawrence shows us Thomas rising to the challenge, fighting "madly, with blind, brute strength," while Severn "lay wrapped on him like a white steel, his rare intelligence concentrated, not scattered; concentrated on strangling Thomas swiftly." Severn continues to move forward, "forcing his landlord's head over the edge of the next flight of stairs," while his "stout and full-blooded" landlord "lost every trace of self-possession": "[Thomas] struggled like an animal at slaughter. The blood came out of his nose over his face; he made horrid choking sounds as he struggled."

The melee only stops when the maid intervenes. "Severn turned away his face, and was wild with shame. He saw his landlord kneeling, his hands at his throat, choking, rattling, and gasping." Then, what was for Lawrence the story's payoff—that moment of intimacy the weaker, younger man wanted to establish with the stronger, older one. "The young man's heart filled with remorse and grief. He put his arms round the heavy man, and raised him, saying tenderly: 'Let me help you up.'" Severn struggles to hold Thomas, barely able to stand, against the wall.

The maid then brings supplies, with which the "young man bathed his landlord's face and temples and throat." The bleeding quickly stopped, but Severn remained "grief-stricken": "He would willingly, at that moment, have given his right hand for the man he had hurt." Thomas is still shaken, looking "like a wounded animal, very pitiable" (84).

Here, Severn quietly moves into the role of caretaker that we have just seen in Aaron Sisson:

> "Come," said Severn, full of pity, and gentle as a woman. "Let me help you to bed." Thomas, leaning heavily on the young man, whose white garments were dabbed with blood and water, stumbled forlornly into his room. There Severn unlaced his boots and got off the remnant of his collar.
>
> (85)

The next morning, there is one final exchange between the combatants, with Thomas apologizing after looking "affectionately, into Severn's eyes." Severn notes his surprise in learning they had been "such essential brutes," men capable of relating to each other with something other than civility, capable of feeling and even expressing a real passion for one another, even if Lawrence's Victorian code of conduct would only allow such feeling to be expressed through a kind of staged violence—or, as Thomas rightly replied, "Oh, I don't know [...] It shows a man's got some fight in him" (86).

Thomas then "looked up in the other's face appealingly. Severn smiled, with a touch of bitterness. The two men grasped hands." "To the end of their acquaintance," Lawrence aptly adds, "Severn and Thomas were close friends, with a gentleness in their bearing, one towards the other."

"The Blind Man" would seem to have the structure of the stories highlighted in the next chapter, featuring a woman protagonist, Isabel Previn, caught between two men—her husband, Maurice, the blind man of the title, his injury the result of a recent wartime injury, and her oldest friend, the barrister Bertie Reid. However, unlike the "other" men we will see in the next chapter, Bertie—here described as "a Scotchman of the intellectual type, quick, ironical, sentimental" (303)— is hardly an erotic ideal for Isabel, being instead more like the young Birkin described by Lawrence in the prologue to *Women in Love*. This Bertie was more comfortable with women than men, someone quick to fall "on his knees before the woman he adored but did not want to marry." Like Birkin and also Edward Severn of "The Old Adam," this new Lawrence stand-in "was ashamed of himself, because he could not marry, could not approach women physically. He wanted to do so. But he could not. At the centre of him he was afraid, helplessly and even brutally afraid" (312).

Bertie's relationship with Isabel was thus much like the one that Lawrence at one time imagined he had had with Jessie Chambers—as a lifelong friend, "like a brother, but better than her own brothers": "She loved him—though not in the marrying sense. There was a sort of kinship between them, an affinity" (302). Bertie seems brought into the story, in other words, to share or somehow test Isabel's love for her husband, Maurice, the story's title character. He was a man Lawrence describes as "passionate, sensitive, perhaps over-sensitive, wincing— a big fellow with heavy limbs and a forehead that flushed painfully" (303). That is, for both Isabel and Bertie, Maurice is something of a cipher: while no simple erotic ideal, a status confirmed by his deep scar— the result of the blast that led to his blindness—he remains a haunting, ultra-male presence throughout the story, what Isabel calls "something strange [...] indefinable." Indeed, Bertie and Isabel are both unnerved by Maurice's physical size, his aloofness, and his uncanny ability to move about "almost unconsciously in his familiar surroundings, dark though everything was"; "seem[ing] to know the presence of objects before he touched them" (308).

Here was a man, "dark and powerful," placed in the story less to attract Bertie by his beauty than to haunt his dreams—a masculine force pleased "to rock thus through a world of things, carried on the flood in a sort of blood-prescience"; a man content as long as "he kept this sheer immediacy of blood-contact with the substantial world"; a man who wanted "no intervention of visual consciousness" (309). Instead, in his blindness, he possessed what Lawrence surely must have wanted for himself—"a certain rich positivity, bordering sometimes on rapture":

> Life seemed to move in him like a tide lapping, and advancing, enveloping all things darkly. It was a pleasure to stretch forth the hand and meet the unseen object, clasp it, and possess it in pure contact. He did not try to remember, to visualize. He did not want to. The new way of consciousness substituted itself in him.

Yet Maurice, it seems, is also insecure, fearful of his rightful place in his marriage, afraid that his disfigurement is too off-putting for his wife. Such concerns in Maurice lead to his making two requests to Bertie that form the story's climax. First, that he be allowed to touch Bertie, a request from which Bertie "shrank away instinctively," only agreeing out of politeness, "suffer[ing] as the blind man stretched out a strong, naked hand to him" (316), in the process knocking off his hat. Maurice then lays his hand on Bertie's head,

> closing the dome of the skull in a soft, firm grasp, gathering it, as it were; then, shifting his grasp and softly closing again, with a fine, close pressure, till he had covered the skull and the face of the smaller man, tracing the brows, and touching the full, closed eyes, touching the small nose and the nostrils, the rough, short moustache, the mouth, the rather strong chin.

Maurice's touches seem free of any erotic intent; how different matters seem with Bertie, the self-composed bachelor who "lived in beautiful rooms overlooking the river, guarded by a faithful Scottish man-servant," the neat, little man, so much like Lawrence himself, who may well have dreamed of such a moment of intimacy but who now finds himself frozen in fear, as the "hand of the blind man" continued his survey, "grasp[ing] the shoulder, the arm, the hand," as if taking Bertie in a "soft, travelling grasp." When Maurice comments on his apparent youth, we are told that Bertie "stood almost annihilated, unable to answer."

Then, that rare, fully realized description of male-to-male touching in Lawrence, the result of Maurice's second request that Bertie touch him—his eyes and especially his scar. Bertie's first response was to "[quiver] with revulsion," at the same time feeling himself succumbing, being unexpectedly drawn "under the power of the blind man, as if hypnotized."

Bertie continues as instructed, "lift[ing] his hand, and la[ying] the fingers on the scar, on the scarred eyes," when

> Maurice suddenly covered them with his own hand, pressed the fingers of the other man upon his disfigured eye-sockets, trembling in every

fibre, and rocking slightly, slowly, from side to side. He remained thus for a minute or more, whilst Bertie stood as if in a swoon, unconscious, imprisoned.

How wonderful it must have seemed to Lawrence to imagine touching such a strong man, and yet how utterly frightful as well—at least as acted out here in the flesh—to be so fearful of the very thing one might most desire! Here is Lawrence at his most gripping, recognizing the complexity of his desires as reflected in Bertie, realizing that when confronted with such a powerful male presence—albeit in a disfigured form and not the beautiful male presence of his erotic dreams—his only response might be panic. We see his stand-in Bertie unable to respond, much less to reciprocate—as he "gazed mute and terror-struck, overcome by his own weakness": "He knew he could not answer. He had an unreasonable fear, lest the other man should suddenly destroy him."

Meanwhile, for Maurice, it was a moment of male bonding, a sign of long-lasting friendship that Lawrence so often proclaimed as an ideal, or, as Lawrence writes, "Maurice was actually filled with hot, poignant love, the passion of friendship. Perhaps it was this very passion of friendship which Bertie shrank from most" (317).

Isabel, who knew Bertie like a brother, recognizes what has happened—that a man, like Lawrence himself, so fearful of intimacy with women, has proven himself just as afraid of intimacy with a man. Fittingly, it is Isabel, in the story's last paragraph, who recognizes Bertie's "desire—to escape from this intimacy, this friendship, which had been thrust upon him." Perhaps this is Lawrence in the role of Aesop's fox, forswearing the sweetness of the grapes he could not reach: "He could not bear it that he had been touched by the blind man, his insane reserve broken in."

"The Prussian Officer" (Lawrence's preferred title was the more playful "Honour and Arms") is the last of our three stories featuring anxiety over man-to-man touching. With only two male characters in this taut tale of illicit desire, Lawrence confronted the structural dilemma of where to locate the repressed homoerotic desire that powers the narrative. At first, Lawrence's answer seems obvious, since his Captain's illicit desire for his orderly is the motive for everything that follows. Nor does this desire seem mutual, with Lawrence so clearly underscoring the orderly's heterosexual nature. We learn, for instance, about his "sweetheart, a girl from the mountains, independent and primitive," about how he went with her "not to talk, but to have his arm round her, and for the physical contact," and about how having to serve under the sexually leering Captain was easier for his being able to "rest with her held fast against his chest" (178). This orderly and his sweetheart—we are told with none of Lawrence's usual equivocations for the young men of his stories—"loved each other."

Nor is it surprising that the Captain's knowledge of his orderly's het- erosexuality made him "mad with irritation," leading him to keep "the young man engaged all the evenings long, and [taking] pleasure in the dark look that came on his face." Thus, on a most basic level, "The Prussian Officer" is a story about the repressed homoerotic desire of an officer (Herr Hauptmann) for his orderly—specifically, how he "tried hard not to admit the passion that had got hold of him," how he refused to admit "that his feeling for his orderly was anything but that of a man incensed by his stupid, perverse servant" (179).

This interpretation leaves one major issue unresolved: what are we to make of the extended passages, containing some of Lawrence's most lyr- ical writing in the story, in which Lawrence displays not the Captain's repressed desire for his orderly but the Captain himself as an erotic ideal for the story's narrator? Such is the situation we have with the story's marvelous opening, with the Captain and his orderly on maneuvers, the orderly having been severely beaten by the Captain the night before. Then, without a hint of irony, we are presented with the narrator's admiration for

the fine figure of the Captain wheeling on horseback at the farm-house ahead, a handsome figure in pale blue uniform with facings of scarlet, and the metal gleaming on the black helmet and the sword-scabbard, and dark streaks of sweat coming on the silky bay horse.

(174–75)

Suppose the story, as just noted, is about the Captain's desire for his orderly. What is the point, then, of Lawrence's playing up the Captain's striking appearance—our being told that this "tall man of about forty, grey at the temples" had "a handsome, finely knit figure," or that his decidedly heterosexual orderly, "having to rub him down, admired the amazing riding-muscles of his loins"?

One possibility is that, despite all the talk of the orderly's sweetheart, Lawrence wanted to explore the orderly's repressed desire for the Captain. Yet Lawrence seems intent on ruling out such a reading, noting, for instance, how the orderly "scarcely noticed the officer any more than he noticed himself." Nonetheless, this lyrical account of the Captain con- tinues, with our learning that he had "reddish-brown, stiff hair, that he wore short upon his skull," that "his moustache was also cut short and bristly over a full, brutal mouth," that "his face was rather rugged, the cheeks thin," that "perhaps the man was the more handsome for the deep lines in his face, the irritable tension of his brow, which gave him the look of a man who fights with life," that "his fair eyebrows stood bushy over light blue eyes that were always flashing with cold fire"?

Lawrence has given us such exquisite, erotically charged writing, but for what purpose, we ask, especially as we are told that the orderly "rarely [...] saw his master's face"? Why these lush, extended descriptions of the Captain when the focus presumably should be on the Captain's psychological state, his repressed desire for his beautiful, young orderly?

But then, what to make of this other puzzler—that Lawrence has little to tell us about the orderly's appearance other than that he was "a youth of about twenty-two, of medium height, and well built"? Alas, Lawrence has about as much interest in the orderly's appearance as he had in his landlord's wife, Mrs. Thomas, in "The Old Adam." Nor is everything about his appearance uniformly positive: tell us that he had "heavy limbs" and a "swarthy" complexion, and "dark, expressionless eyes"?

Perhaps none of this would be surprising if we see "The Prussian Officer" as a story about the repressed homoerotic desire not of one man but of two: the Captain's desire for his orderly and, just barely hidden, the narrator's (or possibly the author's) desire for the Captain. While inventive critics might find a purely aesthetic reason for Lawrence's making his Captain both lover and beloved—the orderly's lover and the narrator's beloved—a more straightforward explanation might lie with the demands of Lawrence's psyche: that, here too, as in "The Blind Man," Lawrence may have been using his story as a warning to himself about the dangers of being aroused, in his case, by an attractive figure like his Captain.

And is this not the point of the story—that any such touching is likely to lead to utter chaos—not to the playful wrestling we just saw between Birkin and Gerald or the character-building exchange between Bertie and his landlord, or even the beating Paul Morel receives from Baxter Dawes, but to the savage kicking that the Captain administers to his orderly and, even worse, the orderly's fatal retaliation against the Captain? Is this not the point of Lawrence's masterful description—how this orderly "did not relax one hair's breadth, but, all the force of all his blood exulting in his thrust, he shoved back the head of the other man, till there was a little cluck and a crunching sensation" (188)? Was this not a lesson for a lifetime about the personal destruction that will surely come for any man who harbors such an illicit desire as this Captain had for his orderly?

And so Lawrence's story ends, a fable with a moral:

> The bodies of the two men lay together, side by side, in the mortuary, the one white and slender, but laid rigidly at rest, the other looking as if every moment it must rouse into life again, so young and unused, from a slumber.
>
> (193)

This lesson at the heart of "The Prussian Officer" about the fearful connection between desire and punishment hovers over Lawrence's essay on Richard Dana's sailing memoir, *Two Years Before the Mast*. Gone is any lingering fascination with physical intimacy between men we see in "The Old Adam" or "The Blind Man," replaced in the Dana essay by a Calvinist-like obsession with the repression of desire as essential to maintaining order on a grand sea voyage, especially one around the treacherous waters of Cape Horn.

The central moment of this crisis involves a flogging administered by the ship's captain. What interests Lawrence in this scene is neither the captain with his whip nor the seaman being flogged, but Dana, the observer who was so shaken by witnessing this flogging. What he experienced was a kind of aberration of his liberal sentiments, what Lawrence calls a "dissolution of his own being," or, in Dana's own words, as quoted by Lawrence, "A man—a human being made in God's likeness—fastened up and flogged like a beast! The first and almost uncontrollable impulse was resistance. But what could be done?—The time for it had gone by—" (109).

Dana's response was to vomit over the side, an action that aroused only contempt from Lawrence, especially given Lawrence's contempt for Dana's idealized notion of the noble individual created in God's image. For Lawrence, we are the children of a different sort of God or, more to the point, a different sort of father—not some aloof, kindly figure interested in our well-being, but a real-life father we respect, even fear, a father who sits on that "other sort of throne" ("a W.C.") and "wipe[s] his own behind"— that is, a real man capable of issuing real penalties. Lawrence's takeaway is clear: "And as long as man has a bottom, he must surely be whipped. It is as if the Lord intended it so."

For Lawrence, there is no escaping the fear that comes with living under such a powerful father, the same image that somehow came to play a key part in Lawrence's emotional life and which, in this essay, he links to the "master and servant" or "master and man relationship" and characterizes as "essentially, a polarised flow, like love": "It is a circuit of vitalism which flows between master and man and forms a very precious nourishment to each, and keeps both in a state of subtle, quivering, vital equilibrium. Deny it as you like, it is so" (109–10).

None of that liberal claptrap about the rights of man and human equality, Lawrence argues, could survive on board a sailing ship. "A master had to be master, or it was hell"; the exact belief in the strong leader that fulfilled what Lawrence wanted as the ever-needy son—"this strange interflow of master-and-man, the strange reciprocity of command and obedience."

What is lacking here is any attempt to envision the Captain as an erotic ideal and, hence, any lyrical prose about the wonders of submission.

Instead, we get more of the prophetic Lawrence, and here with a markedly sadistic edge: "From the poles of will in the backbone of the Captain, to the ganglia of will in the back of the sloucher Sam, runs a frazzled, jagged current, a staggering circuit of vital electricity." Eventually, things snap, with the Captain shouting, "Tie up that lousy swine!" followed by, "[W]hack! whack! down on the bare back of that sloucher Sam comes the cat" (111).

Then, this account of men touching, only now with an unpleasant erotic undercurrent, as Lawrence considers the benefits of such a beating:

By Jove, it goes like ice-cold water into his spine. Down those lashes runs the current of the captain's rage, right into the blood and into the toneless ganglia of Sam's voluntary system. Crash! Crash! runs the lightning flame, right into the cores of the living nerves.

The shipboard beating that Dana observed here is rendered by Lawrence as a simulacrum of human intercourse, albeit here between men—"a natural form of human coition, interchange"—although without a whiff of the wondrous tenderness we have so often seen elsewhere. Instead, he gives us this picture of "the living nerves respond[ing]: "They start to vibrate. They brace up. The blood begins to go quicker. The nerves begin to recover their vividness. It is their tonic." And the result is beneficial for all parties: "The man Sam has a new clear day of intelligence, and a smarting back. The captain has a new relief, a new ease in his authority, and a sore heart." All has been made right in the world: "There is a new equilibrium, and a fresh start. The physical intelligence of a Sam is restored, the turgidity is relieved from the veins of the Captain."

Meanwhile, Lawrence sees the hatred Dana feels for his captain balanced by the charity he feels for the Kanaka boy, called Hope—"a beautiful South Sea Islander" now horribly disfigured and weakened by syphilis. Dana shows great sympathy for this youth, even a kind of love, although not, as is often the case in Lawrence, a love based on a desire for a beautiful male, but one that "was largely pity, tinged with philanthropy"; that is, what Lawrence so thoroughly disliked from his earliest intimacies with Jessie Chambers, a love "elevated" or grossly distorted by ethical considerations, what here he disdainfully labels an "inevitable saviourism" (115).

Two Gay Men in Lawrence's Life—Maurice Magnus and Walt Whitman

In Chapter 2, we looked at Lawrence's most infamous interaction with a gay man—his 1915 visit to Cambridge, when he was shocked to see John Maynard Keynes still in his pajamas at midday. Lawrence's most protracted contact with an openly gay man was likely with the American theatrical manager and bon vivant Maurice Magnus, whom he met on his first night in Florence in November 1919, shortly after arriving from England. Lawrence was immediately attracted to Magnus's energy and high spirits while repelled by his lack of self-discipline, describing him that first night as "about forty, spruce and youngish in his deportment, very pink-faced, and very clean, very natty, very alert, like a sparrow painted to resemble a tom-tit" (30). Very much a character he had never met before—a "little smart man of the shabby world, very much on the spot"—but also one who, in his diminutive size and effeminate manner, was close to the antithesis of the many Greiffenhagen shepherds we have repeatedly encountered.

Their most intimate time together occurred three months later, when Lawrence visited Magnus at the famed Abbey of Montecassino. It is easy to say that Lawrence saw something of his own effeminate nature in Magnus and thus saw time spent with him as a possible means to greater self-understanding, with his visit to Montecassino as a kind of test. If this were the case, it was a test for which Lawrence was ill-prepared, starting with the vague, unwelcome sense of envelopment he experienced almost from the start of his visit. First, there was Magnus's soft-hearted welcome: "So *very* glad to see you"; "I'm so *pleased* you've come," with Magnus "look[ing] into my eyes with that wistful, watchful tenderness rather like a woman who isn't quite sure of her lover" (42, emphasis in original).

Then there was the matter of Lawrence's wardrobe, as it just happened that he had arrived at that mountaintop sanctuary in the middle of February without a proper winter coat. Magnus quickly had a solution, helping Lawrence into one of his magnificent coats—a garment made of "thick, smooth black cloth, and lined with black sealskin, and having a collar of silky black sealskin." Lawrence notes the odd feeling of its "silky fur" and the strange feeling of his solicitous friend "helping me solicitously into this coat, and buttoning it at the throat for me" (45).

"Isn't it wonderful! Ah, the most wonderful place on earth!" Magnus exclaimed, referring to the monastery, seemingly intent on a type of seduction: "'What now could you wish better than to end your days here? The peace, the beauty, the eternity of it.' He paused and sighed."

Lawrence disagreed, finding the monastery "cold as the tomb," sitting as it did on top of a hill just below the snowline. "Now, by the end of January," he continues,

> all the summer heat is soaked out of the vast, ponderous stone walls, and they become masses of coldness cloaking around. There is no heating apparatus whatsoever—none. Save the fire in the kitchen, for cooking, nothing. Dead, silent, stone cold everywhere.
>
> (44)

The following day, Lawrence's magnificent, sun-filled view—"look[ing] down on the farm cluster and the brown fields and the sere oak-woods of the hill-crown, and the rocks and bushes savagely bordering it round"—led him to a reverie on a different sort of life, one lived in "the poignant grip of the past." Lawrence seemed surprised at how this all-encompassing spectacle of a different world spread out below should be such an "agony" to him. One explanation entails his Protestant revulsion at the overwhelming Catholicism of Montecassino and Magnus himself as a devout Catholic. Another entails his aversion to the deeply feminine, womb-like nature of the monastery and its surroundings, landscapes that Lawrence meticulously rendered:

the old farm and the bullocks slowly working in the fields below, and the black pigs rooting among weeds, and [...] a monk sitting on a parapet in the sun, and an old, old man in skin sandals and white-bunched, swathed legs come driving an ass slowly to the monastery gate, slowly, with all that lingering nonchalance and wildness of the Middle Ages.

Such an inviting picture of the past Lawrence produced, even while knowing its anachronistic nature, his being so clearly a "child of the present." "To see all this from the monastery," he continues, summing up his angst, "where the Middle Ages live on in a sort of agony, like Tithonus, and cannot die, this was almost a violation to my soul, made almost a wound" (48).

This same concern dominated their discussion of Italian peasants, with Magnus seeing them as little more than ornamental figures in his all-absorbing Catholic worldview. Lawrence vigorously objected, preferring any of the peasants to Magnus, not because of what the peasants possessed—although he does note their "strong blood-presence"—but because he saw the peasant living free of the conceits of modern life, free of "that complacent mentality that Magnus was so proud of, [...] all the trivial trash of glib talk, [...] all the conceit of our shallow consciousness" (53).

Lawrence also strongly disagreed with Magnus's elevation of friendship over "physical relations," with Lawrence again seeking that central element of attraction to a powerful male that he was often only able to enunciate through euphemisms, as he does here, by referring to *blood*: "If there is no profound blood-sympathy," he responds to Magnus, "I know the mental friendship is trash. If there is real, deep blood response, I will stick to that if I have to betray all the mental sympathies I ever made, or all the lasting spiritual loves I ever felt" (55).

Lawrence expanded upon this point about good and bad male friendships—those with and without "profound blood-sympathy"—in a section dealing with homosexuality in the French Foreign Legion, which was cut from the lengthy biographical introduction that Lawrence wrote for Magnus's *Memoirs of the Foreign Legion*, published in 1924. Lawrence begins by noting how Magnus dismissed out of hand the accepted practice of the Legionnaires, who, in the spirit of pederasty in Ancient Greece, often took on young men as lovers, or, as Magnus called them, *girants*. While Magnus recognizes some level of fellowship, even intimacy, in this practice—for instance, how the Legionnaires would often carry their lovers' packs—he nonetheless dismisses such old-fashioned intimacies as the "withered fig-leaf" of charity, preferring instead the modern simplicity of cash payments. "Just look at the degraded Legionary," he sums up his position, "carrying the pack of his *girant* and doing his chores for him! Wouldn't twenty francs have been *so* much more decent in every way" (94)!

"You spy out a comely looking individual, of the 'lower Classes'"— Lawrence replies with outright ridicule. "[Y]ou invite him to smokes and drinks—and afterwards you pay Him—[...] all nice and in honor, don't you know!—The way you do it!—Oh yes, money will cover multitudes upon multitudes of sins." Lawrence's response is a more expansive critique of the vacuity and the pettiness of reducing human touch, especially between two men, to a mere cash transaction.

Magnus is now condemned as "the little Judas, [who] betrayed everybody with a kiss: coming up with a kiss of love, and then afterwards clearing out triumphant, having got all he wanted, thank you. Cold as a bit of white mud." In such matters, Lawrence finds Magnus far worse "than the poor devils of legionaries," who at least had "their blood-passions and carried them defiantly, flagrantly, to depravity": "To me," Lawrence continues, "the blood-passions are sacred, and sex is sacred: more sacred than mind or spirit or uplift. In the legionaries, even, the recklessness, the blood-recklessness, is sacred"—even if their sexual energies are ultimately self-destructive, "like a snake which should turn and start to gnash at itself and destroy itself, because it is imprisoned or tied up by a cord" (95).

Lawrence ends up praising the passion of the legionaries, only wishing that they could direct it to the proper channel instead of "turn[ing] themselves in defiance against themselves." But what is that "proper channel"? Alas, there is more obscurity in Lawrence as he opines how he wishes the legionaries "could have kept their souls, and honorably stood by the reality which they knew, but were not free to believe in—the reality of passionate blood in the deeps of a man—they would have been great" (95). That is, do as Lawrence did for his entire life, which was basically to abstain from lovemaking, substituting for it a sort of idealized passion between men that entails stopping short of actual touching, recreating in one's own life the platonic attachment of David and Jonathan—an essential reference in Lawrence's iconography, treated at the end of this chapter.

If Lawrence's most protracted physical contact with a gay man was with Magnus, his most protracted intellectual relationship may have been with the American poet Walt Whitman. While Whitman was important to Lawrence's poetry, our focus here is on Lawrence's struggles with Whitman the man, and especially the different ways Lawrence accounted for Whitman's homosexuality. It was never easy for Lawrence to reconcile his general dislike of homosexuality, as far back as his visit to Cambridge in his late twenties, with, at least for most of his life, his great admiration for Whitman. It was a difficult situation that he summed up in a 1919 essay: "In Whitman, at all times, the true and the false are so near, so interchangeable, that we are almost inevitably left with divided feelings" ("Democracy" 85).

We can see Lawrence's back-and-forth feelings in a letter from December 1913, in which he is highly critical of Whitman for insisting that "all men are my brothers, and straightway go[ing] into the wilderness to love them." This was a time, almost two years after his first meeting with Frieda Weekley, during which we often find Lawrence praising himself for having acted like an adult, primarily through, as we have seen in Chapter 3, his hard-won commitment to heterosexuality. Meanwhile, he is quick to criticize Whitman, as he would later criticize E. M. Forster, for continuing to act like a perennial, self-absorbed adolescent—"not at all pouring his seed into American brides to make Stalwart American sons, but pouring his seed into the space, into the idea of humanity" (Vol. 2, 129).

For the Lawrence of 1913, Whitman was "like a human document, or a wonderful treatise in human self revelation"—into "neither art nor religion nor truth," but only a kind of abstract substitute for life itself, a battle with life in which "he never gave his individual self unto the fight." Unlike Paul Morel and Baxter Dawes in *Sons and Lovers* or Birkin and Gerald in *Women in Love*, Whitman was always too self-aware to make such a commitment: "He never fought with another person—he was like a wrestler who only wrestles with his own shadow—he never came to grips. He chucked his body into the fight, and stood apart saying 'Look how I am living'" (130).

This is Lawrence, the Puritan iconoclast, whom we earlier saw condemning homosexuality during his 1915 visit to Cambridge and even in the Mellors of *Lady Chatterley's Lover*, attacking women as overly lustful sexual partners, only here condemning any sexual activity that entails a whiff of self-pleasure. Here is the same Lawrence who, in an essay attacking critics of *Lady Chatterley's Lover* (*Pornography and Obscenity*), opposed the normative, heterosexual lovemaking of Mellors and Connie to the degeneracy of masturbation, calling it "the most dangerous sexual vice that a society can be afflicted with, in the long run." Its "great danger," Lawrence continues, "lies in its merely exhaustive nature," lacking as it does the "give and take" of "all sexual intercourse" (245).

Of particular importance to our current task is Lawrence's 1923 essay on Whitman included in *Studies in Classic American Writers*, as well as three earlier versions of that essay—1921–22, 1922, and a significantly different one from 1919, which has only been available since 2003. In the 1921–22 version, Lawrence continues this attack on Whitman as an onanist who "gives himself to himself," someone committed to "the reaping of the lower body, by the upper." Lawrence does not deny the "mystery of touch"—how our "hands and fingers, those gateways, [...] travel upon the lower body and gather their knowledge of it," in the process "transfer[ring] the control of the lower spontaneous centres to the upper." He even sees an advantage in "an increase in a certain sort of mental consciousness." He also insists that we recognize that other, less fortunate results, including "the vice of masturbation, the vice of the mouth, all the strange vices the modern human being is capable of hav[ing] their explanation here" (408).

The nadir of Lawrence's attack on Whitman comes in the third (1922) and most vitriolic of these four versions of his Whitman essay. Here, he recounts gossip from neighbors accusing the aged Whitman of walking "in his little back yard [...] stark naked and fat and excited with his own nudity and his grey beard" and "stop[ping] the little girls coming home from school, with senile amorousness" (423).

Meanwhile, his most favorable views of Whitman and homosexuality occur in the first two versions, with Lawrence in the first of these (1919) even speaking openly, if in guarded language, about the mechanics of the homosexual act. This account begins with Lawrence noting the high bar necessary for the "sexual consummation between man and woman," calling it "the fiery, electric establishing of the perfect life-current, the vital circuit between the two": "The two poles are brought together and the great life-circuit is established, upon which the very life and being and equilibrium of man and woman depend. Hence the vast mysterious power of sexual love, and of marriage." It is the "sexual act itself," Lawrence continues, "upon which both [men and women] depend for their real, spontaneous living. The whole of mankind is made up of units of man and woman. And therefore all human life rests upon this circuit of vital polarity" (365).

Yet there is something more profound, with Lawrence speaking about *chakras*, or nerve centers of the human body, latching on to the gnostic terminology he discovered in his early thirties—this gnostic Lawrence, in various ways, the convoluted opposite of this volume's lyrical genius. While one Lawrence gives us poetry, the other gives us anatomy lessons, in which we learn that beyond the vagina—what Lawrence refers to as "the advent to the great source of being, and [...] the egress of the bitter, spent waters of the end"—lies "the cocygeal centre." It is there that

> the deepest and most unknowable sensual reality breathes and sparkles darkly, in unspeakable power. [...] Here is the dark node which relates us to the centre of the earth, the plumb-centre of substantial being. Here is our last and extremest reality.
>
> (366)

This place of "egress and ingress," or anus, Lawrence labels "the fundament," contrasting it with the vagina, that "port to the other centre," while labeling "the establishment [...] between the poles of the cocygeal centres"—a euphemism for sodomy—as "the last mystery of established polarity." And for once, Lawrence seems to commend not just male-to-male touching but true sexual intimacy: this

> last perfect balance is between two men, in whom the deepest sensual centres, and also the extreme upper centres, vibrate in one circuit, and know their electric establishment and readjustment as does the circuit between man and woman. There is the same immediate connection, the same life-balance, the same perfection in fulfilled consciousness and being.

With Lawrence, however, nothing involving men touching other men is ever likely to be so unambiguous, and Lawrence's problem with Whitman here morphs into an attack on Whitman's democratic vision of men loving men as a vital part of a world without social hierarchies, one where all men are truly equal. For Lawrence, such a notion of social fusion was "a form of death," so different from the attraction of opposites— the "delicately-adjusted polarity" of the weaker man submitting to the stronger—he so preferred. To strengthen his case against the democratic ideal inherent in Whitman's notion of fusion, Lawrence oddly equates it with the radical, aristocratic asymmetry of Greek pederasty, a world where things get crossed up, and the beloved object now becomes the son, not the father, a boy lacking any social standing who is then "possessed utterly" by the powerful lover intent on "superimposing his will and his intention."

The result for Lawrence is a kind of forced sex similar to the prostitution that he always hated, similar to what we just saw in Magnus's treatment of *girants* in the Foreign Legion. "[P]rostitution," he concludes, means "using one being for the gratification and increase of the other being, without any true duality, true polarised circuit" (367). What Lawrence wanted instead for the world seems an expansion of what he always wanted for himself—the "love between comrades [that] is always and inevitably a love between a leader and a follower," with neither able to live without the other. Such has been the case "of every great manly friendship since time began"—one combining "perfect leadership and perfect liege love," or what Lawrence calls "the very flower and perfection of love." He concluded that it was only

> upon this [that] the next great epoch will be established. Upon the mystery of passionate leadership and passionate answer: the supreme active love relationship between men, when men act in a miracle of unison, making a new world out of the passion of their belief, and in the great inspiration of a culminating leader.
>
> (415–16)

The Limits of Friendship

It should be noted how this "very flower and perfection of love," which Lawrence sees as the basis of one man's highest interaction with another, can be seen as the inverse of the Greek pederasty that he so adamantly condemned. There is still a power differential between the two parties, but the positions have been reversed. The beloved is no longer the powerless boy in thrall to a powerful lover; instead, it is now the powerless boy with whom Lawrence identifies, envisioning him as the ardent admirer of a strong, immobile aristocratic leader—the difference in status making the scopophilic distance between the parties even more essential. It is the senior partner in the Greek paradigm who now becomes the beloved—that calm, manly, often detached father figure, a man much like the bathing Mellors espied by his impassioned, hidden admirer Connie Chatterley.

This reversal of Greek pederasty is just another way of reframing our thesis that the most intensely lyrical part of Lawrence's oeuvre is written almost entirely from the point of view of this younger, "weaker" lover— the sensitive son, if you will—an observation that has two corollaries, each involving an essential term of Lawrence's relating to male intimacy that he coined or borrowed.

The first of these is *Rananim*, Lawrence's fanciful name for a utopian world that he first envisioned during the dark times of World War I. He used it then to refer to his dream that he would

> gather together about twenty souls and sail away from this world of war and squalor and found a little colony where there shall be no money

but a sort of communism as far as necessaries of life go, and some real decency.

About Whitman's notion of fusion or any other intimacy connected to his Rananim, Lawrence has little to say. While the assumption always was that it would consist primarily of men, Lawrence rarely said more than that it was to be established "upon the assumption of goodness in the members, instead of the assumption of [...] badness" (Vol. 2, 259).

While many of his friends seemed to see this notion of Rananim as a kind of parlor game to relieve their wartime miseries, for Lawrence, as he makes clear in a letter from February 1915, it was an essential element in a broad critique of a world that he found profoundly inhibiting, one that kept people like himself from "fulfil[ing] his own nature and deep desires to the utmost." His hope for Rananim was for a world "wherein the ultimate satisfaction and joy is in the completeness of us all as one"—a hope that "the intrinsic part of all of us is the best part, the believing part, the passionate, generous part" (*Letters* 2, 271).

Regarding the need for a leader in this new world, Lawrence urges caution, noting how the "great [destructive] serpent [...] is the will to Power, the desire for one man to have some dominion over his fellow man." Part of this makes perfect sense. As Lawrence himself never felt such a need for "dominion" himself—always more comfortable as the observer than the leader—he wants to fill his Rananim with others like himself: Let anyone who wants to join come "because he knows that his own soul is not the be-all and the end-all, but that all souls of all things do but compose the body of God, and that God indeed shall Be." In other words, individuals will reach fulfillment in Lawrence's Rananim, as in his dreams, by merging with something more extensive and more potent than themselves: "Not self-sacrifice" in this new world,

> but fulfilment, the flesh and the spirit in league together not in arms against one another. And each man shall know that he is part of the greater body, each man shall submit that his own soul is not supreme even to himself.
>
> (272)

The second term is *Blutbruderschaft*, German for "blood brother-hood," and something Lawrence introduces in *Women in Love* through his alter ego, Birkin, as part of his interaction with the more powerful, manly Gerald. Early in the novel, Lawrence had played up the mutual nature of their interaction: how "always their talk brought [the two of] them into a deadly nearness of contact, a strange, perilous intimacy which was either hate or love, or both"; how "the heart of each burned from the other," even if this was something "they would never admit" (28). Then, in the chapter "Man to Man," where Lawrence introduces the term, he mentions how "Gerald really loved Birkin." However, the focus quickly switches from the mutual interaction between the two men to the admiration of one man, Birkin, for the other, Gerald. It is only Gerald whom Lawrence shows us, looking "formal, handsome and *comme il faut*" in his evening clothes: "His hair was fair almost to whiteness, sharp like splinters of light, his face was keen and ruddy, his body seemed full of northern energy" (193).

Again, Lawrence tries to enhance their mutual interaction, noting, for instance, Gerald's awareness of how Birkin could continue without him. Yet the table is quickly switched, with Lawrence showing us Birkin having to deal with the more serious issue of "love and eternal conjunction between two men." It was Birkin, not Gerald, who had to deal with what Lawrence describes as "a necessity inside himself all his life—to love a man purely and fully." And it is to Birkin's problem, of his "loving Gerald all along, and all along denying it," that Lawrence now has Birkin ("with quite a new happy activity in his eyes") ask Gerald the notable question if he knew about how "the old German knights used to swear a *Blutbruderschaft*"—not literally, as the Germans did by making two small cuts in their arms and sharing their blood, but by "swear[ing] to be true to each other, of one blood, all their lives": "That is what we ought to do. [...] swear to love each other, you and I, implicitly, and perfectly, finally, without any possibility of going back on it" (198–99).

It is Birkin who plays the role of lover here, Lawrence tells us, trying "hard to express himself," while Gerald, the passive beloved, "hardly listened": "His face shone with a certain luminous pleasure. He was pleased. But he kept his reserve. He held himself back." Birkin then extends his hand, with Gerald barely touching it, "as if withheld and afraid." The whole exchange is less one between equals than the "delicately-adjusted polarity" that Lawrence praises in the Whitman essay, even if the scene ends with Birkin realizing he had to look past "the physical, animal man, which he usually saw in Gerald, and which he usually he liked so much," to recognize Gerald as someone, for whatever reason, incapable of ever reciprocating.

It has long been noted that the character of Gerald Crich was modeled on Lawrence's close friend during the composition of that novel, the critic John Middleton Murry. It may be more helpful to reverse the observation by noting how Lawrence may have somehow tried to convert Murry, his real-life friend, into the romantic ideal he projected onto his fictional creation, Gerald Crich. Indeed, such an ideal for Lawrence predated Murry's appearance in his life and far outlasted their falling out. As Lawrence confessed to Murry's wife, the short story writer Katherine Mansfield, "I believe tremendously in friendship between man and man, a pledging of men to each other inviolably.—But I have not ever met or formed such friendship" (*Letters* 3, 302).

As noted, one would-be friend—the cynosure of Lawrence's first novel, *The White Peacock*—was Jessie Chambers's older brother, Alan. A second outdoorsman who played a similar role in Lawrence's life was William Henry Hocking, a neighbor for the 18 months Lawrence spent in Cornwall, starting in the spring of 1916. The most moving passage Lawrence wrote about this relationship was in the voice of Richard Lovatt Somers, Lawrence's alter ego in his Australian novel, *Kangaroo*. In the chapter "Nightmare," Lawrence reflects on his difficult time in Cornwall during the war and how Somers "loved working with John Thomas," who at the time "was a year or two older than Somers, and [...] his dearest friend"—"loved working all day among the corn beyond the high-road, with the savage moors all round, and the hill with its pre-christian granite rocks rising like a great dark pyramid on the left, the sea in front" (277).

It was that same perfect blend of work and fellowship that Lawrence had so admired with Alan Chambers, only now it was "a half-philosophical, mystical talking about the sun, and the moon, the mysterious powers of the moon at night, and the mysterious change in man with the change of season, and the mysterious effects of sex on a man." All such talk—and here we see the lyrical Lawrence—while they lay

> in the bracken or on the heather as they waited for a wain. Or one of the girls came with dinner in a huge basket, and they ate all together, so happy with the moors and sky and touch of autumn.

In that novel, Lawrence has Somers admit, "He had all his life had this craving for an absolute friend, a David to his Jonathan, [...] a blood-brother. All his life he had secretly grieved over his friendlessness" (121). Only now, at least when Lawrence was in Australia, did he become unsure about what he wanted, even while various factors combined to heighten his feeling of isolation: "Maybe a living fellowship!" he continues, "but not affection, not love, not comradeship. Not mates and equality and mingling. Not blood-brotherhood. None of that." That is, with none of the fusion of equals he had rejected in Whitman nor with the *Blutbruderschaft* so desired by Birkin in *Women in Love*, but here finally rejected as lacking that "delicately-adjusted polarity" between opposing parties.

At the end of the second version of his Whitman essay (1921–22), Lawrence lashes out against democracy, against the love of comrades, and even against the notion of men as equals, either as political beings or, more to our purpose, as sexual partners. "Let us take our stand on the extreme tip of life," he writes, "where [Whitman] has led us":

> But let us turn round. There is no stride onwards possible, in democracy, in En Masse, in merging. The next stride is the gulf of the bottomless pit. Stride one step further in democracy and merging, and down you go, down the bottomless pit.
>
> (416)

In Whitman's advocacy of fusion, Lawrence seems to have sniffed out something akin to masturbation, a sexual act involving "nothing but loss," with "no reciprocity": "There is merely the spending away of a certain force, and no return. The body remains, in a sense, a corpse, after the act of self-abuse" (*Pornography and Obscenity* 245).

Lawrence is all for "accept[ing] this love of comrades," but not on what he calls "the downward slope": "Not in the Whitman sense of abandon and self-merging. Never. Let us turn round and look each other square in the face. Manly love means action, or it means nothing" (416).

Just what is this action Lawrence is calling for? His first response— "building the world afresh, and smashing the obsolete form"—may seem slightly obscure, as does his second response about one's "profound, passional constructive belief." There should be no surprise, however, where he is heading once he becomes more specific: "It means that one man out of two shall accept the sacred responsibility of leadership, while the other man accepts the joy of liege adherence."

What is this "joy of liege adherence," we note, but another form of the young man's passion for his senior, the lover's passion for his beloved, that we have seen countless times in Lawrence? "That is manly love," he continues. "The glad proposition, and the heroic answer, and men tackling the world like heroes":

> And the love culminates. Each leading soul knows a leader still beyond him. Each leading soul not only leads, but has his own leader whom he follows through a thousand deaths. And this leader again has a greater soul ahead of him; and so on till we reach the last, the final leader of men, the sacred tyrannus.

What then are we to make of Lawrence's lifelong infatuation with that greatest of all such male friendships, the one between the biblical David, the beautiful, courageous claimant to Saul's crown, and the hereditary heir to that crown, Saul's son Jonathan? Lawrence's most complete dramatic rendering of this story is in his play *David*. There, Jonathan is born to a high place, with David's position as future ruler inherent in his superior nature proclaimed by the prophet Samuel:

> Thy strength is at the heart of the world, and thy desires are from thence. The walls of thy breast are the front of the Lord, thy loins are the Deep's, and the fire within them is His. The Lord looketh out of thy eyes and sits on thy lips.
>
> (449)

Here is an arrangement like what we have seen in *Women in Love* between Birkin and Gerald—two men reaching out to form a bond. In Jonathan's words, "our souls [...] as brothers, closer even than the blood," even if this covenant is actively desired by just one party—Birkin in the novel and Jonathan in the play. "O David," Jonathan continues, "my heart hath no peace save all be well between thy soul and mine, and thy blood and mine" (475).

At this point in Lawrence's play, David still questions his ascendancy despite being anointed by Samuel: "In the Lord, I fear nothing. But before the faces of men, my heart misgives me." Might not one who is "suddenly lifted up" end up "as suddenly down"? Here is the opening that Jonathan needs and what Birkin never received from Gerald: that is, the stronger partner opening his heart by exposing his vulnerability, thus placing himself in a position to value the offer of friendship for a lifetime: "I will trust thee, Jonathan," says David, "and cleave to thee till the sun sets on me. Thou art good to me as man never before was good to me, and I have not deserved it. Say thou wilt not repent of thy kindness towards me" (476)!

As a result, the moment of maximum intimacy and trust between the two friends—the swearing of the covenant—appears, at least for this moment, as an exchange between equals. In Jonathan's words, "O brother, give me the oath, that naught shall sunder our souls, for ever." Between equals, but as with the traditional matrimonial proposal, with the more vital partner, here David, assuming the deferential position:

> As the Lord liveth, my soul shall not part for ever from the soul of my brother Jonathan; but shall go with him up the steeps of heaven, or down the sides of the pit. And between his house and my house the covenant shall be everlasting. For as the hearts of men are made on earth, the heart of Jonathan is gentlest and most great.

Surely such a loving response was what Birkin had hoped to receive from Gerald, and, at some level, Lawrence must have hoped for something similar during all the years of complaining about never finding that perfect friend, much less being able to touch that friend, or perhaps that highest of all wishes, having that friend reach out and touch him. For the moment, however, the weaker friend—in Lawrence's play, Jonathan, who is suffering from a leg wound—occupies the higher social standing and thus has the honor of exchanging his royal clothes for David's "herdsman's tunic," a move that more appropriately aligns their emotional standing as follower and leader.

Here, Lawrence's 1925 drama heads off in a different direction, with Lawrence's sympathies now shifted toward the elder Saul as a representative of a heroic past and away from David, his more polished and tactful but ultimately less trustworthy replacement. Indeed, it is in his reworking of his essay "The Crown," also published in 1925, that Lawrence calls David "cunning and triumphant" (269), even comparing him to Judas. Lawrence's treatment of David in both his play and "The Crown" suggests his declining interest in the ideal of male-to-male intimacy.

This loss of interest is even more emphatic in Lawrence's Australian novel, *Kangaroo*, where Somers, his stand-in, struggles with how to respond to a direct offer of male friendship: "He half wanted to commit himself to this whole affection with a friend, a comrade, a mate. And then, in the last issue, he didn't want it at all." Maybe, he realizes, it is the affection itself that he no longer cherishes: "All his life he had cherished a beloved ideal of friendship—David and Jonathan. And now, when true and good friends offered, he found he simply could not commit himself, even to simple friendship" (120).

At one level, it may be a surprise that his alter ego in *Kangaroo* should exclaim that he "didn't want a friend, he didn't want loving affection, he didn't want comradeship." This change he sees as "a revolution in his mind":

> He had all his life had this craving for an absolute friend, a David to his Jonathan [...]: a blood-brother. All his life he had secretly grieved over his friendlessness. And now at last, when it really offered [...] he didn't want it, and he realised that in his innermost soul he had never wanted it.
>
> (121)

On another level, however, much of our analysis suggests that what Lawrence had wanted all along was less friendship with a man than a level of physical intimacy with a strong male—an intimacy that, as we have suggested in *Lady Chatterley's Lover* and will explore in greater detail in a series of works in the next chapter, Lawrence could rarely describe fully except through his female characters. Such is the insight that Lawrence comes to acknowledge in this crucial section of *Kangaroo*—the realization that, while he may have wanted "some living fellowship with other men," he no longer wanted the emotional baggage that comes with such a relationship. Here, in other words, is the same complaint Lawrence made to Jessie Chambers: "Maybe a living fellowship!—but not affection, not love, not comradeship. Not mates and equality and mingling. Not blood-brotherhood. None of that."

"What else?" Somers (or Lawrence) asks. "He didn't know. He only knew he was never destined to be mate or comrade or even friend with any man." But if not friendship, then what else might it be? And here we can see Lawrence circling an insight while never fully alighting—that what he perhaps most wanted was "the thing that the dark races know: that one can still feel in India: the mystery of lordship":

> The mystery of innate, natural, sacred priority. The other mystic relationship between men, which democracy and equality try to deny and obliterate. Not any arbitrary caste or birth aristocracy. But the mystic recognition of difference and innate priority, the joy of obedience and the sacred responsibility of authority.

In a little-known essay from April 1927, "Germans and Latins," we find Lawrence observing two young Germans on a hot day in Tuscany, moving with "strong strides, heedless, marching past the Italians as if the Italians were but shadows." Such perfect young men:

> Strong, heedless, travelling intently, bent a little forward from the rucksacks in the plunge of determination to travel onwards, looking neither to right nor left, conversing in strong voices only with one another [...] in the last golden light of the sun-flooded evening, over the Arno.

Although possibly friends to each other, to Lawrence, they were something entirely different—products of another world, "bring[ing] with them such a strong feeling of somewhere else, of an unknown country, an unknown race, a powerful, still unknown northland. [...] Creatures from the beyond, presaging another world of men" (327, 329). For Lawrence, here is another lesson of a lifetime, one that we shall return to again in Chapter 8—a boy's (and a man's) deeply buried, erotic attachment, less to another man, a would-be friend, than to an ever-distant, idealized male form.

Works Cited

Lawrence, D. H. *Aaron's Rod*. Ed. Mara Kalnins. Penguins Books, 1995.
———. "The Blind Man." In *Selected Short Stories*. Ed. Brian Finney. Penguin Books, 1982: 301–17.

———. "The Crown." In *Reflections on the Death of a Porcupine and Other Essays*. Ed. Michael Herbert. Cambridge UP, 1988: 251–306.

———. "Dana's *Two Years Before the Mast*." In *Studies in Classic American Literature*. Eds. Ezra Greenspan, Ezra, Lindeth Vasey, and John Worthy. Cambridge UP, 2004: 105–21.

———. "*David*." In *The Plays, Part 2*. Eds. Hans-Wilhelm Schwarze and John Worthen. Cambridge UP, 2002: 432–51.

———. "Democracy." In *Selected Essays*. Penguin Books, 1976: 73–95.

———. "Germans and Latins." In *The Bad Side of Books*. Ed. Geoff Dyer. New York Review of Books, 2019: 227–32.

———. *Kangaroo*. Thomas Seltzer, 1923.

———. *Letters of D. H. Lawrence*. Vol. 1: September 1901 – May 1913. Ed. James T. Boulton. Cambridge UP, 1979.

———. *Letters of D. H. Lawrence*. Vol. 2: June 1913 – October 1916. Eds. George J. Zytaruk and James T. Boulton. Cambridge UP, 1981.

———. *Letters of D. H. Lawrence*. Vol. 3: October 1916 – June 1921. Eds. James T. Boulton and Andrew Robertson. Cambridge UP, 1981.

———. *Memoir of Maurice Magnus*. Ed. Keith Cushman. Black Sparrow P, 1987.

———. "The Old Adam." In *Love Among the Haystacks*. Ed. Worthen, John. Cambridge UP, 2001: 71–86.

———. *The Plumed Serpent*. Ed. L. D. Clark. Cambridge UP, 2002.

———. *Pornography and Obscenity*. In *Late Essays and Articles*. Ed. James T. Boulton. Cambridge UP, 2004: 233–53.

———. "Prologue." In *Women in Love*. Eds. David Farmer, Lindeth Vasey, and John Worthen. Cambridge UP, 1987: 489–518.

———. "The Prussian Officer." In *Selected Short Stories*. Ed. Brian Finney. Penguin Books, 1982: 174-93.

———. *The Rainbow*. Ed. Mark Kinkead-Weekes. Penguin Books, 1995.

———. "Review of *The Death in Venice*." In *The Bad Side of Books: Selected Essays*. Ed. Geoff Dyer. New York Review of Books, 2019: 28–34.

———. *Selected Short Stories*. Ed. Brian Finney. Penguin Books, 1982.

———. *Studies in Classic American Literature*. Eds. Ezra Greenspan, Lindeth Vasey, and John Worthen. Cambridge UP, 2003.

———. *The White Peacock*. Ed. Andrew Robertson. Cambridge UP, 2002.

———. *Women in Love*. Heinemann, 1971.

Meyers, Jeffrey. "D. H. Lawrence." In *Homosexuality and Literature, 1890–1930*. McGill-Queen's UP, 1977: 131–64.

7 Hiding in Plain Sight

In Chapter 5, we suggested that in showing Gudrun swooning in Gerald's arms—"everything in her was melted down and fluid, and she lay still, become contained by him, sleeping in him as lightning sleeps in a pure, soft stone"—Lawrence was expressing his own "hidden" thoughts; that in describing Gudrun standing under the same train trestle where he had stood as a boy, watching miners, strong men like his father, their arms tenderly wrapped around a prized companion, Lawrence was essentially recreating the world through the eyes and feelings of a female character.

The claim here is that this narrative from *Women in Love* is not unlike the female voice that Lawrence speaks through in his early poem "Cruelty and Love" (Delphi 7080–81), later given the more subdued title "Love on the Farm." It opens with a striking image of a powerful male who has just strangled, "in his large, hard hands," a rabbit caught in a snare. The speaker, we soon learn, is the man's lover awaiting his return, but also someone not unlike Lawrence's projection of himself in *Sons and Lovers* as a child trembling in fear of his father returning home—a woman (or a child) who "hear[s] his hand on the latch, and rise[s] from my chair / Watching the door open":

> ... he flashes bare
> His strong teeth in a smile, and flashes his eyes
> In a smile like triumph upon me; ...

Then, as with Gudrun and Gerald, there is an embrace as "He flings the rabbit soft on the table board / And comes towards me," his hand an "uplifted sword [...] against my bosom," the "broad / Blade of his hand that raises my face to applaud / His coming [...]."

DOI: 10.4324/9781003495093-7

And again, as with Gudrun and Gerald, and as we saw earlier with Connie and Mellors, there is the same erotic ecstasy in one's surrender—as "he raises my face to him / And caresses my mouth with his fingers which still smell / Of the rabbit's fur!":

> God, I am caught in a snare!
> I know not what fine wire is round my throat,
> I only know I let him finger there
> My pulse of life, letting him nose like a stoat
> Who sniffs with joy before he drinks the blood:
> And down his mouth comes to my mouth, and down
> His dark bright eyes descend like a fiery hood
> Upon my mind: his mouth meets mine, and a flood
> Of sweet fire sweeps across me, so I drown
> Within him, die, and find death good.

In the original version of another early poem, "The Wild Common (Delphi 7124)," Lawrence made the rare move, later erased, of directly comparing his "soul" to "a passionate woman," who "Filled with remorseful terror to the man she scorned.". In "Love on the Farm," he goes past the signaling of a simile to position himself directly inside a female speaker.

Lawrence may have had such transpositions in mind when he began the novel *The Sisters* in 1913, what eventually became *The Rainbow* and *Women in Love*, two works in which Lawrence often deals with his struggle for self-understanding while simultaneously focusing on the love lives of his female characters. These two novels thus follow the pattern we have already seen in *Lady Chatterley's Lover*, where Lawrence has a male character like Mellors or Rupert Birkin as a stand-in, with clear autobiographical and emotional connections with his own life, while freely placing other aspects of his life inside the emotional lives of his female characters—as is the case, for instance, with Ursula's London teaching career so closely mirroring the three years that Lawrence spent at the Davidson Road Boys' School in the London suburb of Croydon or, as we have seen in Chapter 5, with Gudrun's intense, sexual reaction to Gerald under the train trestle.

It was arguably in his short stories and novellas that Lawrence perfected this practice, locating at the center of his narrative the central concern of his own erotic life—namely, how an unhappy protagonist, caught in a troubled relationship or marriage, deals with controlling her disruptive erotic desires, often represented by the appeal of a sexual siren. Of course, such a transposition in gender was not always the norm for Lawrence, something we can see in the early story "The Soiled Rose" (revised and published as "The Shades of Spring"), where the protagonist Syson and his siren, the gamekeeper Arthur Pilbeam, are both male, which was also the case in a second rendering of this situation, "A Modern Lover," considered in Chapter 3.

Here, for instance, is Lawrence's account of his protagonist, Syson, of "The Soiled Rose," eyeing the other male—"a young man of four or five and twenty, ruddy and comely"—presumably dispassionately, with what Lawrence would have us believe was "an artist's impersonal, observant gaze." What struck Syson were the man's "large, dark blue eyes, which now stared aggressively" and "[h]is black moustache, very thick, [...] [and] cropped short over a small, rather self-conscious, almost feminine mouth":

> In every other respect the man was unusually virile. He was just above middle height; the strong forward thrust of his chest, and the perfect ease of his erect, proud carriage gave one the feeling that he was taut with life, like the thick jet of a fountain balanced at ease.
>
> (7)

There was an obvious problem for Lawrence with the narrative structure in these stories, exposing as it does the homoerotic desires of his protagonists, often barely disguised stand-ins for the author, especially when there was so clearly a suitable alternative visible in another early story, "The White Stocking" (discussed in Chapter 5). Here, the siren remains a male, in this case, the business owner Sam Adams, while Lawrence safely places the desire for his dancing prowess in the married Elsie Whiston, who is even allowed to return safely to her husband's good graces at the story's somewhat deflated conclusion.

Lawrence repeats this alternative pattern in another early story, "Samson and Delilah" (1917), about the landlady of a rustic inn who is unable or possibly reluctant to recognize her husband after he has returned after 16 years abroad. When he refuses to leave the inn, a mighty row ensues between them, with the landlady calling on soldiers staying at the inn to help tie up her husband (hence, the story's title):

> The woman clung to his knees. Another soldier ran in a flash of genius, and fastened the strange man's feet with the pair of braces. Seats had crashed over, the table was thrown against the wall, but the man was bound, his arms pinned against his sides, his feet tied.
>
> (118)

Even amid this struggle, there is little doubt about "Samson's" status as a desired sexual object: "The bound-up body began to struggle again. She watched fascinated the muscles working, the shoulders, the hips, the large, clean thighs. Even now he might break the ropes. She was afraid." Here, one sees the same blend of fear and attraction we will see in the female protagonists of the following five stories: "Sun," *The Ladybird*, *The Fox*, "The Princess," and "The Woman Who Rode Away."

A Time in the "Sun"

The late story "Sun" (1925, revised in 1928) is based on the pattern in many of Lawrence's best stories—a push-pull dance between a discontented married wife and a would-be male lover. Our protagonist at the center of "Sun" is Juliet, a woman in her late twenties, unhappily married to an ineffectual husband, Maurice. Juliet remembered, Lawrence writes, "how bitterly they wanted to get away from one another" (19). As seems to have been often the case with Lawrence and Frieda, "[I]n their two lives, the stroke of power was hostile, his and hers. Like two engines running at variance, they shattered one another." And, as with all these stories with the genders reversed, we find the protagonist attracted to or, following the now familiar scopophilic pattern, worshiping from afar a robust, aloof male.

Initially, Juliet's only idol is the bright sun of Sicily, a place that had enthralled Lawrence for two years in his early thirties. Here, like Lawrence, Juliet will find

> a house above the bluest of seas, with a vast garden, or vineyard, all vines and olives, dropping steeply in terrace after terrace, to the strip of coast plain; and the garden full of secret places, deep groves of lemon far down in the cleft of earth, and hidden, pure green reservoirs of water.
>
> (20)

Even in this beautiful setting, Juliet seems depressed, unable "to feel anything real." Still, the sun that boldly illuminated the place was the start of her salvation—"the central sun, his blue pulsing roundness, whose outer edges streamed brilliance. Pulsing with marvellous blue, and alive, and streaming white fire from his edges [...]!" And beside the sun, there was the peasant from the adjoining farm, whom she spied one day, their eyes meeting, with Juliet feeling "the blue fire running through her limbs to her womb, which was spreading in the helpless ecstasy" (29).

Although Juliet, we learn, was naked after sunbathing when the two first met, Lawrence's interest is entirely in her arousal—the peasant himself described as "something over thirty, broad and very powerfully set," someone Juliet had seen before "trimming the olive trees, working alone, always alone and physically powerful, with a broad red face and a quiet self-possession." She even spoke to him, meeting "his big blue eyes, dark and southern hot," as she knew "his sudden gestures, a little violent and over-generous."

Then, what will often be a key component of all these stories, the indecision or demurral of all these protagonists, as if, like Lawrence himself, they too see themselves as the "good" child of a high-minded, Congregationalist mother, someone with deep reservations about such an illicit infatuation. Indeed, Lawrence quickly adds, Juliet "had never thought of him," other than to notice that he was "always very clean and well-cared for." Really! "Such a broad red face, such a great chest, and rather short legs. Too much a crude beast for her to think of, a peasant" (30).

At least now, "mother" was not close, affording our protagonist the freedom to meet "the strange challenge of [the neighbor's] eyes [that] held her, blue and overwhelming like the blue sun's heart," or to observe "the fierce stirring of the phallus under his thin trousers": "with his red face, and with his broad body, he was like the sun to her, the sun in its broad heat." Indeed, Juliet was caught up in the dilemma of Lawrence's life, one we will see played out in all five stories in this chapter: a timid protagonist attracted to while fearing a strange man "so powerfully, that she could not go further from him," yet "paralysed," lacking "the courage to go down to him."

As with Connie's three grand love scenes in *Lady Chatterley's Lover*, Lawrence uses decidedly feminine language to describe Juliet's sexual needs—all terms involving a lover's desire for physical penetration. "Juliet," Lawrence tells us,

> sat late on into the night, watching the moon on the sea. The sun had opened her womb, and she was no longer free. The trouble of the open lotus blossom had come upon her, and now it was she who had not the courage to take the steps across the gully.

Yes, it is a woman's problem here, but change *Juliet* to *Jules*, and "Sun" instantly becomes the story of a gay man's fear of what he most desires—and, given its connection to Lawrence's life, possibly an even more poignant tale.

As expected, Maurice, the dull husband, eventually arrives on the scene—an inappropriate presence "in his dark grey suit and pale grey hat, and his grey, monastic face of a shy business man, and his grey mercantile mentality" (33). Here is a husband portrayed as the antithesis of Juliet's would-be Italian lover—a different sort of man, dressed "in his white cotton trousers and pale pink shirt, [...] so clean, and full of the cleanliness of health." Although "stout and broad, and seem[ing] shortish" like so many of Lawrence's shepherds,

his flesh was full of vitality, as if he were always about to spring up
into movement [...] the type of Italian peasant that wants to make an
offering of himself, passionately wants to make an offering of himself,
of his powerful flesh and thudding blood-stroke.

(36)

Yet it is the spouse who carries the day, saving our protagonist from
herself by asserting his single claim—what for Lawrence in these stories as
well as it seems in his life often turned out to be sufficient—that he was the
protagonist's sole socially sanctioned sexual partner.

Still, it was not easy for Juliet, someone with an ever-active scopophilic
imagination, as she continued watching for her neighbor—a peasant "hot
through with countless suns, and mindless as noon. And shy with a violent, farouche shyness, that would wait for her with consuming wanting,
but would never, never move towards her." What her life might have
been—that is Lawrence's grand theme here and in the four stories that
follow: "With him, it would be like bathing in another kind of sunshine,
heavy and big and perspiring," and with one great, extra advantage—that
"afterwards one would forget" (37).

What joy she might have known—immediate physical gratification
without the emotional entanglement that Lawrence so disliked in his adolescence with his first sexual partner, Jessie Chambers! No! How different
things would be with this new lover! "Personally, he would not exist":

It would be just a bath of warm, powerful life—then separating and
forgetting. [...] She was so tired of personal contacts, and having to talk
with the man afterwards. With that healthy creature, one would just go
satisfied away, afterwards.

Alas, such thoughts are mere fantasy, with our protagonist being
watched over by "a keen-eyed spouse, possessor." And so "Sun" ends,
as did Lawrence's life, with the triumph of domesticity, even with the
protagonist's acknowledgment of her anguish in being unable to "go
across to the peasant." Why? "[S]he had not enough courage, she was not
free enough." Nor would the peasant, weighed down by "the dogged passivity of the earth," ever do more than "wait, wait, only putting himself in
her sight, again and again, lingering across her vision, with the persistency
of animal yearning" (38).

The Ladybird—A Dream of Coming Out

Lawrence's novella *The Ladybird* provides a variation on the dilemma
at the heart of "Sun," starting with another protagonist with obvious

connections with Lawrence, in this case, the rail-thin Lady Daphne Apsley, a woman "threatened with phthisis" (160), living under the constant scrutiny of an officious, high-minded mother and a robust, fun-loving father, all while stuck in a marriage with a well-meaning but sexually unfulfilling partner. While Basil, the husband, is missing in the war, presumably a captured prisoner, Daphne finds herself inexplicably attracted to Count Dionys, in most ways the opposite of the peasant in "Sun." He is both physically unimposing and, as his name suggests, a creature of the night— a man with eyes "dark and haughty"—someone who "seemed to put a shadow between himself and [others], and from across this shadow he looked with his dark, beautifully-fringed eyes, as a proud little beast from the shadow of its lair" (173).

Daphne, someone of high social standing, finds herself in a dilemma: "When she thought of Count Dionys she felt the world slipping away from her." Not unlike Wilde's Dorian Gray, she would sit in front of the mirror, looking

at her blue-green eyes—the eyes of the wild-cat on a bough. Yes, the lovely blue-green iris drawn tight like a screen. Supposing it should relax. Supposing it should unfold, and open out the dark depths, the dark, dilated pupil! Supposing it should?

(182)

And then the fierce rejoinder, the ever-present demurral:

Never! She always caught herself back. She felt she might be killed before she could give way to that relaxation that the Count wanted of her. She could not. She just could not. At the very thought of it some hypersensitive nerve started with a great twinge in her breast; She drew back, forced to keep her guard.

Here, then, is another reworking of the battle between a life protected by a code of domesticity—like the one that Lawrence learned from his mother and did his best to uphold in his marriage—and some dark impulse he seemed intent on repressing except, of course, in the imaginative world of his fiction.

Thus, we see Daphne insisting that she "disliked the thought of the Count": "An impudent little fellow. An impertinent little fellow! A little madman, really. A little outsider." How troublesome such thoughts were, especially when one had such a perfect spouse: for Daphne, "an adorable, tall, well-bred Englishman"; for Lawrence, a "tall, well-bred" German— that is, a spouse "so easy and simple, and with the amused look in his [*or her*] blue eyes." What more could someone want in their sexual partner?

Daphne, Lawrence tells us, couldn't help thinking of her spouse's "strong, easy body—beautiful, white-fleshed, with the fine springing of warm-brown hair like tiny flames." It was her husband to whom she should have been sexually attracted: "He was the Dionysos, full of sap, milk and honey, and northern golden wine: he, her husband. Not that little unreal Count" (182).

Lawrence then ends this passage with an apostrophe to the couple's happy days, similar to his first months together with Frieda, their days spent hiking in Germany and Italy recounted in *Mr. Noon*—here celebrated as "the love-days, and the honeymoon, the lovely, simple intimacy." Daphne speaks of "the marvellous revelation of that intimacy," just as Lawrence could just as readily speak of "the marvellous revelation" of those first weeks with Frieda. Lawrence, like his protagonist, remained a loyal spouse simply because she had given herself to him—or, in the language of his story, the gender roles reversed, that Basil had given himself to her—"so greatly, so generously": "Like an ear of corn [these generous spouses] was there for [the] gathering" (182).

The Count's role here, it turns out, is less as an erotic ideal or source of the scopophilic delight we have seen so often in Lawrence than as an embodiment of the dark, nighttime impulses—impulses that Lawrence's protagonist has such a difficult time controlling before finally submitting to them, at least in a vague, abstract way. This problem, Lawrence writes, comes strictly at night when the Count would sing; the result was pure "a torture" to our protagonist, who, "like a neurotic, was nailed inside her own fretful self-consciousness" (212).

Only in her "upper spirit" could "Daphne" resist. "But underneath," Lawrence tells us, "was a wild, wild yearning, actually to go, actually to be given." Here is a drive that we will see played out to its finality in our last story, "The Woman Who Rode Away," even though the impulse for annihilation here is quite similar: "Actually to go, actually to die the death, actually to cross the border and be gone, to be gone. To be gone from this herself"—or, rendered in the first person, "To be gone from this *myself*, [...] to be gone from father and mother, brothers and ~~husband~~ [*spouse*], and home and land and world: to be gone. To be gone to the call from the beyond: the call. It was the Count calling."

In the original, "He was calling her. She was sure he was calling her" (213). Rendered in the first person, "He was calling *me. I* was sure he was calling *me*. Out of *myself*, out of *my* world, he was calling me."

Even though his language is filled with exotic Orphic references to the underworld, the Count himself is not physically attractive. One result is that his appeal to Daphne lacks many of the rich, sensual details of similar accounts, such as Julie's near-seduction in "Sun." What makes *The Ladybird* special, however, is its strange aftermath, specifically Daphne's unexpected conversation with her husband the morning after she weakened and succumbed to the Count's appeal.

Basil, just recently back in England following the Armistice, immediately noticed something different in his wife—her look of real distress, her "weeping" but without tears, "death pale" with her eyes shut. "Are you in love with the Count" (218), he asks, although less, as one might expect, as an accusation. Indeed, when Daphne cannot answer, Basil appears chagrined and then unexpectedly solicitous, apologizing for even "ask[ing] such a question."

When Daphne then confesses that she could not resist the strange, nocturnal impulses aroused by the Count, the story takes a strange turn with Basil's unexpected response: Your sexual desires are taking you in another direction, Basil seems to say—well, then, no reason to fret. Indeed, Daphne's admission, he tells us, has enabled him "to see clear and feel true for the first time in his life." And what is he now ready to admit? Surprisingly, we learn that he is the one who has lost the "excitement of desire." That he no longer has any interest in seeing Daphne as a sexual object, and maybe never had, indeed, that for all the years of their marriage, she had been more "like a dear, dear sister to him":

> that she was his blood-sister, nearer to him than he had imagined any woman could be. So near—so dear—and all the sex and the desire gone. He didn't want it—he hadn't wanted it. This new pure feeling was so much more wonderful.

As Daphne weeps, Basil continues with the perfect words of solace Lawrence might have imagined being offered to any married person confessing to a lack of heterosexual desire—namely, the acknowledgment that "the sexual part [of our relationship] has been a mistake": "I had rather love you—as I love now. I know that this is true love. The other was always a bit whipped up. I know I love you now, darling: now I'm free from that other" (219)—"that other," an odd, unexpected euphemism for sexual desire.

The Ladybird thus ends as if it were a fairy tale, with the aggrieved spouse magically transformed into what any gay man might want for his wife—what Lawrence might have wanted and indeed likely found in Frieda—that is, a loving, supportive friend for life!

The Fox—Desire and Its Aftermath

The Fox, one of Lawrence's best-known novellas, provides another interesting twist on a similar love triangle, with one half of a lesbian couple, Nellie March, confronting another outdoorsman, the soldier

Henry Grenfel. This arrangement seems to invite the analysis offered by Kate Millett and others in somehow seeing Henry as Lawrence's alter ego—the man who helps correct the sorry condition of the farm tended by two helpless (manless) women, a situation apparent in their inability to protect their farm against the marauding fox. Thus, for Millett, it is Henry who "eliminates his lesbian competition, Jill Banford, murdering her with will power, materially assisted by a tree he fells on her head," and then moves to gain the "total control over [March] he requires so that he may transcend her into the male world of achievement" (265).

The one odd part of this reading is how it reverses everything we have seen about Lawrence so far by identifying him with Henry, the alpha male in the story, intent on subduing an intelligent, introspective woman like Juliet of "Sun" or Daphne of *The Ladybird*, in the process bringing her under his control. It is as if, to go back to *Lady Chatterley's Lover*, Mellors were the active lover intent on subduing Connie instead of running off to live alone the first chance he had. The "married" couple of our story, however, is not unlike those we have seen in both "Sun" and *The Ladybird*, with Jill, the protagonist's spouse, reminiscent of Lawrence's mother, a physically small woman with airs of superiority—"small, thin, delicate thing with spectacles"—and with the protagonist, March, the more active seeker, who, when "out and about, in her puttees and breeches, her belted coat and her loose cap, [...] looked almost like some graceful, loose-balanced young man" (8).

It is also March whose frequent outdoor reveries are so reminiscent of the young Lawrence—for instance, the first time March spotted the fox, "half watching, half musing." Their eyes met, and the effect was like what other "female" protagonists in these stories, Juliet and Daphne, felt when first discovering the male presence that would haunt them for the rest of the story, similar also to the male presence Lawrence describes haunting his alter ego in the suppressed prologue to *Women in Love*—his reference there to "a policeman who suddenly looked up at him, as he inquired the way, or a soldier who sat next to him in a railway carriage." "And he knew her," Lawrence writes in *The Fox*—the speaker, "spellbound": "She knew he knew her. So he looked into her eyes, and her soul failed her. He knew her, he was not daunted." Then he was gone as March "struggled, confusedly" (10) to come to herself.

Nor is it surprising that the novella's most lyrical writing is found in March's accounts of being haunted by this mysterious male presence—how, for example, "he had lifted his eyes upon her, and his knowing look seemed to have entered her brain"; or, the rest rendered in the first person: "*I* did not so much think of him: *I* was possessed by him. *I* saw his dark, shrewd, unabashed eye looking into *me*, knowing *me*. *I* felt him invisibly master *my* spirit." Later, we find March troubled by how the fox "glance[d] over his shoulder at her, half inviting, half contemptuous and cunning" (11). She tried forgetting about him but found herself "more indignant than ever at the impudence of the beggar." Nor was she even conscious of thinking about him, yet "whenever she fell into her half-musing, when she was half rapt and half intelligently aware of what passed under her vision, then it was the fox which somehow dominated my unconsciousness, possessed the blank half of her musing" (12).

Here is a portrait of someone dealing with deep repression of desire, someone feeling haunted "for weeks, and months" by her (or, if a stand-in for the author, *his*) uncontrolled erotic urges—whether this character "had been climbing the trees for the apples, or beating down the last of the damsons, or whether she had been digging out the ditch from the duck-pond, or clearing out the barn." It hardly mattered:

> when she had finished, or when she straightened herself, and pushed the wisps of her hair away again from her forehead, and pursed up her mouth again in an odd, screwed fashion, much too old for her years, there was sure to come over her mind the old spell of the fox, as it came when he was looking at her. It was as if she could smell him at these times.
>
> (12)

A portrait of someone unable to suppress "their" desire:

> And it always recurred, at unexpected moments, just as she was going to sleep at night, or just as she was pouring the water into the teapot to make tea—it was the fox, it came over her like a spell.

The story here takes an unexpected turn, with Henry taking over the role of March's erotic ideal. Initially, March finds herself "already under the influence of his strange, soft, modulated voice, star[ring] at him spellbound":

> He had a ruddy, roundish face, with fairish hair, rather long, flattened to his forehead with sweat. His eyes were blue, and very bright and sharp. On his cheeks, on the fresh ruddy skin were fine, fair hairs, like a down, but sharper. It gave him a slightly glistening look.
>
> (14)

And why not this spell, we might ask? Is this not the type of man we have seen before, for instance, with Tom Vickers in "A Modern Lover," with "down on his cheeks above the razor-line, and the full lips in shadow beneath the moustache"?

Lawrence could hardly be any more transparent, once again with the erotic attraction for Lawrence only minimally disguised by his use of pronouns:

> But to March he was the fox. Whether it was the thrusting forward of his head, or the glisten of fine whitish hairs on the ruddy cheek-bones, or the bright, keen eyes, that can never be said: but the boy was to her the fox, and she could not see him otherwise.

Later, we see March as the attentive homemaker, a role that, as we saw in *Aaron's Rod*, Lawrence delighted in playing himself. What is different here is March's discomfort in having to do so in the presence of her erotic ideal—

> the youth sprawling low on the couch, glanc[ing] up at her, with long, steady, penetrating looks, till she was almost ready to disappear. [...] Her desire to be invisible was so strong that it quite baffled the youth. [...] She seemed like a shadow within the shadow. And ever his eyes came back to her, searching, unremitting, with unconscious fixed attention.
>
> (16)

March could only relax if she could hide in the corner while Jill talked with the newcomer. Who can doubt that this is March's story, as she sits tucked away in "the shadow of her corner [...] [giving] herself up to a warm, relaxed peace, almost like sleep, accepting the spell that was on her"? Here, hidden away, she could avoid being "divided in herself, trying to keep up two planes of consciousness. She could at last lapse into the odour of the fox"—that is, into Henry's animal maleness.

At this point in the story, March, not Henry, is acting as Lawrence's stand-in; she is the one watching "the youth, sitting before the fire in his uniform, [sending] a faint but distinct odour into the room, indefinable, but something like a wild creature." March, the stand-in, who "no longer tried to reserve herself from it"; March, who delighted in this scopophilic moment—sitting "still and soft in her corner like a passive creature in its cave" (18).

Once again, we see Lawrence at his most lyrical, recounting a character's intense psychic battles, here vivid dreams not unlike Daphne's in *The Ladybird*. Here it is Marsh who hears "a singing outside which she could not understand, a singing that roamed round the house, in the fields, and in the darkness," moving Lawrence's protagonist so that "she felt she must weep" or in the first person, "*I* felt *I* must weep":

She went out, and suddenly she knew it was the fox singing. He was very yellow and bright, like corn. She went nearer to him, but he ran away and ceased singing. He seemed near, and she wanted to touch him. She stretched out her hand, but suddenly he bit her wrist, and at the same instant, as she drew back, the fox, turning round to bound away, whisked his brush across her face, and it seemed his brush was on fire, for it seared and burned her mouth with a great pain.

(20)

The dreamer—here, nominally March—"awoke with the pain of it, and lay trembling as if she were really seared."

Ascribing this dream to Lawrence may be too intrusive into someone's privacy, especially given the phallic implications of March's interaction with the fox after Henry has killed it—how Lawrence's protagonist "passed her hand softly down it":

And his wonderful black-glinted brush was full and frictional, wonderful. She passed her hand down this also, and quivered. Time after time she took the full fur of that thick tail between her fingers, and passed her hand slowly downwards. Wonderful, sharp, thick, splendour of a tail.

(41)

In such a scene, we see the reappearance of Greiffenhagen's shepherd from Chapter 5, with March now the maiden, curiously subdued by this strange male figure with his fur talisman. One is reminded of that dark male figure of the early poem "Cruelty and Love"—another powerful man who kills rabbits with his bare hands: "Ah soon in his large, hard hands she dies, / And swings all loose to the swing of his walk." And a third killer of rabbits, that other erotic ideal, George Saxton of *The White Peacock*, whom Lawrence describes as rushing upon the rabbit as it "darted into some fallen corn, but he had seen it, and had fallen on it. In an instant he was up again, and the little creature was dangling from his hand" (49).

One might wish that Lawrence had kept the focus on March's dilemma in *The Fox*, as he did with the young wives in both "Sun" and *The Ladybird*, with *The Fox* thus continuing as a study of March's quest for a different sort of emotional fulfillment. Instead, Lawrence opts to domesticate March's shepherd in the second half of his story. Once Henry starts actively courting March and interacting with the two women, his status changes, as did Mellors's in *Lady Chatterley's Lover*, from an erotic ideal to a potential lifetime partner, with all the baggage that Lawrence saw entailed in such a lifetime commitment. Thus, after Banford's "accidental" death, Lawrence closes *The Fox* by giving Henry and March a series of extended monologues on the pitfalls of marriage.

The first of these is Henry's, soon after he has finished badgering March to marry him. Just as he "realized that [March] was a woman, and vulnerable, accessible," Lawrence notes, there was a change in Henry—"a certain heaviness had possessed his soul." There is a reason that neither passionate feelings nor lyrical passages in Lawrence rarely involve a man looking at a woman, as Henry is doing here. No longer March's "fox"— someone being looked at—Henry is here transformed into another one of Lawrence's reluctant lovers of women: a man who, like Mellors in *Lady Chatterley's Lover*, finally "did not want to make love to [a woman]. [...] [who] shrank from any such performance, almost with fear." As a result, "he held back from that which was ahead, almost with dread. It was a kind of darkness he knew he would enter finally, but of which he did not want as yet even to think" (53).

Nor is March, once she sees her erotic ideal in the daylight, especially excited about the prospects of Henry as a potential lifetime partner. The moment allows Lawrence to use March as a vehicle for his public persona, the one ever ready to wax poetic about the drudgeries entailed in marriage. "Something was missing," Lawrence muses through March:

> Instead of her soul swaying with new life, it seemed to droop, to bleed, as if it were wounded. [...] If he spoke to her, she would turn to him with a faint new smile, the strange, quivering little smile of a woman [or *anyone*] who has died in the old way of love, and can't quite rise to the new way.
>
> (67)

March's thoughts form a devastating attack on the impact of marriage and domesticity on one's erotic life—the social pressure felt that one "ought to do something, to strain [oneself] in some direction. And there was nothing to do, and no direction in which to strain [oneself]." The problem is apparent—an unwillingness to "accept the submergence which [this] new love put upon [one]." It is possible to read Lawrence as a proto-feminist, here voicing a woman's fear of losing her independence in marriage, when the tone and message reflect the same complaint Lawrence first made with Jessie Chambers—why did love have to be so difficult? Who can doubt the ultimate source of this familiar complaint here about "the weary need of our day to *exert* [oneself] in love"?

What follows is a brilliant passage about the level of repression that Lawrence felt the unfulfilled partner must accept in a marriage, learning to live "submerged under the surface of love." One had to be "like the seaweeds," March muses, that she saw as she peered down from the boat, swaying forever delicately under water, with all their delicate fibrils put tenderly out upon the flood, sensitive, utterly sensitive and receptive within the shadowy sea, and never, never rising and looking forth above water while they lived.

Likewise, the degree of pessimism that follows would seem to be a more accurate reflection of Lawrence's experience than March's: A repressed life, one lived underwater: "Never. Never looking forth from the water until they died, only then washing, corpses, upon the surface."

But while they lived, always submerged, always beneath the wave. Beneath the wave they might have powerful roots, stronger than iron; they might be tenacious and dangerous in their soft waving within the flood. Beneath the water they might be stronger, more indestructible than resistant oak trees are on land. But it was always under-water, always under-water.

(67)

Here, the passage ends—"And she, being a woman, must be like that"— but one also feels the force of an alternate ending: "And *I*, being *married*, must live like that."

What is evident is the sympathy, based on his life, that Lawrence felt for a woman like March contemplating the prospects—literally the bonds—of married life. "But at the very point where she most wanted success, in the anguished effort to make some one beloved human being happy and perfect, there the failure was almost catastrophic" (68). Note how this passage continues without reference to the speaker's gender, with Lawrence again intent on bewailing the incompatibility of men and women as sexual partners:

You wanted to make your beloved happy, and his happiness seemed always achievable. If only you did just this, that, and the other. And you did this, that, and the other, in all good faith, and every time the failure became a little more ghastly. You could love yourself to ribbons and strive and strain yourself to the bone, and things would go from bad to worse, bad to worse, as far as happiness went. The awful mistake of happiness.

Such lyrical brilliance from Lawrence, again hidden in a female character, although focused here on the frustration of desire, not its fulfillment:

The more you reached after the fatal flower of happiness, which trembles so blue and lovely in a crevice just beyond your grasp, the more fearfully you became aware of the ghastly and awful gulf of the precipice below you, into which you will inevitably plunge, as into the bottomless pit, if you reach any farther. You pluck flower after flower—it is never the flower. The flower itself—its calyx is a horrible gulf, it is the bottomless pit.

(69)

What Lawrence calls this "whole history of the search for happiness" ends, he glumly adds, "in the ghastly sense of the bottomless nothingness."

While Lawrence may have given March the best lines about marital unhappiness, he saves the last word for Henry, noting how he "chafed, feeling he hadn't got his own life."

Although Henry's final plea in *The Fox* may seem to be a call for March's submission—that she "would not be a man any more, an independent woman with a man's responsibility"—there is little sign that what Henry was seeking here was anything other than avoiding the "awful straining" Lawrence saw as the result of women and men constantly placing impossible demands on their partners, men and women refusing to accept that they would always be two separate people. While Henry does call for March's submission, his one condition seems to be her accepting that "he would have all his own life as a young man and a male, and she would have all her own life as a woman and a female." Here, Henry seems similar to Lawrence's other recalcitrant bachelor, Oliver Mellors, suggesting that if he were condemned to live with a woman, his greatest wish would be for one willing to leave him alone.

"The Princess"—The Fear of Being Touched

In Chapter 5, we noted the extent to which Lawrence's complex relationship with his father mirrors ideas Freud was exploring at about the same time under the rubric of the "negative" or "passive" Oedipus conflict. For Freud, this entailed the son adopting "a feminine attitude towards his father," with the boy placing himself in his mother's position, finding himself in a situation not unlike Greiffenhagen's maiden, at once both aroused and fearful when observing the half-clothed shepherd. Not noted then was how Freud saw this "negative" Oedipus conflict, occurring at what he called the "meeting place between the sense of guilt and sexual love," as the basis for a boy's masochistic fantasies—the passive condition in a boy where "being beaten also stands for being loved" ("A Child" 116–17).

Five years later, Freud expanded upon this idea in the essay "The Economic Problem of Masochism," identifying what he calls *feminine masochism* in men, marked by fantasies of "being gagged, bound, painfully beaten, whipped, in some way maltreated, forced into unconditional obedience, dirtied and debased." The most "richly elaborated" masochistic fantasies, Freud continues—and significant for our analysis here—are ones that "place the subject in a characteristically female situation" (162).

What is crucial for understanding Lawrence is the distinction between a scopophilic stage, present in so many of the narratives we have already reviewed, where the protagonist's pleasure is almost entirely from watching the strong male, and a more active (and often far less pleasant) masochistic phase, in which often female protagonists find themselves erotically attracted to male violence. We have seen this condition in Paul Morel's odd relationship in *Sons and Lovers* with his putative rival, Baxter Dawes, especially in his fight with Baxter, in which Paul seems eager to accept being beaten. We also saw this pattern in "The Old Adam" and *Women in Love*, where Lawrence's stand-ins seem to welcome losing fights against more powerful antagonists to whom they are physically attracted.

Our focus in our final two stories, "The Princess" and "The Woman Who Rode Away," will likewise focus on the controversy and mayhem involved when Lawrence uses female protagonists to explore his erotic attraction to strong and, in each of these stories, increasingly violent men.

As with our other stories in this chapter, and *The Ladybird* in particular, it is easy to see Lawrence's identification with his heroine, Dollie Urquhart, the "Princess" of the title. As with Daphne from the earlier story, there is her stature—"small, nearly tiny in physique"—that made her look "like a changeling beside her big, handsome, slightly mad father." Lawrence, in his biographical essay, "Getting On," referred to himself as "the most delicate: a pale-faced, dirty-nosed frail boy" (29). But more to the point is the lifelong damage that Lawrence shared with his heroine from growing up under an overbearing parent constantly harping on the family's moral superiority. For Lawrence, it was his mother, Lydia Lawrence, who, even at the start of his career in 1910—before meeting Frieda and before *Sons and Lovers*—he could praise only as "a clever, ironical delicately moulded woman, of good, old burgher descent," that is, as a woman with airs, compared to his father's "sanguine temperament, warm and hearty," but "unstable [...] lack[ing] principle," that is, "as my mother would have said" (*Letters* 190).

By the time Lawrence got around to describing his mother in the essay "Getting On"—some 17 years after this letter and two years after "The Princess"—the slight critical edge visible in his early assessment of her had turned into an all-out critique. There she is still "a shrewd and ironical woman," yet now one who looked up to a neighbor, Henry Saxton, whom Lawrence despised as a self-inflated blowhard, especially compared to his warm-hearted father. Still, he was the man whom his mother insisted on treating "with tender respect": "And, since I was foreordained to accept all her values," he bitterly complains, "I had to look up to Henry Saxton too." Here, with greater insight into his life, Lawrence acknowledges how his mother "deceived" him: "

> stood for all that was lofty and noble and delicate and sensitive and pure, in my life. And all the time, she was worshipping success, because she hadn't got it. She was worshipping a golden calf of a Henry Saxton

—all while belittling his father, a man, Lawrence adds, who "had charm and a certain warm, uncurbed vitality that made a glow in the house" (28).

Lawrence's Princess, the protagonist of his tale, lacked the exuberant presence of Lawrence's father—her sole parent, Colin Urquhart, being very much in the mode of Lawrence's supercilious mother: "My little Princess," Dollie's father warned, "must never take too much notice of people and the things they say and do." His one admonition was to keep yourself above "any of the people in the world." Why? Because, like Lawrence's mother, he believed that "their demons are all dwindled and vulgar. They are not royal. Only you are royal, after me. Always remember that" (161). That is, the very sort of admonition that Lawrence sensed kept him captive for much of his life to his mother's narrow, Congregationalist morality— an attitude that may explain his insistence on marrying Frieda at the earliest possible moment, then remaining faithful to her (except possibly with Rosalind Baynes) while ignoring her repeated liaisons, and, of course, most pertinent of all, living most of his life in intense dread of homoerotic desire.

Here, in a nutshell, is the shadow under which Lawrence lived his life, the family secret that he finally could reveal only under the mythic structure of his tales such as "The Princess," with its own ghostly parent conveying such inhibitions to his frightened child as if an execration from a fairy tale: that she must live alone and unfulfilled, simply because she was better than everyone else. "It is our great secret," this "god-father" tells his daughter:

> I am a prince, and you a princess, of the old, old blood. And we keep our secret between us, all alone. [...] you must never forget that you alone are the last of Princesses, and that all other are less than you are, less noble, more vulgar.

It is no accident that Dollie is 38, Lawrence's age when he wrote the story, or that he would devote far less text to describing Dollie than her erotic ideal, Domingo Romero, the Mexican guide at the Rocky Mountain retreat Dollie visits. He was "a tall, silent fellow," Lawrence writes, "with a heavy closed mouth and black eyes that looked across at one almost sullenly" (167)—that is, a man with that mixture of qualities. First is the attraction: "From behind he was handsome, with a strong, natural body, and the back of his neck very dark and well-shapen, strong with life"; then, the danger: "his dark face was long and heavy, almost sinister, with that peculiar heavy meaninglessness in it, characteristic of the Mexicans of his own locality" (168).

Indeed, one senses an ambivalence in Lawrence, perhaps the result of an incipient racism that distinguished Romero from the alabaster men more closely associated with his father. On the one hand, there is Romero, who was "almost a typical Mexican to look at, with the typical heavy, dark, long face, clean-shaven, with an almost brutally heavy mouth," and with "black and Indian-looking" eyes, with only at their center a slight "spark of pride, or self-confidence, or dauntlessness": "Just a spark in the midst of the blackness of static despair." On the other, there was this spark, which gave him "a certain alert sensitiveness to his bearing and a certain beauty to his appearance"—with his "low-crowned black hat, instead of the ponderous headgear of the usual Mexican and [...] clothes [that] were thinnish and graceful."

The concrete details suggest that Lawrence may have had a specific person in mind—how, for instance, he spoke English "like a foreign language, rather slow, with a slight hesitation, but with a sad, plangent sonority lingering over from his Spanish"; how he was "always perfectly shaved; his hair [...] thick and rather long on top, but always carefully groomed behind";

And his fine black cashmere shirt, his wide leather belt, his well-cut, wide black trousers going into the embroidered cowboy boots had a certain inextinguishable elegance. He wore no silver rings or buckles. Only his boots were embroidered and decorated at the top with an inlay of white suède. He seemed elegant, slender, yet he was very strong.

(170)

It is hard not to see Dollie's confusion as a projection of Lawrence's: how Romero's smile "suddenly creased his dark face, showing the strong white teeth. [...] creas[ing] his face almost into a savage grotesque": "And at the same time there was in it something so warm, such a dark flame of kindliness for her, she was elated into her true Princess self." Yet, Lawrence admits, Dollie could never consider marrying the kind, helpful Romero even though he was "in himself a gentleman, and she had plenty of money for two"—in other words, "there was no actual obstacle." Then, this strange passage reflecting what Lawrence may have thought while looking at his original Romero, namely, the odd sense that the two men may have been married already, at least spiritually (their "daemons may have been"), even while their historical selves—the handsome Mexican and his cautious Anglo admirer—were "for some [practical] reason incompatible." Surely, Lawrence ponders, "a peculiar subtle intimacy of inter-recognition between" two such people would not "in the least [...] lead to marriage" (171).

Another thing Dollie shared with Lawrence was a zest for exploring the inner recesses of the high mountain passes, of "want[ing] to descend to the cabin below the spruce trees, near the tarn of bright green water. [...] [of wanting] to see the wild animals move about in their wild unconsciousness." We know Lawrence relished such high-altitude rides:

> Sometimes, crossing stream, she would glance upwards, and then always her heart caught in *my* breast. For high up, away in heaven, the mountain heights shone yellow, dappled with dark spruce firs, clear almost as speckled daffodils against the pale turquoise blue lying high and serene above the dark-blue shadow where she was.
>
> (175)

What started as a three-person travel party was soon reduced to two, Dollie and Romero, when their host could not continue. Meanwhile, Dollie reasons that "Romero was not the kind of man to do anything to her against her will." Besides, she wanted both "to go over the brim of the mountains, to look into the inner chaos of the Rockies," and to do this with Romero, whom she felt "had some peculiar kinship with her." Wasn't being alone, one might say, exposing oneself to danger—lost in "mountains, ponderous, massive, down-sitting mountains, in a huge and intricate knot, empty of life or soul"—the very point of the journey? "It frightened her, it was so inhuman," as it might have frightened Lawrence:

> she had not thought it could be so inhuman, so, as it were, anti-life. And yet now one of her desires was fulfilled. She had seen it, the massive, gruesome, repellent core of the Rockies. She saw it there beneath her eyes, in its gigantic, heavy gruesomeness.
>
> (181)

At the end of their long ride, Dollie and her guide settle into a deserted miner's cabin. After dinner, Dollie, shaking with cold, tries to sleep on the lone bunk while Romero sleeps on the floor. Here, we see the one question of this story and, to some extent, of Lawrence's life: "What did she want? Oh, what did she want?" The one thing she knew she wanted was "warmth, protection, [...] to be taken away from herself." Here we hear a familiar refrain in Lawrence—the grand desire for the unknown hemmed in by an even greater fear:

And at the same time, perhaps more deeply than anything, she wanted to keep herself intact, intact, untouched, that no one should have any power over her, or rights to her. It was a wild necessity in her that no one, particularly no man, should have any rights or power over her, that no one and nothing should possess her.

(188)

Shivering with cold, Dollie finally asks Romero to provide the much-desired warmth, something Lawrence's protagonist could only do under the most extenuating circumstances:

She had never, never wanted to be given over to this. But she had *willed* that it should happen to her. And according to her will, she lay and let it happen. But she never wanted it. She never wanted to be thus assailed and handled, and mauled. She wanted to keep herself to herself. (emphasis in original)

Still, "she had willed it to happen, and it had happened," with Dollie "pant[ing] with relief when it was over."

Nor is such intimacy in Lawrence likely without regret, a disappointment here that quickly morphs into Dollie feeling "like a victim": "And he was exulting in his power over her, his possession, his pleasure" (189).

Matters are no better the next morning, with Dollie intent on escaping and Romero suddenly sounding something like Jessie Chambers, seeking a modicum of emotional warmth after their physical intimacy. And it is here that the tone of the story changes, becoming shrill, not unlike *The Fox*, with Romero transformed like Henry, from an erotic ideal to an over-ardent suitor, and with Dollie uttering familiar Laurentian bromides about resisting having "anybody's will put over me": "You can never get me under your will" (192).

Alas, for Lawrence's Princess, such assertions become the equivalent of a lifetime sentence. Romero, unreconciled to Dollie's rejection, is eventually shot dead by forest rangers while she drifts back into the safety of her father's world, with even her virginity miraculously restored. "[S]lightly crazy," Lawrence tells us, "she married an elderly man, and seemed pleased."

"The Woman Who Rode Away"—No Turning Back

The last story in this chapter, "The Woman Who Rode Away," is in some ways the most difficult to discuss, partly as it has been marked by Millett's scathing remarks in her 1970 treatise, *Sexual Politics*. Nor is this the place to defend Lawrence against all of Millett's charges. As already noted, his attitude toward women was negatively affected by a dislike for his mother, which he had difficulty acknowledging even as he expended so much psychic energy playing the twin roles of the good ("straight") son and the good ("faithful") husband. In his essays, Lawrence often felt freer to air many of his grievances against modern life, including the new roles for women and the changing status of gays, Jews, and people of color. And some of these grievances show up in "The Woman Who Rode Away," including its grotesque last sentence—suggesting that this has been a tale about the "mastery that man must hold, and that passes from race to race" (71). In addition, Millett is right that parts of the story have the glossy, obsessive feel of what she calls "a pornographic dream," noting how one such scene was "shot in MGM technicolor" (288).

Where Millett is least helpful is in her locating Lawrence's presence in this story where we rarely ever find him—as an omniscient narrator or outsider intent on watching, even enjoying his female protagonist brutalized and, at the story's brutal climax, ritually murdered by her Indian captors; as someone, in Millett's words, content to observe "a death which is astounding in the sadism and malice with which it is conceived" (285). Still, we must ask why we should expect to find Lawrence as an observer of such a scene here when, everywhere else we look, we see his feelings deeply entwined with those of his conflicted female protagonists. Such has been the case with the other four stories from this chapter, all involving women who, like the protagonist of "The Woman Who Rode Away," find themselves sorely tempted by a male erotic ideal into leaving a safe but stultifying relationship.

Such was a dilemma that seems to have haunted Lawrence throughout his married life and that also haunts the protagonist of this story—an unnamed 33-year-old woman (Lawrence was 39 during the composition) whose "conscious development had stopped mysteriously with her marriage, completely arrested": "Her husband had never become real to her, neither mentally nor physically" (40). In this complaint, we can hear echoes of the gay adolescent who came to dislike his mother for inhibiting his sensual development, now the adult who seems to feel a similar resentment for a spouse, or, as his protagonist here complains, "Only morally her husband swayed her, downed her, kept her in an invincible slavery."

Yet there is one moment in her analysis of this story where Millett recognizes Lawrence as more than a gleeful observer of his protagonist's degradation, far more than a sadist. Here we come to a second reason that makes this such a peculiar story—namely, Millett's observation that much of the power of this story derives from "needs deep in Lawrence's own nature": "There is as much attention lavished upon the masochistic as upon the sadistic" (288)—that is, from Lawrence's intense identification here with the plight of his unnamed female protagonist.

One difficulty has to do with how quickly Millett seems to dismiss this need in Lawrence as "perverse": "[O]ne perceives a peculiar relish for the [masochistic over the sadistic] in the author," she continues,

> a wallowing in the power of the Indian male, his beauty and indifference and cruelty, exerted not only on the silly woman, his victim, but on Lawrence too. It is the author himself standing fascinated before this silent and darkly beautiful killer, enthralled, aroused, awaiting the sacrificial rape.

Millett thus makes "The Woman Who Rode Away" a problematic story to discuss in two contradictory ways: on the one hand, by relegating Lawrence to the role of sadistic observer and, on the other, by almost gleefully dismissing as "perverse" Lawrence's emotional and psychosexual needs as expressed through his unnamed protagonist. Millett's dismissive, even homophobic claim is that "The Woman Who Rode Away" was written by a disturbed soul—both a sadist who gleefully watches his protagonist suffer and a masochist who gleefully shares her suffering. Our claim, as outlined below, is that this is yet another tale in which Lawrence is using his female protagonist to confront the same obstacle as in these other four stories—the trauma of a life unlived.

There is one element in "The Woman Who Rode Away" that separates it from our first four tales—namely, its overriding feeling of desperation, a raising of the stakes, as it were, that gives the story the quality of a perverse fairy tale in which Lawrence has eliminated the possibility of his protagonist changing her mind—that is, has removed the chance given to Julie in "Sun" to return to her husband even before meeting her would-be lover, or that March in *The Fox* had to equivocate about getting married, or even the chance the Princess of our last story had to turn against her Mexican lover, condemning him to death and herself to a sterile afterlife. Here, in "The Woman Who Rode Away," matters were finally going to be different, with Lawrence creating a narrative structure akin to pornography, where under no circumstance would his stand-in have the option of turning back, where what one wants to happen—even if, or especially if, one is reluctant to admit it—will in due course happen.

Here, then, are two alternate readings of this puzzling story. The first takes the story literally, as an account of an unhappily married woman, 20 years younger than her husband and with two children—the story of a woman whose life is turned upside down simply by overhearing a casual conversation about wild tribes of Indians who inhabit the most remote regions of the nearby mountains. "But don't you suppose it's wonderful, up there in their secret villages?" a young visitor opines, to which her cynical husband demurs: "Savages are savages, and all savages behave more or less alike: rather low-down and dirty, unsanitary, with a few cunning tricks, and struggling to get enough to eat" (42).

This literal reading assumes that this unnamed wife had numerous reasons for disliking her husband, for wanting "to break the monotony of her life," but that Lawrence, ever the astute psychological analyst, has almost nothing else to say about her married life, focusing instead on her fanciful response to an offhand remark by a young visitor—noting how "his peculiar vague enthusiasm for unknown Indians found a full echo in the woman's heart."

Indeed, the story's fairy-tale quality partly derives from this lack of a psychological motive in Lawrence's protagonist. Instead of giving us insight into her past life, Lawrence tells us how she was "overcome by a foolish romanticism more unreal than a girl's": "She felt it was her destiny to wander into the secret haunts of these timeless, mysterious, marvellous Indians of the mountains." And the specific appeal of these particular Indians, the Chilchuis, "living in a high valley to the south, who were the sacred tribe of all the Indians"? Only that they were "descendants of Montezuma and of the old Aztec or Totonac kings [who] still lived among them, and the old priests still kept up the ancient religion, and offered human sacrifices—so it was said" (42).

What follows in this first reading is what Lawrence calls the protagonist's "crazy plans," as noted in the story's title, to ride away, to seek out these Indians literally as a human sacrifice for their ritualistic needs—while the Native Americans, in turn, for a host of unclear reasons, seem eager to murder a blond white woman as a necessary step in recapturing the power of the sun. Taken literally, this is an odd tale of a middle-aged woman's death wish, with little sense of why she is so miserable or why these Indigenous people would be so willing to oblige her—so odd a tale that one can understand why Millett might see it primarily as an outlet for Lawrence's misogyny, a means for creating a scenario whereby he can vicariously put himself in the place of the Chilchui as they ritually and sadistically torture his female protagonist.

There is also an alternate, nonliteral reading of "The Woman Who Rode Away," one that focuses on the similarity between this story and the four previous tales, that is, as another story in which Lawrence was using the plight of his female protagonist to work through a key component of his own complex, unfulfilled sexual life—specifically, the attraction and the fear associated with succumbing to a distant, male erotic ideal. What makes this story different from the other four, as noted before, is the "all-in" quality of the protagonist's relationship with that ideal. Plainly stated, in "The Woman Who Rode Away," Lawrence has created a tale in which, bluntly, there is no turning back from the fate that the protagonist has chosen—the deep bodily penetration that will serve as the story's conclusion.

As noted, Millett was correct in seeing a pornographic element in the story, although this second reading deals entirely with a masochistic, not a sadistic, fantasy. The Indians may be sadistic toward the protagonist's horse. Still, all the sexual energy in the story is in how Lawrence's protagonist responds to the Indians' coldness and the subsequent depersonalization "she" experiences in watching them—for instance, in meeting this Indian's "black, large, bright eyes, [...] for the first time her spirit really quailed." Here, in a sense, was what Lawrence seems to have desired his whole adult life—a cold, distant sexual partner, one with no interest in emotional intimacy, a partner whose "eyes were not human to her"—a partner, in other words, representing the depersonalization that can be such a desired element in sadomasochistic sex, especially for the bottom, for the penetrated partner: "He looked at her with a black, bright inhuman look, and saw no person in her at all. As if she were some strange, unaccountable *thing*, incomprehensible to him, but inimical" (47).

Lawrence's protagonist continues to protest, but her captor is relentless in mistreating her horse: "The woman was powerless. And along with her supreme anger there came a slight thrill of exultation. She knew she was dead" (48)—that is, she knew that finally this adventure would have its climactic end.

The mistreatment continues as our protagonist is directed to a shelter for the night: "She crept in and lay inert. She did not care what happened to her, she was so weary, and so beyond everything." From there, she could see "three men squatting round the fire on their hams, chewing the tortillas they picked from the ashes with their dark fingers, and drinking water from a gourd. They talked in low, muttering tones, with long intervals of silence"—these men who were "not interested in her nor her belongings." And then, that now-familiar mixture of fear and excitement:

> There they squatted with their hats on their heads, eating, eating mechanically, like animals, the dark sarape with its fringe falling to the ground before and behind, the powerful dark legs naked and squatting like an animal's, showing the dirty white shirt and the sort of loin-cloth which was the only other garment, underneath. And they showed no more sign of interest in her than if she had been a piece of venison they were bringing home from the hunt, and had hung inside a shelter.
> (49)

Later, she is questioned; when she offers no resistance, she senses "an extraordinary thrill of triumph and exultance passing through the Indians": "Then they all looked at her with piercing black eyes, in which a steely covetous intent glittered incomprehensible" (52).

If Lawrence is hiding in this protagonist, her plight does take on the gleam of sadomasochistic pornography. With his protagonist "the more puzzled," he writes, "as there was nothing sensual or sexual in [this] look": "It had a terrible glittering purity that was beyond her. She was afraid, she would have been paralysed with fear, had not something died within her, leaving her with a cold, watchful wonder only."

Millett is correct that such scenes have the feel of technicolor pornography:

> a drum started on a high beat, and there came the deep, powerful burst of men singing a heavy, savage music, like a wind roaring in some timeless forest, many mature men singing in one breath, like the wind; and long lines of dancers walked out from under the big house:
>   Men with naked, golden-bronze bodies and streaming black hair, tufts of red and yellow feathers on their arms, and kilts of white frieze with a bar of heavy red and black and green embroidery round their waists, bending slightly forward and stamping the earth in their absorbed, monotonous stamp of the dance, a fox-fur, hung by the nose from their belt behind, swaying with the sumptuous swaying of a beautiful fox-fur, the tip of the tail writhing above the dancer's heels.
>
> (59)

And what of Lawrence's protagonist? Watching "for hours and hours," we learn—"spell-bound, and as if drugged." There, amid "the terrible persistence of the drumming and the primeval, rushing deep singing, and the endless stamping of the dance of fox-tailed men," she "seemed at last to feel her own death; her own obliteration."

What initially might look like blatant misogyny—"Her kind of womanhood, intensely personal and individual, was to be obliterated again"—can be readily rewritten in non-gendered language to suggest that Lawrence's principal concern here is the erotic excitement connected to the loss of one's ego, that sense of hollowing out experienced by the submissive sexual partner, male or female. What follows then is that "intensely personal and individual [self waiting] [...] to be obliterated": "the great primeval symbols were to tower once more over [one's] fallen individual independence."

Meanwhile, the "sharpness and the quivering nervous consciousness of [our] highly-bred [selves] was to be destroyed again," our distinct sense of self "cast once more into the great stream of impersonal sex and impersonal passion": "Strangely, as if clairvoyant, she saw the immense sacrifice prepared. And she went back to her little house in a trance of agony."

Later, Lawrence's protagonist is given an herbal drink that would "numb her mind altogether, and release her senses into a sort of heightened, mystic acuteness and a feeling as if she were diffusing out deliciously into the harmony of things."

What one sees here are the various preparations for an implicit sexual event, all without a hint of the emotional intimacy that the young Paul Morel seemed to blame for ruining his first sexual experiences with Jessie Chambers. Such is the realization of Lawrence's protagonist here—what "at length became the only state of consciousness she really recognised: this exquisite sense of bleeding out into the higher beauty and harmony of things" (62).

What follows is a ceremonial bath, also with unmistakable erotic overtones:

In the darkness and in the silence she was accurately aware of everything that happened to her: how they took off her clothes, and, standing her before a great, weird device on the wall, coloured blue and white and black, washed her all over with water and the amole infusion.

(66)

Then, more on the excitement of anticipation, heightened by this abiding sense of detachment.

What follows is, for Lawrence's protagonist, unmistakably, a thrill: "They were so impersonal, absorbed in something that was beyond her. They never saw her as a personal woman: she could tell that." But it is also the feeling of anyone who welcomes being stripped of his or her personhood: "She was some mystic object to them, some vehicle of passions too remote for her to grasp."

Then, still more technicolor sadism or, more aptly, masochism, as Lawrence's protagonist finds herself in a trance, "watch[ing her captors'] faces bending over her, dark, strangely glistening with the transparent red paint, and lined with bars of yellow." As always, Lawrence returns to the captors' detachment—their "unchanging steadfast gleam, and the purplish-pigmented lips [...] closed in a full, sinister, sad grimness":

The immense fundamental sadness, the grimness of ultimate decision, the fixity of revenge, and the nascent exultance of those that are going to triumph—these things she could read in their faces, as she lay and was rubbed into a misty glow, by their uncanny dark hands. Her limbs, her flesh, her very bones at last seemed to be diffusing into a roseate sort of mist, in which her consciousness hovered like some sun-gleam in a flushed cloud.

(67)

It is hardly original to suggest a general connection between Lawrence and the French philosopher Michel Foucault. If so, one prescient connection is in this celebration of pleasure—anal pleasure, particularly—thoroughly detached from any form of morality or "love," a pleasure instead associated with the near-total loss of self-consciousness. This is less the Foucault of his voluminous histories of sexuality than the man who frequented and wrote about the leather bathhouses of San Francisco's Castro District, well chronicled in James Miller's *The Passion of Michel Foucault*. It was here that Foucault could live out what Lawrence seems only to have imagined and then could write about only in the coded form we have just examined—only here, Miller contends, that Foucault could fulfill his "lifelong fascination with 'the overwhelming, the unspeakable, the creepy, the stupefying, the ecstatic,' embracing 'a pure violence, a wordless gesture' ": "I think the kind of pleasure I would consider as *the* real pleasure," Foucault continues, as if providing a gloss on Lawrence's story, "would be so deep, so intense, so overwhelming that I couldn't survive it"; or as he explained in another interview, "Complete total pleasure [...] for me, it's related to death" (27, emphasis in original).

Or, as Lawrence writes in "The Woman Who Rode Away," with only slightly more circumspection, although again hiding behind the third-person pronoun:

> She knew the gleam would fade, the cloud would go grey. But at present she did not believe it. She knew she was a victim; that all this elaborate work upon her was the work of victimising her. But she did not mind. She wanted it.
>
> (67)

The final triumph in this story thus belongs, not as Millett suggests, to the captors, but to Lawrence's protagonist and her willing surrender to the "oldest man" among her captors, one who stood in "absolute motionlessness," one whose eyes "in their black, empty concentration [revealed] power, power intensely abstract and remote" (71).

Lawrence's fascination with male-to-male anal sex is best seen like Foucault's in terms of what psychiatry professor Jeffrey Guss deems its universal, boundary-breaking nature—what he labels a practice of "complex erotic rituals [...] embodied through enactments of power, surrender, trust, transgression, pleasure, arousal and release." The pleasure in such an activity, Guss continues, is "derived not only from internal sensation and its meanings, but also relationally, through the trust and body boundary transgressions that constitute anal sex itself." One result of these "often difficult and arduous sex practices" is a sort of "spiritual transformation"—

the top and bottom co-creat[ing] a sacred, ecstatic celebration of masculinity, rugged and tender, intimate and transcendent, Dionysian and
reverent. The result is homoerotic redemption, as outlawed desire is
transformed into an erotic brotherhood in which abjected sexuality and
desire become a path toward acceptance and community.

(41)

Regardless of how one feels about Guss's interpretation, it is hard to
deny the connection between the notion of brotherhood and community enunciated here and the cosmic affiliation that Lawrence sought
after for so much of his life—the germ, for instance, at the heart of his
vision of Rananim, his much-discussed but futile plan for a community of
like-minded souls. It is in this dream of Rananim, as well as in his many
beautifully rendered texts, that we can see something deeply humane and
far-reaching in Lawrence's complex emotional nature—and what Millett
seems to miss in her critique—namely, the sense in which Lawrence did
indeed live up to that key term from *Lady Chatterley's Lover*, "tender-
hearted," although, perhaps most accurately, in his idealized relations
with other men.

Nor, to repeat, was man-to-man sodomy for Lawrence likely ever more
than a deeply repressed impetus for his extraordinary imagination. Or as
Plato notes in *The Republic*,

Of our unnecessary pleasures and appetites there are some lawless ones,
[...] which probably are to be found in us all, but which, when controlled by the laws and the better desires in alliance with reason, can in
some men be altogether got rid of, or so nearly so that only a few weak
ones remain.

(798)

—especially for a sickly boy reared in a small mining community, while
closely nurtured by a hypervigilant, prudish mother fixated on respectability—
his first 16 years of life under the reign of Queen Victoria herself.

Such are the desires, Plato continues,

that are awakened in sleep when the rest of the soul, the rational, gentle
and dominant part, slumbers, but the beastly and savage part, replete
with food and wine, gambols and, repelling sleep, endeavors to sally
forth and satisfy its own instincts

—or, for a great writer with an unfathomable literary imagination,
sallies forth in his writings, and, at least for Lawrence, most often and
most explicitly expressed in the struggles of a female protagonist.

Works Cited

Freud, Sigmund. "A Child Is Being Beaten." In *Sexuality and the Psychology of Love*. Basic Books, 1997: 97–122.

———. "The Economic Problem of Masochism." In *The Ego and the Id and Other Works*. Standard Edition, Vol 19. London: Hogarth P, 1961: 155–70.

Guss, Jeffrey. "Men, Anal Sex and Desire: Who Wants What?" Psychoanalysis, *Culture & Society*, 12, 2007: 38–43.

Lawrence, D. H. *Complete Works*. Delphi Classics, 2015.

———. *The Fox; The Captain's Doll; The Ladybird*. Ed. Dieter Mehl. Penguin Books, 1994.

———. "Getting On." In *Late Essays and Articles*. Ed. James T. Boulton. Cambridge UP, 2004: 25–32.

———. "The Ladybird." In *The Fox ; The Captain's Doll; The Ladybird*. Ed. Dieter Mehl. Penguin Books, 1994: 155–222.

———. *Letters of D. H. Lawrence*. Vol. 1: September 1901 – May 1913. Ed. James T. Boulton. Cambridge UP, 1979.

———. "The Princess." In *St. Mawr and Other Stories*. Ed. Brian Finney. Cambridge UP, 2002: 157–95.

———. "Samson and Delilah." In *England, My England and Other Stories*. Ed. Bruce Steele. Cambridge UP, 2002: 108–22.

———. "The Soiled Rose." *The Blue Review*. May 1913: 6–23. Online text: https://repository.library.brown.edu/studio/item/bdr:452099/PDF/

———. "Sun." In *The Woman Who Rode Away and Other Stories*. Eds. Dieter Mehl and Christa Jansohn. Cambridge UP, 2002: 19–38.

———. *The White Peacock*. Ed. Andrew Robertson. Cambridge UP, 2002.

———. *The Woman Who Rode Away and Other Stories*. Eds. Dieter Mehl and Christa Jansohn. Cambridge UP, 2002: 39–71.

Miller, James. *The Passion of Michel Foucault*. Simon & Schuster, 1993.

Millett, Kate. *Sexual Politics*. Touchstone Book, 1990.

Plato. *The Collected Dialogues*. Eds. Edith Hamilton and Huntington Cairns. Princeton UP, 1961.

8   His Father's Body

Early in *The White Peacock*—a novel that Lawrence began when he was 20 and published five years later—Cyril Beardsall, the first of his many fictional stand-ins, and a friend were on an evening stroll when they were disturbed by a strange murmur from "where a great tree had fallen," its "crooked bough [making] a beautiful seat for two." However, instead of finding hidden lovers interrupting their peaceful walk, they stumble across a man "muttering through his sleep"—a man who might be considered the antithesis of Lawrence's erotic ideal. His clothing was "good, but slovenly and neglected," while his face was "pale and worn with sickness and dissipation." Lawrence's intent here was to show the harmful effects of alcohol, as this old man's "grey beard wagged, and his loose unlovely mouth moved in indistinct speech." This odd figure seemed to be "acting over again some part of his life [...] He would give a little groan, gruesome to hear and then talk to some woman. His features twitched as if with pain, and he moaned slightly" (22).

Such was the introduction of Lawrence's father into print—the first appearance of arguably the most important figure in his imaginative life, one who would reappear in the guise of Greiffenhagen's shepherd and countless other forms. Only this time, the father is not recognized by the son and, later in the novel, is dismissed as a reprobate by the rest of his family, even as they are summoned to his deathbed. Cyril, we learn, has to strain to remember him—his only positive memory was that of "a tall, handsome, dark man with pale grey eyes [that] was made up from my mother's few words, and from a portrait I had once seen" (33).

What else Cyril remembers is mainly negative, often reflecting his mother's view of her husband's character—as a man "of frivolous, rather vulgar character [...] a liar, without notion of honesty, [who] [...] had deceived my mother thoroughly": "One after another she discovered his mean dishonesties and deceits, and her soul revolted from him, and

DOI: 10.4324/9781003495093-8

because the illusion of him had broken into a thousand vulgar fragments," his mother turned away "with the scorn of a woman who finds her romance has been a trumpery tale." His mother, we learn, "rejoiced bitterly" when his father left home, moving on to "other pleasures" some 18 years earlier (33).

By the time Cyril and his mother arrive, "the man [he] had seen in the woods" is already dead, "the puffiness gone from his face," and now the tone changes, with Cyril feeling "the great wild pity, and a sense of terror, and a sense of horror, and a sense of awful littleness and loneliness among a great empty space" (37). As Keith Cushman has indicated, here we can see a premonition of his father's first commanding role in Lawrence's literary imagination, far more visible in his early short story "Odour of Chrysanthemums," drafted and revised during the final stages of *The White Peacock*.

"Odour of Chrysanthemums"

"Odour of Chrysanthemums" is the story that seems to fulfill Paul Morel's wish, or perhaps nightmare, as a child that his father would somehow stop terrorizing his mother and family, although not in the manner of this story, by dying in a mining accident and having his body carried home to be prepared for burial. Walter Bates, the deceased miner, has a young son and daughter, but unlike with *Sons and Lovers*, Lawrence has no interest in telling this story from the boy's perspective. Instead, he displays his lyrical genius here at the start of his career, as he will do throughout his career, by placing himself in the role of the strong man's admirer—in this story, reimagining himself here as the miner's wife, Elizabeth, and giving to her solely an expanded sense of wonder and sympathy that we just glimpsed in Cyril's response in *The White Peacock* to seeing his father's corpse.

Elizabeth, assisted by Mrs. Bates, Walter's mother, begins by disrobing the body. As the two women "saw him lying in the naïve dignity of death," Lawrence writes, they "stood arrested in fear and respect"—the wife overcome by "how utterly inviolable he lay in himself." Because of the mine's heat, Walter was still warm: "Elizabeth embraced the body of her husband, with cheek and lips. She seemed to be listening, inquiring, trying to get some connection. But she could not. She was driven away. He was impregnable" (103).

Mrs. Bates watched as Elizabeth "carefully washed [her husband's] face, carefully brushing the big blond moustache from his mouth with the flannel." "He was a man of handsome body," Lawrence notes, "and his face showed no traces of drink. He was blonde, full flushed, with fine limbs." "White as milk he is, clear as a twelve-month baby," Mrs. Bates adds, "bless him, the darling! [...] Not a mark on him, clear and clean and white, beautiful as ever a child was made" (104).

Before looking at Elizabeth's soaring monologue that concludes this story, turning it into an early triumph of Lawrence's lyrical imagination, we first briefly consider three other scenes involving the eroticized ideal of a miner's body: two from *Sons and Lovers* and one from the short story "Daughters of the Vicar."

The first scene from *Sons and Lovers* involves a conversation that Paul has with Miriam about the "real joy and satisfaction" that he now believes his otherwise priggish mother must have formerly had from his father: "I believe she had a passion for him; that's why she stayed with him." This attitude differs from Lawrence's summary in *The White Peacock* of the discord that the father supposedly wrecked upon Cyril's family. It is almost as if Lawrence now has Paul imagining what he would have felt had he been in his mother's place. " 'That's what one must have, I think,' [Paul] continued—'the real, real flame of feeling through another person—once, only once, if it only lasts three months' " (317).

The "woman" in this passage sounds less like Gertrude Morel or Lydia Lawrence than the young Lawrence breaking free of his mother's control and imagining what a vibrant young person might have felt in the presence of such a man. "And with my father, at first," he continued, "I'm sure she had the real thing. She knows; she has been there." Paul believes such a feeling had to be reciprocal:

> You can feel it about her, and about him [...] [It's] something big and intense that changes you when you really come together with somebody else. It almost seems to fertilize your soul and make it that you can go on and mature.
>
> And you think your mother had it with your father?" Miriam asks, clearly placing the focus where Lawrence wants it—oddly, on the sexual feeling his mother must have felt with his father, which Paul agrees his mother must have been grateful for "even now, though they are miles apart.

Miriam now senses that this is what Paul must also be seeking—"a sort of baptism of fire in passion." She seems to see Paul's remarks as a regular part of a boy's growing up, as something that was "essential to him, as to some men, to sow wild oats," thus glossing over the fact that the entire subject of this discussion about sexual initiation—something about which "he would never be satisfied till he had it" (318)—had been entirely focused not on his father's sexual satisfaction but his mother's. Here, in other words, we see the germ of what this study has tried to show as the dominant thread in Lawrence's life—seeing his erotic ideal not in a woman like his mother but in a man like his father, that is, in Freud's notion of the negative Oedipus complex noted in the previous chapter, where the boy behaves more like a girl, "display[ing] an affectionate feminine attitude to his father."

The second scene from *Sons and Lovers* depicts his father's Friday night bathing ritual. On this night, his father complains about the cold of the scullery blowing through his thin frame and his mother teasing him for no longer having a young man's figure. Paul's mother laughs off the father's retort, saying that he's "nobbut a sack o' faggots," with Lawrence's narrator ready to take sides, carefully noting how his father

> had still a wonderfully young body, muscular, without any fat. His skin was smooth and clear. It might have been the body of a man of twenty-eight, except that there were, perhaps, too many blue scars, like tattoo-marks, where the coal-dust remained under the skin, and that his chest was too hairy.
>
> (197)

And his mother then seconds his observation, adding, "Never a man had a better start, if it was body that counted" (236).

One can hardly overstate the importance of this short scene of the young Paul Morel watching his father bathe, much as Connie would later watch Mellors. It is a scene that Lawrence would recreate, often from the point of view of an admiring female. Such was the case in "Daughters of the Vicar," a story Lawrence composed while working on *Sons and Lovers*. In it, the main character and observer of the bathing miner is one of the title's daughters, Louisa Lindley, a young woman struggling to break free from her family's petty gentility: from her Vicar father and, more to the point, his wife, a censorious woman very much in the mold of Lawrence's mother—a woman, "[w]ounded to the quick of her pride, [who] found herself isolated in an indifferent, callous population." One result of her isolation was her seeing "herself hating her husband"—a condition liable to wreck her entire family:

> she knew that, unless she were careful, she would smash her form of life and bring catastrophe upon him and upon herself. So in very fear, she went quiet. She hid, bitter and beaten by fear, behind the only shelter she had in the world, her gloomy, poor parsonage.
>
> (107)

When Louisa's older sister safely marries another cleric, a weak, tiny man "scarcely larger than a boy of twelve," Louisa's means of escape involves her eventual attachment to a man in the mold of Lawrence's father, the miner Alfred Durant. Lawrence's plot has Louisa nursing Durant's mother, who has fallen seriously ill with a tumor, as Alfred returns from his shift at the mine, and thus becomes responsible for helping with his dinner—something she found "strange and exciting." "She was strung up tense," Lawrence notes, as she watched him "turned away from his food, looking in the fire":

> Her soul watched him, trying to see what he was. His black face and arms were uncouth, he was foreign. His face was masked black with coal-dust. She could not see him, she could not even know him. The brown eyebrows, the steady eyes, the coarse, small moustache above the closed mouth—these were the only familiar indications.
>
> (136)

At the request of Alfred's mother—"He can't bear if his back isn't washed"—Louisa agrees to assist with his bath. When she enters, she finds Alfred "kneeling on the hearthrug," like Mellors and Greiffenhagen's shepherd, "stripped to the waist," washing as he did every evening, "in a large panchion of earthenware." All this felt strange, even threatening to Louisa—"the almost repulsive intimacy being forced upon her"—as she watched Alfred

> mechanically rubbing the white lather on his head, with a repeated, unconscious movement, his hand every now and then passing over his neck. [...] She had to brace herself to this also. He bent his head into the water, washed it free of soap, and pressed the water out of his eyes.
>
> (137)

Louisa is not unlike Connie Chatterley in her most intense lovemaking moments, "los[ing] her own distinctness." Louisa, however, is far from certain she is ready for such abandonment, remembering her mother's warning about "the difference between her [daughter] and the common people." Still, what follows can be seen as a prequel to Connie's passion so apparent in *Lady Chatterley's Lover*, with Lawrence's presence throughout this scene palpable even in the third-person narration.

As Alfred's bath continues, he plunges his arms into the dark water, with Louisa "scarcely [able to] conceive him as human." Acting out of habit, Alfred "groped in the black water, fish[ing] out soap and flannel, and hand[ing] them backward to [her]": "Then he remained rigid and submissive, his two arms thrust straight in the panchion, supporting the weight of his shoulders. His skin was beautifully white and unblemished, of an opaque, solid whiteness."

Louisa was fascinated: "this also was what he was"—not just a miner but a man. "Her feeling of separateness passed away: she ceased to draw back from contact with him and his mother." Here, she realized, was a different sort of "living centre":

> Her heart ran hot. She had reached some goal in this beautiful, clear, male body. She loved him in a white, impersonal heat. But the sunburnt, reddish neck and ears: they were more personal, more curious. A tenderness rose in her, she loved even his queer ears. A person—an intimate being he was to her. She put down the towel and went upstairs again, troubled in her heart. She had only seen one human being in her life—and that was Mary. All the rest were strangers. Now her soul was going to open, she was going to see another. She felt strange and pregnant.
>
> (137)

This bathing scene from "Daughters of the Vicar" is a beautiful evocation of a scene that seems to have haunted Lawrence—that of someone, nominally a woman, letting go, experiencing for the first time the wonder of what it is to love a man. Even as Lawrence was finding such an expressive outlet for his genius, he was also hard at work (given its labored quality, likely harder at work) on a far different sort of text, *The Study of Thomas Hardy*, an unpublished treatise, nominally on the English novelist, but containing lengthy musings on a different matter that we have already seen which also preoccupied Lawrence—namely, the various difficulties men endure in living with women. It is as if the lyrical diamond that is Lawrence's treatment of Alfred's bath—this miner as another scopophilic ideal—turns to coal dust once the object of sexual arousal is no longer a man.

While Lawrence's goal in such a tract might be noble—to praise marriage and heterosexuality—his tone quickly becomes didactic, even hectoring, much as we saw in Chapter 4 in his letter to his Croydon colleague, Arthur McLeod. Just who is the subject of this discourse? Who is it that needs to be convinced that the

> supreme desire of every man is for mating with a woman, such that the sexual act be the closest, most concentrated motion in his life, closest upon the axle, the prime movement of himself, of which all the rest of his motion is a continuance in the same kind?

Or that

> the vital desire of every woman is that she shall be clasped as axle to the hub of the man, that his motion shall portray her motionlessness,

convey her static being into movement, complete and radiating out into infinity, starting from her stable eternality, and reaching eternity again, after having covered the whole of time?

(*Study* 56)

What are we to make of two such texts—one intensely lyrical, the other argumentative? The question returns us to where we began in Chapter 1, looking at Charlotte Brontë's struggle to write about the joys of spring with the same passion and dazzling lyricism with which she describes the pain of winter. Poor Lawrence, one might add, never escaping Brontë's dilemma! At least he recognized a certain futility in his role as prophet, adding this graceless observation about the futility of "this complete movement: man upon woman, woman within man": "This is the desire, the achieving of which, frictionless, is impossible, yet for which every man will try, with greater or less intensity, achieving more or less success."

The final published version of Lawrence's story "Odour of Chrysanthemums" ends with an early example (from 1911) of the *hidden* Lawrence—a grand interior monologue nominally recording the thoughts of Elizabeth Bates, the dead miner's wife and, like so many of Lawrence's most lyrical and erstwhile autobiographical passages, written in the third person. This selection is so moving, less for what either Elizabeth Bates or Lydia Lawrence lost—his mother predeceased his father by 14 years—than for what it says about Lawrence's nascent realization of what his father's presence came to mean in his psychic life.

"For as she looked at the dead man, her mind, cold and detached," this central passage begins. "Who am I? What have I been doing?" the wife asks. "I have been fighting a husband who did not exist"—or, possibly in Lawrence's mind, "fighting a father," one who had "existed all the time." "What wrong have I done?" the passage continues, the speaker filled with regret over never having "seen him" for who he was, the two of them only meeting and fighting "in the dark, not knowing whom they met nor whom they fought." The wife's words might as well have been the son's:

And now she saw, and turned silent in seeing. For she had been wrong. She had said he was something he was not; she had felt familiar with him. Whereas he was apart all the while, living as she never lived, feeling as she never felt.

(104)

The whole passage can be readily rendered in the first person—"And now *I* saw, and turned silent in seeing"—recording that often repeated sense of anguish in Lawrence emanating from that feeling of some distant but deeply fulfilling attachment having been forever ripped out of his life. Nor is it a coincidence that the story itself was one of Lawrence's earliest successes, perhaps the first instance of his giving a palpable form to his longing to recapture such a broken connection, in this case, if not with his actual father—Arthur Lawrence was very much alive and would remain alive another 11 years—then with that distant sense of male power his father came to stand for in his imagination.

"In fear and shame," Lawrence wrote, again nominally about the deceased miner's wife,

> she looked at his naked body, that she had known falsely. [...] Her soul was torn from her body and stood apart. [...] Now he was dead, she knew how eternally he was apart from her, how eternally he had nothing more to do with her. She saw this episode of her life closed. They had denied each other in life. Now he had withdrawn. An anguish came over her.
>
> (105)

In the story, Elizabeth eventually dresses her dead husband—"almost ashamed to handle him," questioning anyone's right "to lay hands on him":

> It was hard work to clothe him. He was so heavy and inert. A terrible dread gripped her all the while: that he could be so heavy and utterly inert, unresponsive, apart. The horror of the distance between them was almost too much for her—it was so infinite a gap she must look across.

Then the two women covered the father with a sheet "and left him lying, with his face bound," tidying the kitchen with the same home-making skills that visitors remarked upon seeing in Lawrence. And it is Lawrence, the son, who matters the most here, the young Lawrence who must have sensed, even as he penned this wondrous story, the lifetime of estrangement awaiting him. The story ends with this recognition, spoken through the miner's wife, of death as our "ultimate master," from which one recoils "with fear and shame."

In Italy, Dreaming of Men

From Lawrence's first book of travel essays, *Twilight in Italy* (1916), based on travels with Frieda soon after their elopement, comes this ethereal portrait of an Italian local, Faustino or *Il Duro*—a "very handsome" man, Lawrence writes, "beautiful rather, a man of thirty-two or -three, with a clear golden skin, and perfectly turned face, something godlike." "His hair," he continues, "was jet black and fine and smooth, glossy as a bird's wing, his brows were beautifully drawn, calm above his grey eyes, that had long dark lashes." And, as one might expect with any of Lawrence's manly shepherds, *Il Duro's* beauty is hardly without its sinister side. His eyes, for instance, had "a sinister light in them, a pale, slightly repelling gleam, very much like a god's pale-gleaming eyes, with the same vivid pallor. And all his face had the slightly malignant, suffering look of a satyr. Yet he was very beautiful" (173).

Everything about this erstwhile simple Italian fascinates Lawrence, starting with his quick walk,

> with his head rather down, passing from his desire to his object, absorbed, yet curiously indifferent, as if the transit were in a strange world [...] Yet he did it for his own pleasure, and the light on his face, a pale, strange gleam through his clear skin, remained like a translucent smile, unchanging as time.

Lawrence cannot quite understand the effect *Il Duro* has on him, other than knowing that he was "curiously attractive and curiously beautiful"— that is, at least to Lawrence. He was

> like stone in his clear colouring and his clear-cut face. His temples, with the black hair, were distinct and fine as a work of art. [...] [H]is eyes had this strange, half-diabolic, half-tortured pale gleam, like a goat's, and his mouth was shut almost uglily, his cheeks stern. [...] He was clear and fine as semi-transparent rock, as a substance in moonlight. [...] like a crystal that has achieved its final shape and has nothing more to achieve.
>
> (177)

Here again, we see the same scopophilic delight in viewing an imposing man—"All the morning and the afternoon he was among the vines, crouching before them, cutting them back with his sharp, bright knife, amazingly swift and sure, like a god"—albeit now, in a travel memoir:

> It filled me with a sort of panic to see him crouched flexibly, like some strange animal god, doubled on his haunches, before the young vines, and swiftly, vividly, without thought, cut, cut, cut at the young budding shoots, which fell unheeded on to the earth. Then again he strode with his curious half-goatlike movement across the garden, to prepare the lime [...] He was not a worker. He was a creature in intimate communion with the sensible world, knowing purely by touch the limey mess he mixed.

Watching *Il Duro* like this, as "he strode over the earth, a gleaming piece of earth himself, moving to the young vines," reminds Lawrence of something in his distant past or possibly something near-mythic in our more expansive collective past, as if one were watching "God grafting the life of man upon the body of the earth, intimately conjuring with his own flesh."

Here was a creature, "bestial, and yet godlike crouching before the plant, as if he were the god of lower life," a mythic, Greiffenhagen-like figure living in isolation: "So he could not marry, it was not for him. He belonged to the god Pan, to the absolute of the senses"—that rare, uneasy blending of attraction and fear associated with fathers. "All the while his beauty, so perfect and so defined, fascinated me, a strange static perfection about him," but then to see him

> crouched before the vines on his haunches, his haunches doubled together in a complete animal unconsciousness, his face seeming in its strange golden pallor and its hardness of line, with the gleaming black of the fine hair on the brow and temples

—to see all that was too unsettling, "like the reflecting surface of a stone that gleams out of the depths of night" (178).

Finally, Lawrence decides—and here one senses a great sigh of relief, caught as he was describing this attraction for the Italian laborer—that there was "nothing between us except our complete difference," the two of them, "like night and day flowing together."

Then, five years later, in a second travel book, *Sea and Sardinia*, Lawrence recounts his first day in Cagliari, having tea with Frieda at a local café. At one point, he becomes fascinated by a nursemaid, "bright as a poppy," who has accompanied a large family, describing her attire with a novelist's attention to detail, noting her "rose-scarlet dress of fine cloth, with a curious little waistcoat of emerald green and purple, and a bodice of soft, homespun linen with great full sleeves" (62). Interesting observations, to be sure, and made with the same attention to women's clothes we have seen before—that is, without a hint of desire.

How quickly matters change when Lawrence looks across the road and sees his "first peasant"—"an elderly, upright, handsome man, beautiful in the black-and-white costume." Just as seeing the dexterous worker years later in Ceylon would trigger thoughts of his father, Lawrence is shaken by spying this peasant in his "full-sleeved white shirt and the close black bodice of thick, native frieze, cut low." Almost immediately, there is a flow of details: of the "short kilt or frill, of the same black frieze, a band of which goes between the legs, between the full loose drawers of coarse linen"; how these drawers "are banded below the knee into tight black

frieze gaiters," and his "long black stocking cap, hanging down behind."
Whereas he was a neutral observer in his earlier account of the nursemaid,
he does nothing to hide his feelings here: "How handsome he is, and so
beautifully male!" he adds. "He walks with his hands loose behind his
back, slowly, upright, and aloof."

Nor is it surprising that what he finds attractive should be distant and
slightly menacing—"The lovely unapproachableness, indomitable." In
part, it was the colors—"the flash of the black and white"; in part, the
man's insouciance—

> the slow stride of the full white drawers, the black gaiters and black
> cuirass with the bolero, then the great white sleeves and white breast
> again, and once more the black cap—what marvellous massing of the
> contrast, marvellous, and superb, as on a magpie.

All summed up in this unguarded expression of delight: "How beautiful
maleness is, if it finds its right expression."

Then Lawrence sees a second peasant, this time "a young one with a
swift eye and hard cheek and hard, dangerous thighs. [...] [who] wears a
close knee breeches and close sleeved waistcoat of thick brownish stuff that
looks like leather." "How fascinating it is," Lawrence adds, "after the soft
Italians," to see something else, something that reverberates within him—
"to see these limbs in their close knee-breeches, so definite, so manly, with
the old fierceness in them still" (63).

As noted by Dennis Porter, it seems as if something about a "curious,
flashing, black-and-white costume" has struck a deep chord in Lawrence,
a note similar to what we have just seen in the grieving wife's lament in
"Odour of Chrysanthemums," something haunting the very presence of
Greiffenhagen's shepherd. "I seem to have known it before," Lawrence
continues—"to have worn it even: to have dreamed it. To have dreamed
it: to have had actual contact with it. It belongs in some way to something
in me—to my past, perhaps." He admits not knowing: "But the uneasy
sense of blood-familiarity haunts me. I know I have known it before."

Here, Lawrence may be echoing Aristophanes's speech from Plato's
Symposium about the intense nostalgia we feel having been cut off from our
other half, how, when we suddenly meet that person, we are "wondrously
struck with friendship, attachment, and love," not knowing exactly what
it is we want from that other person: "What it is, it is incapable of saying,
but it divines what it wants and speaks in riddles."

Such perhaps is the conundrum at the center of his comments on
"a persistent passionate fear-dream about horses" in *Fantasia of the
Unconscious*—a dream we might have of those majestic animals with
"powerful, almost beautiful physical bodies." What does it mean, he

asks, if someone like myself "suddenly finds himself among great, physical horses, which may suddenly go wild. Their great bodies surge madly round him, they rear above him, threatening to destroy him. At any minute he may be trampled down" (199).

Here is Lawrence possibly confronting his only brittle nature, albeit still speaking only of a generic *man*, someone whose "greatest desire" is here represented by "a menace"—"The spontaneous self [...] secretly yearning for the liberation and fulfillment of the deepest and most powerful sensual nature." Then comes an even more probing insight, also encased in generic terms, suggesting that such a man is possibly dealing with "an element of father-complex"—the individual horse "refer[ring] to the powerful sensual being in the father. The dream may mean a love of the dreamer for the sensual male who is his father" (200).

One wonders if such a horse might not be part of the herd of horses that blocked Ursula's path, "burst[ing] before her," at the end of *The Rainbow*—"In a sort of lightning of knowledge their movement travelled through her, the quiver and strain and thrust of their powerful flanks, as they burst before her and drew on, beyond." Lawrence knew what it was to be conscious of their sexual power—

> their red nostrils flaming with long endurance, and of their haunches, so rounded, so massive, pressing, pressing, pressing to burst the grip upon their breasts, pressing for ever till they went mad, running against the walls of time, and never bursting free.

To be conscious of "their great haunches [...] smoothed and darkened with rain"; of "the darkness and wetness of rain [that] could not put out the hard, urgent, massive fire that was locked within these flanks, never, never" (452).

The following morning in Cagliari, we again find Lawrence attending to the routine inconveniences of tourist life, this time searching for milk for his coffee—when he stops to comment on a group of workers hauling a heavy chest using tiny Sardinian donkeys, animals so small that they make "a boy walking at their side look like a tall man." Such small talk stops when he suddenly sees not Ursula's horses but two more peasants dressed in that same black and white outfit as he had seen the day before, only now realizing that his "dream of last evening was not a dream"— that these men in these costumes had awakened a sense of a distant, unacknowledged desire, a powerful but comforting male presence that he had once known but now seems to have forgotten. Or, as Lawrence continues,

And my nostalgia for something I know not what was not an illusion. I feel it again, at once, at the sight of the men in frieze and linen, a heart yearning for something I have known, and which I want back again.

(64)

"Something I have known [...] which I want back again"! Yes—don't we all?

Works Cited

Cushman, Keith. "D. H. Lawrence at Work: The Making of 'Odour of Chrysanthemums.'" *Journal of Modern Literature*, 2 (Winter), 1971–72: 367–92.

Freud, Sigmund. "The Ego and the Id." In *The Freud Reader*. Ed. Peter Gay. W.W. Norton, 1989: 628–58.

Lawrence, D. H. "Daughters of the Vicar." In *Selected Stories*. Ed. Brian Finney. Penguin Books, 1982: 106–51.

———. "Odour of Chrysanthemum." In *Selected Short Stories*. Ed. Brian Finney. Penguin Books, 1982: 88–105.

———. *Psychoanalysis and the Unconscious and Fantasia of the Unconscious*. Viking P, 1960.

———. *The Rainbow*. Ed. Mark Kinkead-Weekes. Penguin Books, 1995.

———. *Sea and Sardinia*. Ed. Mara Kalnins. Cambridge UP, 1997.

———. *Sons and Lovers*. Viking P, 1971.

———. *Study of Thomas Hardy and Other Essays*. Ed. Bruce Steele. Cambridge UP, 1985.

———. *Twilight in Italy and Other Essays*. Paul Eggert. Cambridge UP, 2002.

———. *The White Peacock*. Ed. Andrew Robertson. Cambridge UP, 2002.

Porter, Dennis. "The Other Italy: D. H. Lawrence." In *Haunted Journeys: Desire and Transgression in European Travel Writing*. Princeton UP, 1991: 202–22.

9 In Australia

Man Alone

Lawrence and Frieda arrived in Australia in May 1922, as he was working on the "honeymoon" section of the unfinished *Mr. Noon*, describing events some ten years earlier when the two of them had run off together to Germany and Italy. The novel he completed that year, *Kangaroo*, was based on that three-month visit to Australia and featured another set of close stand-ins for Lawrence and Frieda in Richard Lovatt Somers and Harriet, his wife. In many ways, they provide an update to *Mr. Noon* regarding their strained marital relations, with both works revealing the plight of a man still struggling to accept a life of thwarted desire. The intense passion of *Lady Chatterley's Lover* still lay four years in the future, with the passion there, as we have seen, presented almost entirely from a woman's point of view, hence directed toward a male sexual object—Lawrence happily finding in his last novel a vehicle for writing openly about desires that, at least based on the confessional sections of *Kangaroo*, his stand-in had long since forgone as a viable option for himself.

Lawrence's take on his marriage in *Kangaroo* can be seen as an outgrowth of the more realistic reckoning of his newlyweds that he first signals in *Mr. Noon*. It was a change that, given the prophetic nature of Lawrence's thinking, he outlined in that unfinished novel as an aspect of any man's relationship with any woman, although, in *Mr. Noon*, rendered in a mock-heroic tone. For instance, there is Lawrence's winking that he is going "to let the cat out of the bag" about marriage, supposedly confessing to us how a couple is not at all like a pair of doves in a cage; instead, they are more likely to be complete opposites, even adversaries. A couple, expressed in terms of Lawrence's absolutes, is like the "whole universe rest[ing] on the magical opposition of fire and water, sun and rain." "Is not the marriage bed," he continues,

> a fiery battle field, as well as a perfect communion, both simultaneously. Till we know this, we know nothing. And till we fight our fights like

DOI: 10.4324/9781003495093-9

splendid royal tigers, in the wonderful connubial rage, we are nothing. We are at a dead-lock: either water-logged, or gone woody and dry. Water-logged and fat, or woody and dry and sapless.

(186–87)

Here, in a nutshell, is Lawrence's notion of the permanent, adversarial nature of men and women: that they are separate beings with different natures who come together out of a search for perfection or, as Lawrence learned from his youthful study of Schopenhauer, out of biological necessity. On this, Lawrence never seems entirely certain. What he is sure about is that men and women are happier living in their separate spheres, experiencing freedom in the only way possible, by being true to their distinct natures. Again, men and women are like "two terrible opposites, fire and water"—"two eternal, universal enemies [...] the man and the woman of the material universe, father and mother of all things." The obvious result for Lawrence was the realization that "mating" itself was "always half a fight. At least half a fight. Is not the very embrace at least half a fight" (186).

There is a fatalistic aspect to Lawrence's view of the sexes that he seemed able to overcome on only a couple of memorable occasions, each featuring a striking image of a man and woman acting in harmony. One, from *Women in Love*, depicts a woman "hung in a pure rest, as a star is hung, balanced unthinkably," anticipating intimacy: "she would touch the reality in him, the suave, pure, untranslatable reality of his loins of darkness." Meanwhile, the man too is in a suspended state, knowing her "darkly, with the fullness of dark knowledge"; waiting, yes, but also free within himself—"night-free, like an Egyptian, steadfast in perfectly suspended equilibrium, pure mystic nodality of physical being. They would give each other this star-equilibrium which alone is freedom" (311)—a beautiful image, for sure, even if the underlying meaning emphasizes Lawrence's sense of the irreconcilable differences between the sexes, that is, Mellors's view of the sexes, not Connie's.

And a second from *Aaron's Rod*, a reworking of Whitman's striking rendering of "two eagles in mid-air":

grappling, whirling, coming to their intensification of love-oneness there in mid-air. In mid-air the love consummation. But all the time each lifted on its own wings: each bearing itself up on its own wings at every moment of the mid-air love consummation. That is the splendid love-way.

(167)

Opposed to such lyrical accounts of physical intimacy between men and women is the more common mock-heroic treatment of conjugal difficulties we see in *Mr. Noon*, an approach that Lawrence continues in *Kangaroo*, notably in the chapter "Harriet and Lovatt at Sea in Marriage." Here, Lawrence offers yet another attempt to sum up the prosaic state of his marriage, again placing it in the broader context of the general battle between the sexes. It is an argument that begins with the assertion that husbands can play only one of three roles in a marriage, alas, all unsatisfactory: "the lord and master who is honoured and obeyed," "the true friend and companion," or what is considered "the crux of all ideal marriage to-day," and perhaps the least appealing of the three, "the perfect lover." "Not even the lord and master," Lawrence continues, "turns out such a fiasco as does the perfect lover, ninety-nine times out of a hundred," ending as it usually does "in a quite ghastly anti-climax, divorce and horrors and the basest vituperation" (196).

Here is Lawrence, the putative satirist, likening "the perfect-love business" to

a wildly stormy strait, like the Straits of Magellan, where two fierce and opposing currents meet and there is the devil of a business trying to keep the bark of marriage, with the flag of perfect-love at the mast, from dashing on a rock or foundering in the heavy seas.

The husband and wife are like "two fierce and opposing currents meet[ing] in the narrows of perfect love. [...] when the albatross hovers in the great sky like a permanent benediction, and the sea shimmers a second heaven." Such a calm can never last long: "The seas will soon begin to rise, the ship to roll. And the waters of perfect love—when once this love is consummated in marriage—become inevitably a perfect hell of storms and furies" (196–97).

The conceit at the heart of this commentary becomes an account not just of Lawrence's married life but his broader relationship with heterosexuality—with the "hymeneal bark either founder[ing], or dash[ing] on a rock, or more wisely get[ting] out of the clash of meeting oceans and tak[ing] one tide or the other." In other words, it is the wife who is the true "captain of the marriage bark," steering it either "into the vast Pacific waters of lord-and-masterdom" or "much more frequently [...] into the rather grey Atlantic of true friendship and companionship," in both instances acting as if all is well by "keeping the flag of perfect love bravely afloat."

What follows, then, is Lawrence's hardy recommendation for "all those married couples who truly and sincerely want to get on" to opt for "perfect companionship" (198). It is a recommendation, however, that finally does not seem acceptable to Lawrence, reducing as it does the compelling questions of sexual expression and identity—issues that finally produced his most extraordinary writing—to uninspired satire about boats at sea.

Somers, Lawrence's stand-in, has trouble accepting this conclusion that the best he can do in life is this lukewarm friendship between the sexes. So it was that, in part, *Kangaroo* becomes a study of a man's struggle against the shallowness of his marriage—an account of why he was willing to "refute her, deny her, and imagine himself a unique male." Nor is he in doubt over the goal of this struggle—"to be male and unique, like a freak of a phœnix" (204). Accomplishing such a goal, Somers senses, may require his breaking free from the constraints of domesticity and heterosexuality—being the "lord and master" of a marriage ultimately seems to be of little interest either to Somers or Lawrence.

What did matter was the same straining for emotional or sexual fulfill-ment that we have seen repeatedly in Lawrence, here expressed as the pos-sibility of "open[ing] the doors of his soul and let[ting] in a dark Lord and Master for himself, the dark god he had sensed outside the door":

> Let him once truly submit to the dark majesty, break open his doors to this fearful god who is master, and enters us from below, the lower doors; let himself once admit a Master, the unspeakable god: and the rest would happen.

This vision of submission would haunt Somers throughout a series of dreams in *Kangaroo*, all of which have the ring of truth for a writer who regularly drew upon his experiences during his three-month stay in Australia. There was, for instance, Somers's attractive Aussie neighbor, Jack Callcott—a "handsome, well-built [man] with strong, heavy limbs"—but maybe not quite the configuration to attract Somers, in part because of a sort of mismatch, with his "long lean, rather pallid face really [not seeming] to belong to his strongly animal body" (62). The result was a male offering himself to Somers as a friend or mate, not as a sexual ideal to whom he might willingly submit. As we saw in Chapter 6, the aging Lawrence seems to have lost interest in the emotional entanglements associated with male friendships.

Lawrence also offers us a rare glimpse into a lurking heterosexual desire with Jack's wife, Victoria, who one day looked at Somers "with her dark eyes dilated into a glow, a glow of offering." At least for a moment, the result was Somers being unexpectedly aroused—"his limbs full of desire, like a power. [...] like bitter smouldering that at last leaps into flame." This was "not love," Lawrence is quick to tell us—"just weapon-like desire," perhaps something like that strong urge for sexual completion that led him to pressure Jessie Chambers and other women for sex in his early twenties. Here, again, was the "god Bacchus": "She had the sacred glow in her eyes. [...] And the fire was very clean and steely, after the smoke. And he felt the velvety fire from her face in his finger-tips" (164).

Yet, no sooner was Somers aroused than "his old stubborn self intervened," ending the moment, Lawrence adds, "almost involuntarily," telling the woman "Good-night" while admitting, "Perhaps it was fear." Yet, Lawrence admits, neither of their spouses—Victoria or Harriet— would have objected to their having a discreet affair. "Why not follow the flame, the moment sacred to Bacchus?" Lawrence has Somers ask. "Why not, if it was the way of life" (165)?

It all seemed a puzzle to Somers, especially given his knowledge of the Greek gods and their goings-on—those "swift short moments of Io or Leda or Ganymede": "Should not a man know the whole range?" he asks. "And especially the bright, swift, weapon-like Bacchic occasion, should not any man seize it when it offered?"

As Lawrence readily admits, perhaps the problem was that his "heart of hearts was stubbornly puritanical." However, even this seems like a hedge in his effort to account for how his being aroused by "[t]hese flashes of desire for a visual object" was insufficient to "carry him into action." For Lawrence, at this stage of his life, the answer seems to be that the only sex he wanted was akin to what in a few years he would show Connie experiencing with Mellors: what is here described as part of "a downslope into Orcus, and a vast, phallic, sacred darkness, where one was enveloped into the greater god as in an Egyptian darkness"—that is, sexual experience entailing the loss of boundaries, the dissolution of the self: "He would meet there or nowhere. To the visual travesty he would lend himself no more." To the other aspects of physical intimacy—especially "the visual travesty"—he would "lend himself no more."

Surprisingly, the same night Somers repudiated his neighbor's sexual advance, he was awakened "almost at once from a vivid little dream," an unusual occurrence as Lawrence tells us that ordinarily, Somers only dreamt in the morning. Nor is it surprising that this dream had a distinct sexual dimension, with Somers imagining himself in his rented bungalow, "bending forward" doing regular household chores, "when suddenly a violent darkness came over him, he felt his arms pinned, and he heard a man's voice speaking mockingly behind him, with a laugh." Strange things can happen in a dream: in this case, Somers seeing "the man's face too—a stranger, a rough, strong sort of Australian," perhaps not unlike Victoria's rugged husband, Jack, a man Lawrence had described as having "a certain slow, dark, lingering look of the eyes, which reminded one of [...] some patient, enduring animal with an indomitable but naturally passive courage" (64–65).

Then Somers realized "with horror" that they had "put a sack over my head, and fastened my arms, and I am in the dark, and they are going to [...]." Amid this masochistic fantasy, Lawrence seems not quite ready to imagine the stark fate that a few years hence would await his "woman who rode away," instead allowing matters to change course suddenly: Somers's great fear, we learn, was his being robbed, not of his virginity but of his "little brown handbag from the bedroom," which had all their money. But still with an overwhelming shock: "If the thing had really happened," Lawrence concludes, "it could hardly have happened to him more than in this dream" (166).

Somers had another sexually charged dream earlier in the novel, this one, which he had such trouble admitting, about his intense dislike of the two most influential women in his life—his wife and his mother—and the rigid boundaries he felt both had erected around him, in the process protecting him from his desires and, thus, in ways he had trouble articulating, preventing him from reaching his full potential. In this earlier dream from *Kangaroo*, there is only one woman whom he loved, "something like Harriet, something like his mother," and yet, he claims, still the good son protective of both, this woman of his dream was "unlike either" but was instead "a woman sullen and obstinate against him, repudiating him" (108).

Part of Somers's resentment in the novel comes from Harriet's opposition to his carving out a special space for himself, with her just laughing off, as a "bit of little boy's silly showing off," his wanting to become close "mates" with his neighbor Jack or with the novel's title character, Kangaroo, the leader of a secret nationalist movement. While Somers accuses Harriet of being unfair, he is not entirely clear about what he may want out of such friendships, with the lurking sense that his proclaimed reason—for "doing some work with men alone, sharing some activity with men"—may only be a placeholder for a different level of intimacy he was incapable of confronting directly, a desire for a "pure male activity [that] should be womanless, beyond woman" (108).

Another part of his resentment is toward his mother's overprotective ways and snobbishness—apparent when the 22-year-old Lawrence showed her an early draft of a scene from *The White Peacock* that featured a bride running up a church path. His mother, Lawrence continues, carefully "put on her spectacles, and read with an amused look on her face": " 'But my boy,' she said, amused and a bit mocking, as she put down the book and took off her spectacles, 'how do you know it was like that?' "

"How did I know?" writes the flabbergasted Lawrence: "My heart stood still"—his mother had treated him as if he had written "a school essay and she were the teacher: kindly and sceptical." It was only then, he continues, that he saw "the slight contempt she had for me: nay, even more, the slight hostility to my presumptuousness"—how she envisioned he

> might 'get on' in the ordinary rut, and even become a school-master at three pounds a week. Which would be a great rise above my father. But that I should presume to 'know' things off my own bat!—things I had not learned at school!—well, it was presumption in me.
>
> ("Getting On" 30)

Here was the source of Lawrence's raw resentment against both women: "Bitter the woman [in this strange dream] was grieved beyond words, grieved till her face was swollen and puffy and almost mad or imbecile, because she had loved him so much, and now she must see him betray her love." Betray, of course, only because that was what this dreamer himself wanted: to live without this woman, without any woman, as the first step in living with men, or, more to the point, as the first step in loving a man, or, an even greater taboo, allowing oneself to be loved by one. At least, Lawrence continues in *Kangaroo*, "that was how the dream woman put it: he had betrayed her great love, and she must go down desolate into an everlasting hell, denied, and denying him absolutely in return, a sullen, awful soul" (108).

And what a nightmare it was for this sensitive son and obedient husband—this one dream image that reminded him of his wife,

> and of his mother, and of his sister, and of girls he had known when he was younger—strange glimpses of all of them, each glimpse excluding the last. And at the same time in the terrible face some of the look of that bloated face of a madwoman which hung over Jane Eyre in the night in Mr Rochester's house.
>
> (108–09)

As Lawrence notes, we can readily believe Somers was "a great enemy of dreams," considering them "devils" that routinely overcame his otherwise sturdy daytime defenses.

> When he was asleep and off his guard, then his own weaknesses, especially his old weaknesses that he had overcome in his full, day-waking self, rose up again maliciously to take some picturesque form and torment and overcome his sleeping self.

Dreams, Lawrence knew, are the "revenge which old weaknesses took on the victorious healthy consciousness, like past diseases come back for a phantom triumph."

Surely, Somers reasoned, his mother and wife were both supporters; "both believed in him terribly," believed in him "with all the intensity of undivided love." Yet such complete acceptance was only for the man they knew, what Lawrence calls the "personal man." His nightmares were all connected to that other, less familiar side, the hidden man, the one who "would go beyond them, with his back to them, away from them into an activity that excluded them, in this man they did not find it so easy to believe" (110).

In some sense, *Kangaroo* is a novel filled with such dreams, a confessional work about the thwarted desires of its author—a married man in his mid-thirties, deeply unsure where to turn for satisfaction, emotional or sexual. Here we can see Lawrence in possibly his quintessential role: less the explorer of passion between lovers—after all, he likely was never physically intimate with a man, nor did he ever write about such an intimacy, at least openly—than the chronicler of how one can remain both fully alive and entirely alone in the world. This is the Lawrence we have seen throughout this monograph—the lyrical chronicler of what might seem an unfulfilled life, except for the intense beauty he regularly found in the world around him.

Such is the case with Somers's first great soliloquy that occurs after he has been weighing the possibility of accepting the offer to assist Kangaroo and, at least for the moment, deciding that, "As for loving mankind, or having a fire of love in his heart, it was all rot" (142)—a state of mind that Somers labels "almost fierily cold." Then, we see that other, open-hearted Lawrence, the artist who found his greatest passion not in another person but in the beautiful coldness of the ocean: in "the pale sea of green glass that fell in such cold foam," a scene that mirrors the fierce coldness of heart that Lawrence so wants for himself: literally to know what it is like to stand

> at the edge looking at the waves rather terrifying rolling at him, where he stood low and exposed, far out from the sand-banks, and as he watched the gannets gleaming white, then falling with a splash like white sky-arrows into the waves, he wished as he had never wished before that he could be cold, as sea-things are cold, and murderously fierce.

Perhaps there had always been a connection between Lawrence's dislike of emotional entanglements with others and the recompense he sought in nature. Here, then, is Somers ready to celebrate what it is like "[t]o have oneself exultantly ice-cold, not one spark of this wretched warm flesh left, and to have all the terrific, icy energy of a fish. To surge," this reverie continues, "with that cold exultance and passion of a sea thing!"

Now he understood the yearning in the seal-woman's croon, as she went back to the sea, leaving her husband and her children of warm flesh. No more cloying warmth. No more of this horrible stuffy heat of human beings. To be an isolated swift fish in the big seas, that are bigger than the earth; fierce with cold, cold life, in the watery twilight before sympathy was created to clog us.

(142)

Such is the beauty of solitude—"The cold, lovely silence, before crying and calling were invented"—and of being a poet: "His tongue felt heavy in his mouth, as if it had relapsed away from speech altogether."

Or in a second monologue from the following chapter, this one also about the attraction of a cold desire, one that perhaps afforded a particular sort of pleasure, just not the cloying sort, the kind that was always "fretting like a tugged chain":

Why not break the bond and be single, take a fierce stoop and a swing back, as when a gannet plunges like a white, metallic arrow into the sea, raising a burst of spray, disappearing, completing the downward curve of the parabola in the invisible underwater where it seizes the object of desire, then away, away with success upwards, back flashing into the air and white space.

(158–59)

The implication we have seen before: Why should we not be allowed to have sex free of emotional entanglements? "Why shouldn't meeting be a stoop as a gannet stoops into the sea, or a hawk, or a kite, in a swift rapacious parabola downwards, to touch at the lowermost turn of the curve, then up again?" Why shouldn't our meetings be "down, down in the invisible," with us still free as individuals when it is over? "Beneath every gannet that jumps from the water ten thousand fish are swimming still. But they are swimming in a shudder of silver fear. That is the magic of the ocean. Let them shudder the huge ocean aglimmer" (159).

Despite this praise of existential solitude, Lawrence describes two occasions of Somers's lovemaking with Harriet, albeit each time in only a single sentence and only following an extended account of what amounted to foreplay for Somers—time alone with nature. Before their first encounter, Lawrence shows us Somers's exhilaration from swimming naked in the ocean—his "walk[ing] straight into the fore-wash, and [falling] into an advancing ripple":

At least it looked a ripple, but was enough to roll him over so that he went under and got a little taste of the Pacific. Ah, the fresh cold wetness!—the fresh cold wetness! The water rushed in the back-wash and the sand melted under him, leaving him stranded like a fish. He turned again to the water. The walls of surf were some distance off, but near enough to look rather awful as they raced in high white walls shattering towards him.

(168)

Before the second encounter, Somers, in a torpor as the result of a recent marital spat, has turned to confront the immensity of the world and especially "the old, old influence of the fern-world": Man

breathes the fern seed and drifts back, becomes darkly half vegetable, devoid of pre-occupations. Even the never-slumbering urge of sex sinks down into something darker, more monotonous, incapable of caring: like sex in trees. The dark world before conscious responsibility was born.

(206)

He first tries to get the attention of a kookaburra, a bird like him seemingly "sunk in unutterable apathy." "Ah well," he thought, "life is so big, and has such huge ante-worlds of grey twilight. How can one care about anything in particular" (207)! As he heads home, his thoughts "drifted away into the grey pre-world where men didn't have emotions. Where men didn't have emotions and personal consciousness, but were shadowy like trees, and on the whole silent, with numb brains and slow limbs and a great indifference."

Once home, he found a "rather wistful" partner who loved him "rather quiveringly." But, no surprise, the outcome of this second act of lovemaking was that "even in the quiver of her passion [he found] some of this indifference, this twilight indifference of the fern-world."

Here, then, is the second great source of Lawrence's lyricism, which, unlike his erotic desire, was never hidden—namely, his eagerness to celebrate the stark beauty of "Man's isolation." What he saw as "always a supreme truth and fact, not to be forsworn"—to be alive in isolation filled with a "dark, unexplained blood-tenderness that is deeper than love, but so much more obscure, impersonal." What Lawrence found in nature was this unending sense of wonder—"an indwelling magnificence, direct flow from the unknowable God" (384–85). In comparison, the human love between a man and a woman seemed more like "fighting for candle-light, when the dark is so much better." And then the most wondrous possibility of all, that "best of human meetings," something far beyond "absolute human love": "To meet another dark worshipper" (328).

One is reminded of another of Lawrence's loners, the music teacher and violinist Siegmund from his second novel, *The Trespasser*—a married man who goes on vacation to the Isle of Wight with a student of his, Helena, nominally as her lover, only to spend his most intense, sensual moments, just as Somers does in *Kangaroo*, alone in the ocean. One such instance was the morning when Siegmund, usually a cautious swimmer, "feeling a delight in his triumph over the waves," swam through an archway to a bay that was "inaccessible from the land," a place where "the water ran like a flood of green light over the skin-white bottom." Once there, he "waded out of the green, cold water on to sand that was pure as the shoulders of Helena, out of the shadow of the archway into the sunlight, on to the glistening petal of this blossom of a sea-bay." He was proud of himself for having made his way to this sea-cave "like a white bee into a white virgin blossom that had waited, how long, for its bee" (63).

Here, Lawrence paints the portrait of a man in love, with nature as his partner: "The sand [...] warm to his breast, and his belly, and his arms. [...] like a great body he cleaved to." There was a warmth he sought— "his hands again on the warm body of the shore, let[ting] them wander, discovering, gathering all the warmth, the softness, the strange wonder of smooth warm pebbles"—but, as with Somers in *Kangaroo*, the greatest attraction is with the darkness and especially the "cold mystery of the deep sand [...] He pushed in his hands again and deeper, enjoying the almost hurt of the dark, heavy coldness."

What a clear lineage: from the 22-year-old Lawrence we saw in Chapter 3 writing to Blanche Jennings about working in the fields—where "the willows have glittered like hammered steel in the morning"; to the 26-year-old Lawrence we see here in *The Trespasser*; to the 37-year-old Lawrence of *Kangaroo*, standing on the beach, looking in amazement at "the fins of dolphins ... [that] seemed almost over the sea edge. And then, suddenly, oh wonder, they were caught up in the green wall of the rising water"!

> ... and there for a second they hung in the watery, bright green pane of the wave, five big dark dolphins, a little crowd, with their sharp fins and blunt heads, a little sea-crowd in the thin, upreared sea. They flashed with a sharp black motion as the great wave curled to break. They flashed in-sea, flashed from the foamy horror of the land. And there they were, black little school, away in the lacquered water, panting, [Somers] imagined, with the excitement of the escape. Then one of the bold bucks came back to try again, and he jumped clean out of the water, above a wave, and kicked his heels as he dived in again.
>
> (386–87)

Such is Somers's state of mind here at the end of the novel, when he breaks off contact with the visionary leader Kangaroo, acknowledging that it was time for him to leave Australia for good—yet not before one final visit to the seashore.

And what a night he chose—one "full of moonlight as a mother-of-pearl": "The light on the waves [...] like liquid radium swinging and slipping. Like radium, the mystic virtue of vivid decomposition, liquid-gushing lucidity."

> The sea too was very full. It was nearly high tide, the waves were rolling very tall, with light like a menace on the nape of their necks as they bent, so brilliant. Then, when they fell, the fore-flush rushed in a great soft swing with incredible speed up the shore, on the darkness soft-lighted with moon, like a rush of white serpents, then slipping back with a hiss that fell into silence for a second, leaving the sand of granulated silver.
>
> (399–400)

The foam of the waves struck Somers as "the hissing, open mouths of snakes."

> A huge but a cold passion swinging back and forth. Great waves of radium swooping with a down-curve and rushing up the shore. Then calling themselves back again, retreating to the mass. Then rushing with venomous radium-burning speed into the body of the land. Then recoiling with a low swish, leaving the flushed sand naked.

"That was the night," Lawrence continues. "Rocking with cold, radium-burning passion, swinging and flinging itself with venomous desire." And amidst this deserted scene, there's Lawrence's frail persona—"a bit of human wispiness in thin overcoat and thick boots": "Only, when he came past the creek on the sands, rough, wild ponies looking at him, dark figures in the moonlight lifting their heads from the invisible grass of the sand, and waiting for him to come near," then to continue grazing, reassured by his gentle voice:

> [Somers] rocking with the radium-urgent passion of the night: the huge, desirous swing, the call clamour, the low hiss of retreat. The call, call! And the answerer. Where was his answerer? There was no living answerer. No dark-bodied, warm-bodied answerer. He knew that when he had spoken a word to the night-half-hidden ponies with their fluffy legs. No animate answer this time. The radium-rocking, wave-knocking night his call and his answer both.
>
> (400–01)

Kangaroo may not be Lawrence's most beloved novel; still, it is one in which he speaks to us with rare directness about the beauty of the unknown, of what it is like to worship a "God without feet or knees or face," what it is like to be overcome with desire for that which always lies just beyond our grasp:

> This sluicing, knocking, urging night, heaving like a woman with unspeakable desire, but no woman, no thighs or breast, no body. The moon, the concave mother-of-pearl of night, the great radium-swinging, and his little self. The call and the answer, without intermediary. Non-human gods, non-human human beings.

It is a novel in which he again tells us what it is like to live free and live alone. Or, as Lawrence writes in his poem "The Uprooted" (Delphi 7824), about what we must all do when confronted with the common fate of our loneliness—and that is, "in solitude slowly and painfully put forth new roots / into the unknown, and take root by oneself."

Works Cited

Lawrence, D. H. *Aaron's Rod*. Ed. Mara Kalnins. Penguins Books, 1995.
———. *Complete Works*. Delphi Classics, 2015.
———. "Getting On." In *Late Essays and Articles*. Ed. James T. Boulton. Cambridge UP, 2004: 25–32.
———. *Kangaroo*. Thomas Seltzer, 1923.
———. *Mr. Noon*. Ed. Lindeth Vasey. Cambridge UP, 1984.
———. *Trespasser*. Ed. Elizabeth Mansfield. Cambridge UP, 1982.
———. *Women in Love*. Heinemann, 1971.

Index